SEE ME! HEAR ME! DIVINE/HUMAN RELATIONAL DIALOGUE
IN GENESIS

Elizabeth B. Tracy

SEE ME! HEAR ME! DIVINE/HUMAN RELATIONAL DIALOGUE IN GENESIS

PEETERS

LEUVEN – PARIS – BRISTOL, CT

2015

A catalogue record for this book is available from the Library of Congress.

© 2015 — Peeters, Bondgenotenlaan 153, B-3000 Leuven

ISBN 978-90-429-3048-3
D/2015/0602/28

"The Jews are not so much God's chosen people as his argumentative ones. They don't take things on faith. Abraham, Moses and Job all argued with God. And sometimes won."

Benjamin Netanyahu
Time Magazine 5/28/12

TABLE OF CONTENTS

CHAPTER 1

INTRODUCTION

A. INTRODUCTION

1. Why this topic?

I come rather late to my PhD studies of the Hebrew Bible. I spent over fifteen years in film and television production where I read and analyzed books, stories and scripts. When I decided to pursue an advanced degree in Biblical Studies it seemed a complete 180 degree turn and yet the methodical tools of script analysis have served me well. While reading a biblical text I see character motivation, scenes, and dialogue that inform both the character and the action.

In scripts, while location and wardrobe set the scene, it is the dialogue that most often defines the character. Since beginning my studies I have spent a good deal of my time "listening" to the biblical text, who speaks, where and when they speak, how the questions, concerns and responses are formed. Dialogue between humans plays out relatively straight forward like most movies we view. It is the conversation between the Divine[1] and human that stretches my imagination. I wonder, if we had nothing else but these few Divine/human relational dialogue exchanges, what would be our opinion of the Deity?

Consider the Divine/human relational dialogues to be covered in this thesis: The Divine speaks to the angry murderer Cain.[2] In the wilderness, the foreigner and slave Hagar is found by a messenger of the Deity who

---

[1] Throughout this thesis I will be investigating the personal relationship between God and mankind as revealed in dialogue. In each of the conversations the entity referred to as divine in nature is portrayed (or titled) in a slightly different manner. According to my research the form of the manifestation of the Deity does not have a great effect on the interpersonal nature of the conversation. To refer to the Hebrew God differently in each case would distance the reader from the conclusions that will be drawn. For this purpose I will refer to any divine manifestation as either "the Divine" or "the Deity" to avoid confusion.

[2] Genesis 4:3-15.

calls her by name.[3] In relational dialogue with Abram/Abraham the focus of conversation is not the patriarch but Sarah, Ishmael, Isaac and Eliezer.[4] When Jacob wrestles at Peniel he demands and is given a blessing by his divine attacker.[5]

The juxtaposition of these stories fascinates me. The first to commit murder is the first to converse with the Deity. The foreigner is seen as a unique individual by the Divine while the chosen mother receives a divine rebuke. Potential heirs are dismissed and the legitimate successor only promised as humans argue, cry, laugh and demand response from their Deity. A former professor of mine used to say, "There's something there, there."[6] What is there, for me, are questions. Fokkelman states, "The Bible does not contain one single instance of *small talk*; almost every word by a character is existentially revealing or rooted."[7] If this is true, is it possible to find an interpersonal relationship model between lowly humans and the Divine as contained within conversation in the Hebrew Bible?

The aim of this thesis is to examine instances of relational dialogue between the Deity and human individuals in the book of Genesis by separating the conversations from the narrative through lines that most often inform biblical analysis. Instead of watching a movie complete with music, chase sequences and explosions I am interested in those snapshots of character developed in what is called a two-shot — when everything else is pushed to the background and face to face dialogue takes center stage. Through this line of inquiry, I will develop a model of Divine/human dialogue that will then inform a model of the Divine/human relationship.

2. Why just Genesis?

This thesis will limit the scope of research on Divine/human dialogue to the book of Genesis. In order to understand this choice the focus must be narrowed by degrees.

---

[3] Genesis 16:7-14.
[4] Genesis 17:15-22; 18:9-15; 15:1-17.
[5] Genesis 32:25-31.
[6] My thanks to Prof. Tammi Schneider of Claremont Graduate University.
[7] J. P. Fokkelman, *Reading Biblical Narrative: An Introduction* (Louisville, Ky.: Westminster John Knox, 1999), 69. Emphasis original.

Much of the Hebrew Bible is considered historical and, while not historiographical in the strictest sense of the word, the collection of books does concern itself with the history of the Deity's people. The narratives then, reflect a "history of a people to whom God has spoken and through whom he has acted."[8] The three main subdivisions of the Hebrew Bible are Torah, Prophets and Wisdom. According to Speiser, the first five books[9] were "intimately attributed to God and emerged thus as a body of teachings comprising the one Torah above all others."[10] If the Greek term *Pentateuch* describes the external detail of the first portion of the canon, then the Hebrew title Torah addresses the content.[11] Coates states that the term Torah is derived from "the history of the canon established within a specific religious community. It connotes something about function within a specific community of faith."[12] The function of this instruction within a unique narrative is to record what the Deity expects of its people and who exactly those people are.

[8] J. Alberto Soggin and John Bowden, *Introduction to the Old Testament: From Its Origins to the Closing of the Alexandrian Canon*, 2nd ed. (London: SCM, 1976), 37.
[9] Some scholars argue for a Hexateuch configuration suggesting that "the unity of narration does not cease with the death of Moses but moves into the traditions of conquest in Joshua." George W. Coats, *Genesis*, FOTL 1 (Grand Rapids, Mich.: Eerdmans, 1983), 13-26. Although the term is still used by some scholars, it has been in decline since Noth proposed a completely new theory, i.e., the Deuteronomistic Historian, in 1943. Gerhard von Rad, *Genesis: A Commentary*, OTL (Philadelphia, Pa.: Westminster, 1972), 13-24. Also see Soggin and Bowden, *Introduction to the Old Testament: From Its Origins to the Closing of the Alexandrian Canon*, 79-98.
[10] E. A. Speiser, *Genesis*, AB 1 (Garden City, N.Y.: Doubleday, 1964), xix. According to Soggin the first five books of the Bible are considered the most important part of the canon. Soggin and Bowden, *Introduction to the Old Testament: From Its Origins to the Closing of the Alexandrian Canon*, 79.
[11] Note that nowhere within the Pentateuch does the content call itself "Torah." "There are occasions when the Pentateuch speaks explicitly of a written *tōrā*. Yet this usage does not of itself narrow down the meaning of the word; each occurrence has to be judged from its own context... The only Pentateuchal passage that refers comprehensively to a written *tōrā* is Deut xxxi 9, where we are told that 'Moses wrote down this *tōrā*.' This particular statement points either to the portions of Deuteronomy that precede, as most moderns assume, or to the poetic sections which follow, as some scholars believe. In neither event could the Pentateuch as a whole be at issue. Yet it is this one ambiguous reference, more than anything else, that eventually gave rise to the doctrine of the Mosaic authorship of the entire Pentateuch." Speiser, *Genesis*, xviii-xix. Also see Soggin and Bowden, *Introduction to the Old Testament: From Its Origins to the Closing of the Alexandrian Canon*, 80-83.
[12] Coats, *Genesis*, 15.

Within the Torah are three basic narrative units:[13] the Primeval Saga[14], the Patriarchal Sagas[15] and the Moses Saga.[16] Genesis contains the first two. The Primeval saga (sometimes called the Primeval History) has a universal quality describing the early history of a family that will one day become a treasured people. The Patriarchal saga shows strife within the family. The Moses saga portrays discord within the nation. Contained in these sagas are intimate moments where the Deity and humans interact. These instances are not confined to sacred institutions or cultic spheres of sacrifice. They are not mediated by priests or specific prophets and yet they still contain themes of divine promise, protection and fulfillment.[17] The sagas of Genesis are, from the beginning, concerned "not with man who with his desires and despair believes himself to be alone in the world, but rather with man to whom the living God has been revealed and who therefore has become the object of divine address, a divine act, and therefore a divine judgment and divine salvation."[18] Genesis offers a unique narrative window with which we can observe humankind's intimate relationship with the Deity through dialogue.

3. Possible Results

In this thesis I am interested in three potential results. The first is the identification of latent elements which may be considered present in all or most dialogues between the Deity and humans which will lead to

---

[13] Von Rad and Speiser separate the Primeval Sagas (Gen 1:1-11:32) from the Patriarchal Sagas (Gen 12:1-50:26). See von Rad, *Genesis: A Commentary*, 45-163.; Speiser, *Genesis*, 3-81. Coats includes the Primeval Saga within the Patriarchal Sagas. Coats, *Genesis*, 27-34.

[14] Genesis 1:1-11:32. Coats defines saga (sage) as "a long, prose, traditional narrative having an episodic structure developed around stereotyped themes or objects. It may include narratives that represent distinct genres in themselves. The episodes narrate deeds or virtues from the past insofar as they contribute to the composition of the present narrator's world." Coats, *Genesis*, 319.

[15] Genesis 12:1-50:26. "The patriarchal sagas narrate stories about the fathers and their families in their life setting in Canaan. In this literature the culture appears to be semi-nomadic, the religion a mobile one tied not to a particular place, but rather to a particular tribal patriarch. Whenever the patriarch moves, the God of the patriarch moves with him." Claus Westermann, *Genesis 1-11: A Commentary*, trans. John J. Scullion (London: SPCK, 1974), 15.

[16] Exodus 1:1-Deut 34:12. The Moses saga "recounts the events of Moses in Egypt, the process that brought him to his people, *the sons of Israel*, the formation of the group into a working unit, and the events of trial and victor that brought them to the land of Canaan." Ibid., 15. Emphasis in the original.

[17] Von Rad, *Genesis: A Commentary*, 29-31. Also see Coats, *Genesis*, 22.

[18] Von Rad, *Genesis: A Commentary*, 25.

a second goal, the development of a potential formula identifiable as Divine/human relational dialogue. The final outcome I hope to achieve is the application of these results to a better understanding of the Divine/ human relationship through the examination of dialogue.

4. Translations

All translations contained in this thesis are my own. Also note that I differentiate Abram from Abraham in my writing when results stem from before or after Gen 17:5. I do not, however, correct other author's quotes when they do not make this same distinction which, in some cases, leads to a paragraph where the patriarch is identified as both Abram and Abraham.

B. METHODOLOGY

The dialogues discussed in this thesis vary in size, content, and form. They are similar but divergent. In order to study them properly it will be necessary to combine two modes of biblical criticism. Form criticism allows a text to be examined and defined as an individual narrative dialogue between humankind and the Deity. The emphasis on typical features of the texts we will be inspecting will be employed to tie them together. To counter-point form criticism's natural tendency to concern itself with what is common, narrative criticism will be utilized when investigating distinct and dissident elements within each text. These unique elements, combined with those found through form criticism, will serve to define the genre of Divine/human dialogue in Genesis. For this reason it is important that we examine the constitutional facets of both form and narrative criticism.

1. Form Criticism

For biblical scholars, formulating a concise definition of form criticism is as easy as achieving a consensus on the characterization of the Trinity. The *Handbook of Biblical Criticism* defines form criticism as "the analysis of the typical forms by which human existence is expressed linguistically."[19]

---

[19] Richard N. Soulen, *Handbook of Biblical Criticism* (Atlanta, Ga.: John Knox, 1976), 62.

The Blackwell Companion to the Hebrew Bible admits that "form criticism may be the most elusive of the creatures in the garden of Older Testament scholarship."[20] Early modern biblical scholarship focused on historical and documentary questions. John Hayes and Carl Holladay explained that "historical criticism had come to recognize that many biblical writings 'grew' out of certain historical contexts over periods of time, and literary and documentary criticism sought especially to detect various sources which underlay the final form of the biblical texts."[21] These approaches, while expanding our understanding of the text, did not encourage investigation into individual literary units using genre[22] recognition, expound on sociological factors surrounding given passages or attempt to identify the significance of faith practices expressed in given segments of a text. As scholars sought to move beyond documentary and historical analysis, form criticism began to take shape.

In 1901 Gunkel, regarded as one of the most creative and influential biblical scholars of the twentieth century,[23] published his commentary on Genesis. Building on research of the day, Gunkel employed new methods[24] that pioneered work which would later be expanded by the likes of von Rad (1938) and Noth (1948). In the process he became known as the founder of biblical form criticism.[25] The minutia of the study of the

---

[20] Antony F. Campbell, "Preparatory Issues in Approaching Biblical Texts," in *The Blackwell Companion to the Hebrew Bible*, ed. Leo G. Perdue (Oxford: Blackwell, 2001), 9. Also see Erhard Blum, "Formgeschichte—a Misleading Category? Some Critical Remarks," in *The Changing Face of Form Criticism for the Twenty-First Century*, ed. Marvin A. Sweeney and Ehud Ben Zvi (Grand Rapids, Mich.: Eerdmans, 2003), 32.

[21] John H. Hayes and Carl R. Holladay, *Biblical Exegesis: A Beginner's Handbook* (Atlanta, Ga.: John Knox, 1982), 78.

[22] In this thesis, form is defined as the overall shape or structure of the text. Genre is defined as a conceptual "ideal" or "typical" form.

[23] For example see: Blum, "Formgeschichte—a Misleading Category? Some Critical Remarks," 33. Roy F. Melugin, "Recent Form Criticism Revisited in an Age of Reader Response," in *The Changing Face of Form Criticism for the Twenty-First Century*, ed. Marvin A. Sweeney and Ehud Ben Zvi (Grand Rapids, Mich.: Eerdmans, 2003), 46. Von Rad, *Genesis: A Commentary*, 31.

[24] Hermann Gunkel, *Genesis*, trans. Mark E. Biddle (Macon, Ga.: Mercer University Press, 1997), [4]. Also see Blum, "Formgeschichte—a Misleading Category? Some Critical Remarks," 41.

[25] John Barton, *Reading the Old Testament: Method in Biblical Study* (Philadelphia, Pa.: Westminster, 1984), 35. Soulen, *Handbook of Biblical Criticism*, 62. Marvin A. Sweeney and Ehud Ben Zvi, eds., *The Changing Face of Form Criticism for the Twenty-First Century* (Grand Rapids, Mich.: Eerdmans, 2003), 2. Antony F. Campbell, "Form Criticism's Future," in *The Changing Face of Form Criticism for the Twenty-First Century*, ed. Marvin A. Sweeney and Ehud Ben Zvi (Grand Rapids, Mich.: Eerdmans, 2003), 16. Blum contends that Gunkel did not coin or use the term "form criticism" himself. Blum, "Formgeschichte—a Misleading Category? Some Critical Remarks," 32.

history of the text, as Wellhausen[26] had done, was too narrow for Gunkel. His new approach gave more attention to the form (*Gattungen*) of the text. He enhanced the field of biblical scholarship with what he termed the study of "literary history" (*Literaturgeschichte*).[27] His work "paid close attention to literary, historical, and cultural parallels from Egypt, Babylon, and even later Arab cultures[... *added by ET*] He was especially cognizant of the importance of the Babylonian discoveries made in the late nineteenth century."[28] As Gunkel studied he became convinced that each individual scriptural unit "originally had a separate life of its own before it became part of a source in the Pentateuch, and that these stories and laws were handed down by *oral tradition* from the earliest period of Israelite history until they became fixed in writing."[29] The interest, for Gunkel, lay not in identifying the personality of the original writer but in "identifying literary 'types' that lie deeper than any

---

[26] Julius Wellhausen, a contemporary of Gunkel's, synthesized and clarified generations of scholarly research in a new construction of Israel's history by concentration on source-criticism and the dating of the literary sources J, E, P, and D. His book *Geschichte Israels*, I, first appeared in 1878. Later editions were issued under the title *Prolegomena zur Geschichte Israels* (translated into English in 1957 under the title *Prolegomena to the History of Ancient Israel*). Subsequent books, *Abriss der Geschichte Israels und Judah* (1894) and *Israelitische und Jüdische Geschichte* (1894) expanded on his reconstruction of Israel's history.

[27] Gunkel, *Genesis*, [6]. Also see "Fundamental Problems of Hebrew Literary History," in *What Remains of the Old Testament? And Other Essays* (London, 1928) 57-68, originally published as "Die Grundprobleme der israelitischen Literaturgeschichte," *Deutsche Literaturzeitung* 27 (1906).

[28] Hermann Gunkel, *Water for a Thirsty Land: Israelite Literature and Religion*, ed. K. C. Hanson, trans. A.K. Dallas and James Schaaf (Minneapolis, Minn.: Fortress, 2001), x. The following is a quick survey of biblical discoveries that may have influenced Gunkel's scholarship: Napoleon Bonaparte's invasion of Egypt in 1798 included scientists who virtually founded modern archaeology. In the 1830s Sir John Wilkinson copied paintings and inscriptions. By 1842 Frenchman Paul Emile Botta was sent to Mosul to begin excavations in the ruins of Nineveh. Subsequent digs revealed the palace of Sennacherib and the famous pictures of the siege of Lachish. In 1843 a German team lead by Richard Lepsius began investigating and making exact records of tombs and monuments. In 1872 George Smith discovered the *Epic of Gilgamesh* and identified it as a story very similar to the story of Noah's flood. Sir William Flinders Petrie went to Egypt in 1880 to survey the pyramids and began an almost 40 year study of Egyptian archaeology. During the last quarter of the nineteenth century, French scholars working in Babylonia uncovered remains of the Sumerian culture. In 1887 a team from the University of Pennsylvania excavated the Sumerian religious center of Nippur uncovering thousands of cuneiform tablets, including many myths and hymns.

[29] John Van Seters, "The Pentateuch," in *The Hebrew Bible Today: An Introduction to Critical Issues*, ed. Steven L. McKenzie and M. Patrick Graham, 1st ed. (Louisville, Ky.: Westminster John Knox, 1998), 10. Emphasis in the original.

individual effort."[30] Gunkel made biblical scholars aware of the importance of the relationship of genres (*Genre*), setting in life (*Sitz im Leben*)
and the intention (*Intention*) of texts. His influence on the field and subsequent scholarship has not faded with time.[31]

The first major attempts to expand on Gunkel's new approach were
made by von Rad[32] and then by Noth.[33] While their styles differed, both
sought to understand how the authors of the final source documents shaped
the tradition and theology now at their disposal. Both began by examining
larger literary units with von Rad focusing on the Hexateuch and Noth on
the Deuteronomistic History. The research was "an effort to trace the later
growth of earlier traditions and theological reflection on them."[34]

Von Rad's interest in form-criticism was revealed in his concern with
the forces shaping the Hexateuch. He saw the books of Genesis to Joshua
as one large connected narrative but did not focus on whether they were
the result of individual narrative sources or a final redactor who combined
the sources. He felt that "the reader must keep in mind the narrative as a
whole and the contexts into which all the individual parts fit."[35]

Noth, on the other hand, studied the remote origins of the Pentateuch.
His purpose was to "trace the history of Pentateuchal traditions from
their earliest formulations in the preliterary period down to the time of
their composition in successive literary stages"[36] with the final result
being the Pentateuch as we now have it. Noth saw Wellhausen's source
analysis as a provisional starting point but rejected the uni-linear reconstruction he had espoused. He believed that Gunkel's form-criticism
provided crucial access to the pre-literary period[37] but concentrated on
units rather than the configuration of materials. Noth stated that early

---

[30] Gunkel, *Genesis*, [7].

[31] Kim, in his essay "Form Criticism in Dialogue with Other Criticisms" poetically
describes Gunkel's influence as being "like the root of a tree, it has produced many
branches of subdisciplines. As a parent, it has yielded many children." Hyun Chul Paul
Kim, "Form Criticism in Dialogue with Other Criticisms: Building the Multidimensional Structures of Texts and Concepts," in *The Changing Face of Form Criticism for
the Twenty-First Century*, ed. Marvin A. Sweeney and Ehud Ben Zvi (Grand Rapids,
Mich.: Eerdmans, 2003), 102-03.

[32] See Gerhard von Rad, *The Problem of the Hexateuch and Other Essays*, trans. E. W. Trueman Dicken (New York: McGraw, 1966).

[33] See Martin Noth, *A History of Pentateuchal Traditions*, trans. Bernhard W. Anderson
(Chico, Calif.: Scholars Press, 1981).

[34] Sweeney and Ben Zvi, eds., *The Changing Face of Form Criticism for the Twenty-First
Century*, 2.

[35] Von Rad, *Genesis: A Commentary*, 13.

[36] Noth, *A History of Pentateuchal Traditions*, xiv.

[37] Ibid., xviii.

traditions were formulated "in small units and in concise style in contrast to later material which tends to appear in large units composed in discursive (*ausgeführt*) style."[38]

As Noth surveyed the units within the Pentateuch for clues as to their origin, von Rad looked for an internal connection between these individual narratives. He felt sagas were all subordinate to the overarching theme of the 'promise to the patriarchs' with special emphasis on the promise of land and descendants.[39] Von Rad felt that knowledge of the "specific character of the literature"[40] would have an imperceptible effect on the understanding of the text.

For Richter, von Rad and Noth's use of genre led to crisis. Richter criticized *Formgeschichte* for "determining textual genres too hastily on the basis of a combination of material and sociolinguistic arguments: form = content = *Sitz im Leben*."[41] Richter argued that form criticism, while being quick to determine genre, overlooked and even disregarded a proper description of the grammatical[42] and literary form of an individual text. His alternative was based on strictly formal and hierarchically organized criteria.[43]

Richter's approach advocated taking an analytical route from "form" to "content." He developed a scientific approach that allowed the scholar to go from word to sentence to text.[44] The attempt to create clear exegetical techniques "in which analysis of the form has priority over that of the content, synchrony comes before diachrony and the individual text before genre determination"[45] led to what one commentator has called, "the most rigorous attempt to put form-critical study on a thoroughly scientific basis."[46] Unfortunately, Richter's detailed analysis was sometimes too myopic for scholars.[47]

---

[38] Ibid., xxiii-xxiv.

[39] Von Rad, *Genesis: A Commentary*, 22.

[40] Ibid., 11.

[41] E. Talstra, *Solomon's Prayer: Synchrony and Diachrony in the Composition of I Kings 8, 14-61*, CBET 3 (Kampen: Kok Pharos, 1993), 261.

[42] Richter's link with grammar is even more underlined in his three volume grammatical study Wolfgang Richter, *Grundlagen einer Althebräischen Grammatik* (St. Ottilien: EOS-Verlag, 1978).

[43] Talstra, *Solomon's Prayer: Synchrony and Diachrony in the Composition of I Kings 8, 14-61*, 260.

[44] Ibid., 17.

[45] Ibid., 260-61.

[46] Campbell, "Preparatory Issues in Approaching Biblical Texts," 10.

[47] Childs, in his commentary on Exodus, observed that Richter's analysis of the burning bush text (Exod 3:1-4:17) was "too hair-splitting and as a result [had, *added by ET*] unduly atomized the text. For example, Richter eliminates the appearance of the angel

Gunkel rejected Wellhausen's diachronic source fragmentation in favor of a synchronic approach to the study of texts. Von Rad took the approach that more was better and focused his studies on forces shaping not just the first five books of the Hebrew Bible but included the book of Joshua in his Hexateuch study. Noth, in turn, examined individual units of texts but offered no intertextuality theories. Richter applied his scientific approach to form criticism by dissecting Noth's texts to their smallest details, using the hexateuchal inclusion of von Rad, and looking for Gunkel's 'earliest period of Israelite history' within the exacting genres he had formulated. So the problem of defining form criticism remains: how should a scholar travel from language to text? If we accept that form criticism allows the interpreter freedom to look beyond a specific transmission stage and examine certain thematically connected texts side by side, then we must next determine how this is to be done.

In his guide to methodology Steck states that "form criticism is meaningful in oral as well as written transmission stages, for a text (component genre) within a larger section of text (framing genre), and for an independent text. It is meaningful for a small unit as well as a more comprehensive text complex (such as Yahwistic work or the Deuteronomistic History)."[48] He goes on to explain that form criticism is the ability to set a text in its "existing *linguistic* world."[49] He argues:

> Form critical work does not just constitute the investigation of the linguistic shape of an *individual* text and the parallel examples which appear during the investigation... the task of form criticism also includes, in principle, research into the Hebrew (or Aramaic) *linguistic world as a whole* and illumination of the history of text patterns (*genre history*). In this case, work on individual texts is not the goal but is the means and the material of the investigation.[50]

For Steck the linguistic world is broken down into four parts,[51] the *tonal level* which highlights the sound of the text; the *word level* investigates individual words of the text; the *sentence level* examines the structure of

---

of Yahweh in v. 2 as being sequentially out of place and reconstructs a 'smooth text'. But this move has failed to reckon with the literary style of the biblical author, paralleled in Gen 18.1, in which v. 2 serves as a type of superscription to the narrative." Brevard S. Childs, *Exodus, a Commentary*, OTL (London: SCM Press, 1974), 52.

[48] Odil Hannes Steck, *Old Testament Exegesis: A Guide to the Methodology*, 2nd ed. (Atlanta, Ga.: Scholars Press, 1998), 115.

[49] Ibid., 96. Emphasis original.

[50] Ibid., 100. Emphasis original.

[51] Ibid., 97.

the individual sentence and finally the *text level* treats the identified text as a whole by folding in the previous three investigations. The size of an examined text does not matter in Steck's form criticism. The advantage to this definition of form criticism at the language level is that the devices he employs allows the scholar to dissect individual texts into their foundational linguistic elements. It is in the analysis of these elements that theories can then be identified and tracked.[52]

If Steck's definition of form criticism allows for some freedom within a regimented investigation, Alter cautions that form criticism is "set on finding recurrent regularities of pattern rather than the manifold variations upon a pattern that any system of literary convention elicits; moreover, form criticism uses these patterns for excavative ends — to support hypotheses about the social functions of the text, its historical evolution, and so forth."[53] With the emphasis on patterns (or genre) it is incumbent on the scholar not to allow the desire for 'tidy classification'[54] to rob form criticism of its creativity. According to Barton "criticism is a descriptive pursuit, analyzing, explaining and codifying the questions that perceptive readers put to the text; not a prescriptive discipline laying down rules about how the text ought to be read."[55] If applied correctly, with attention to limit overzealous formulation, form criticism can welcome the investigator into a wider world view of the text in question. It can lead the scholar "to understand and appreciate the role and significance of the faith and practices of the believing community in the formation of the traditions that the community would hold sacred and declare canonical."[56]

As we embark on biblical scholarship in the twenty-first century the invaluable contributions of form criticism as a tool for study has not diminished.[57] It has however, according to Campbell, lost some of its dynamism. Misunderstandings have developed over the years and need to be dispelled before form criticism can regain its original vigor. Campbell states that two things must be clearly understood. "First, the decision about the literary type (genre) is not an understanding imposed on the

[52] Ibid., 104. Emphasis added.
[53] Robert Alter, *The Art of Biblical Narrative* (New York: Basic Books, 1981), 47-48.
[54] Campbell warned that "two trends particularly militate against the successful application of form criticism. One is the security given by focus on detail; outreach to the whole is dangerous. The other is the difficulty of putting persuasive words on the perceptions that underlie an intuitive conviction." Campbell, "Preparatory Issues in Approaching Biblical Texts," 10-11.
[55] Barton, *Reading the Old Testament: Method in Biblical Study*, 6.
[56] Hayes and Holladay, *Biblical Exegesis: A Beginner's Handbook*, 80-81.
[57] Melugin, "Recent Form Criticism Revisited in an Age of Reader Response," 46.

text; it is a decision that emerges out of the understanding of the text. Second, the question of the shape and structure of the text is to be asked of the passage in the present biblical text; it is not asked of some remote, uncertain original form putatively assumed from the past."[58]

In 1968 Muilenburg commented on these same concerns in his SBL presidential address. He maintained that form criticism suffered due to its emphasis on what was common to all the representatives of a genre and that "unique features of the particular pericope [were, *added by ET*] all but lost to view."[59] Melugin agreed. He stated that "analysis of typicalities in the form and usage of language cannot adequately be formulated without also taking into account the unique features of individual texts."[60] Concern for the individual nature of the text combined with concern for its shape or structure must be paramount to the modern form critic.[61] Campbell subscribes to a rather postmodern definition of form criticism stating that "whatever is regarded as an individual text, whether shorter or longer, needs to be treated as a whole, and each individual whole will be affected by the influence of the typical."[62] For this purpose we will now turn to an examination of narrative criticism.

2. Narrative Criticism

In the field of biblical studies narrative criticism[63] is still in its infancy (or at least its early adulthood).[64] As mentioned in the last section, Muilenburg's

---

[58] Campbell, "Form Criticism's Future," 24. I follow Campbell in this respect. The object of this thesis is not to date these conversations, reflect on the history of Israel, Israel's religious institutions or how these conversations might have affected said religious institutions. Since diachronic source criticism is not advantageous in this study the synchronic method will be applied as the texts are delineated and studied. The exercise here is to take the divine conversations (as they will be defined) and address the relationship described within the text between humanity and the Divine.

[59] James Muilenburg, "Form Criticism and Beyond," *JBL* 88 (1969): 5.

[60] Melugin, "Recent Form Criticism Revisited in an Age of Reader Response," 48.

[61] Campbell, "Form Criticism's Future," 16.

[62] Ibid., 23.

[63] To clarify, in older studies the terms "narrative criticism" and "literary criticism" are sometimes interchangeable. In Hebrew Bible studies "literary criticism" is most often recognized as the antiquated term for "source criticism." For the purposes of this thesis "literary criticism" and/or "narrative criticism" will encompass the study of the literary structure of a passage as defined by current narrative critics. The term "source criticism" will be substituted for "literary criticism" (outside of direct quotes) when referring to Wellhausen's groundbreaking work and with that of his subsequent followers. If, at any time, there is possible confusion a footnote will be listed with clarification.

[64] "Infancy" as in approximately twenty years compared with other biblical scholarship traditions. See Mark Allan Powell, *What Is Narrative Criticism? A New Approach to*

presentation paved the way for literary approaches such as structuralism[65] and rhetorical analysis.[66] By the mid 1970s the influence of the philosophically based study of structuralism dominated many discussions of biblical passages.[67] However, there were problems with the discipline. The specialized vocabulary and philosophical orientation hampered its application by a wide audience of interpreters.[68]

In his introduction to *The Art of Biblical Narrative* Alter recalls his initiation into the study of Bible as literature. He states, "The earliest idea for this project began with an invitation in 1971 from the Department of Religion at Stanford University to give an informal colloquium on the literary study of the Bible."[69] Alter records that the session was more successful than anticipated; however, he filed his notes away and did not return to them. Four years later he resurrected the lecture notes for the editors of *Commentary*, turning them into an article on the need for a literary approach to the Bible.[70] Five additional articles followed in quick succession most of which became the basis for his seminal book, mentioned above, published in 1981. Alter succeeded where structuralism failed. By shifting the interest from structuralism to a more formalistic analysis Alter appealed to a wider audience and proved the value of literary criticism.[71] Formalism, especially American formalism, focuses on examining the main elements of plot, structure, character and themes[72]

---

the Bible (London: SPCK, 1993), 1.; David M. Gunn and Danna Nolan Fewell, *Narrative in the Hebrew Bible*, Oxford Bible Series (Oxford: Oxford University Press, 1993), 9-11.

[65] Structuralism developed primarily in France during the 1950s and 1960s. The object of structural criticism is to analyze literature from the standpoint of modern linguistic theory. The writings of Levi-Strauss, Barthes and Ricoeur were particularly significant. See Powell, *What Is Narrative Criticism? A New Approach to the Bible*, 12-14.

[66] Rhetorical criticism focuses on the means through which a work achieves a particular effect on its reader. See ibid., 14-18.

[67] Paul R. House, "The Rise and Current Status of Literary Criticism of the Old Testament," in *Beyond Form Criticism: Essays in Old Testament Literary Criticism*, ed. Paul R. House (Winona Lake, Ind.: Eisenbrauns, 1992), 4.

[68] For a detailed analysis and explanation of terms see Richard Jacobson, "The Structuralists and the Bible," *Int* 28 (1974): 146-64.

[69] Alter, *The Art of Biblical Narrative*, x-xi.

[70] Robert Alter, "In the Community: A Literary Approach to the Bible," *Commentary* 60, (1975) page 5.

[71] House suggests that Alter produced a scholarly book that gained a measure of popular success. He maintains that the influence of the book for the growth of the literary methods of biblical interpretation 'can hardly be overestimated.' House, "The Rise and Current Status of Literary Criticism of the Old Testament," 15-16.

[72] Ibid., 12.

within the narratives which allowed Old Testament critics the opportunity to develop theories on how the narratives worked together.[73]

Narrative criticism emerged in response to the historical and structural investigations that had been 'normative' for more than a century.[74] While many scholars believed they now knew more about the Hebrew Bible's composition than ever before, not all considered these results to be an advancement in understanding or application.[75] The influences of inter-disciplinary studies led many to conclude that "the standard means of biblical analysis had almost run its course."[76] Because the Bible's literary qualities had not been a typical subject for investigation,[77] narrative criticism was able to open the door to a new approach to scripture. The focus now became the connecting threads that held the text together instead of the dissected blocks that supposedly created it.

---

[73] See Frye's book *The Great Code: The Bible and Literature* which traces major themes and archetypes through the whole Bible. Frye concludes that any literary analysis of the Bible must include a unified reading of the text. He notes that "those who do succeed in reading the Bible from beginning to end will discover that at least it has a beginning and an end, and some traces of a total structure." Northrop Frye, *The Great Code: The Bible and Literature* (New York: Harcourt Brace Jovanovich, 1982), xiii.

While Alter had been working primarily in the Hebrew Bible, scholars of the New Testament were also discovering the advantages of narrative criticism. Mark Powell reports that, in 1977 at Carthage College, professor David Rhoads, a Bible scholar, invited a colleague from the English department to instruct students how to read one of the Gospels the way one would read a short story. Rhoads was impressed by the presentation and in 1982 he and Don Michie, the English professor, published *Mark As Story* which demonstrated a literary approach to New Testament studies. According to Powell it is Rhoads who decided to call the new approach "narrative criticism." Powell, *What Is Narrative Criticism? A New Approach to the Bible*, 6.

Rhoads' book was followed the next year by two other works on the New Testament that consciously followed this approach. They were R. Alan Culpepper's *Anatomy of the Fourth Gospel: A Study in Literary Design* and Jack Dean Kingsbury's *The Christology of Mark's Gospel*. Completing the initial comprehensive literary treatment of the New Testament's five narrative books were Kingsbury's *Matthew as Story* and Robert C. Tannehill's *The Narrative Unity of Luke-Acts: A Literary Interpretation*.

Rhoads' original paper "Narrative Criticism and the Gospel of Mark" was delivered during the 10th Markan Seminar at SBL in 1980. Others involved in the seminar were Norman Perrin and Werner Kelber as chairs, Thomas Boomershine, Joanna Dewey, Robert Fowler, Norman Petersen, Robert Tannehill and Mary Ann Tolbert. David M. Rhoads, "Narrative Criticism and the Gospel of Mark," *JAAR* 50 (1982) page 5.

[74] Paul R. House, *Beyond Form Criticism: Essays in Old Testament Literary Criticism*, Sources for Biblical and Theological Study 2 (Winona Lake, Ind.: Eisenbrauns, 1992), 6.

[75] Ibid., 7.

[76] Ibid., 3. Scholars began to see that source criticism, while dividing texts, had a tendency to atomize it as well. These methodologies obscure the unity of texts. The overemphasis of historical detail often costs readers a proper understanding of plot, theme and character.

[77] Powell, *What Is Narrative Criticism? A New Approach to the Bible*, 1.

Narrative criticism was not created *ex nihlo*, however. It is based on ideas that have been used in the study of other forms of literature. Among biblical scholars it is well established that the stories of the Pentateuch, and even through 2 Kings, are a literary work of art which is why Fokkelman states that "these stories can be readily analyzed as works for fiction."[78] For these scholars, however, what had to be accomplished first was to define the method of analysis.

Within the study of literature, narrative criticism is primarily concerned with any work that tells a story.[79] In the broadest sense of the field, narrative criticism is the study of events, "whether actual or fanciful, reported in any way for any reason."[80] Elements within, but sometimes distinguished from narrative, may be exposition and dialogue "though any one or two of these may be set within the other. In this view, narrative is understood as that which advances action, whereas exposition informs the reader of what has already occurred as background to that action."[81] Contemporary scholarship is, therefore, most engaged with the question of the characteristic elements of narrative. "The tendency among scholars is to define narrative as the relating of an event in which there is a buildup (*desis*) and a release (*lysis*) of tension, or, to define it as a plot with a beginning, a middle, and an end."[82]

With regards to form criticism, narrative is determined by style, i.e., "the verbal forms of the sentences and their connectedness throughout a text – as distinguished from those kinds of texts that either describe permanent conditions or define attitudes or express commands, prohibitions, admonitions, exhortations, and even laws and prophetic announcements in which narrative style is also used."[83] Bar-Efret argues that the biblical world, as presented in the scriptures, is brought to life purely by the power of the words chosen to create it. He states:

> its entire existence rests upon language. Since the way language is used determines the nature of the world of the narrative, including that of the characters populating it, and since it is upon the linguistic design that all the meanings embodied in the narrative are dependent, it is necessary to examine the way in which the writers have used their

---

[78] J. P. Fokkelman, *Narrative Art in Genesis: Specimens of Stylistic and Structural Analysis* (Assen: Van Gorcum, 1975), 6-7.

[79] Powell, *What Is Narrative Criticism? A New Approach to the Bible*, 23.

[80] Soulen, *Handbook of Biblical Criticism*, 110.

[81] Ibid., 110-11.

[82] Ibid., 111.

[83] George W. Coats, *Exodus 1-18*, FOTL 2A (Grand Rapids, Mich.: Eerdmans, 1999), 165.

medium and how they have exploited the various linguistic possibilities in each case. In other words, we must investigate the style of the
narrative.[84]

In general, however, narrative criticism is too broad a term. It becomes
necessary to find a way to narrow the focus.

Powell states that objective types of criticism should be viewed as the
literary product of "a self-sufficient world in itself. The work must be
analyzed according to intrinsic criteria, such as the interrelationship of
its component elements."[85] The passages to be examined in this thesis
encompass moments when the Divine and humankind interact on a very
personal level. Outside the biblical narrative setting these events would
be considered fantastic. Yet within scriptural literature the Deity and
humankind speak "face to face," internal dialogue becomes audible,
divine visitations by angels or messengers of the Deity are common
occurrences and humankind is known by name to its otherwise distant
creator. "Narrative criticism is not interested in questioning the accuracy
of such reports or in determining what historical occurrences might have
inspired the tales."[86] Instead, it allows the scholar to make inquiries into
a world that exists, fundamentally, within the language.[87] "Consequently,
it is appropriate to pay attention to even the minutest details of biblical
narratives and to their linguistic features."[88] Narrative criticism then
"takes these details and looks for elements within a story that show a
logical progression of cause and effect."[89]

[84] Shimon Bar-Efrat, *Narrative Art in the Bible*, 2nd ed. (Sheffield: Almond, 1989), 197-98.
[85] Powell, *What Is Narrative Criticism? A New Approach to the Bible*, 11. Powell is distilling M.H. Abram's 1958 analysis of poetic literary theory which is defined by four basic types of criticism. The types are defined as: (1) Mimetic: theory involving imitation in literature from influences surrounding the work. (2) Pragmatic: theory which views literature as a means to an end and judges its success at achieving said aim. (3) Expressive: theory in which the author not only creates the work but also regulates the criteria by which it is judged. And (4) Objective: theory which literature is judged not through external elements but 'solely by criteria intrinsic to its own mode of being.' M. H. Abrams, *The Mirror and the Lamp: Romantic Theory and the Critical Tradition* (New York: Norton, 1958), 8-29.
[86] Mark Allan Powell, "Literary and Structuralist/Postmodernist Approaches Methods," in *Methods of Biblical Interpretation*, ed. John H. Hayes (Nashville, Tenn.: Abingdon, 2004), 171.
[87] Fokkelman, *Narrative Art in Genesis: Specimens of Stylistic and Structural Analysis*, 6.
[88] Bar-Efrat, *Narrative Art in the Bible*, 199.
[89] Powell, *What Is Narrative Criticism? A New Approach to the Bible*, 42.

Narrative content is often defined as having two main characteristics: story and discourse.[90] "A story consists of such elements as events, characters, and settings, and the interaction of these elements comprises what we call the plot. Discourse refers to the rhetoric of the narrative, how the story is told."[91] Narrative criticism also seeks order within the composition of the narrative content. The emphasis, however, is not on exact replication of language but on concepts or allusions created by the language.[92] Bar-Efrat states that:

> In every narrative it is possible to discern three strata: 1. the stratum of language — the words and sentences of which the narrative is composed; 2. the stratum of what is represented by those words, namely the 'world' described in the narrative: the characters, event and settings; 3. the stratum of meanings, that is the concepts, views and values embodied in the narrative, which are expressed principally through the speech and actions of the characters, their fate and the general course of events.[93]

A conceptual approach to narrative criticism opens the scholar up to comparative passages. The sometimes rigid requirements developed under form criticism are relaxed somewhat to allow "similar yet different" to be included as part of the analysis. "As a result, narrative critics find there is a wealth of information already available on this important aspect of literary study."[94] Narrative criticism, therefore, interprets a text from the point of view of an 'implied author.'[95] An "implied author," invokes

---

[90] Powell, "Literary and Structuralist/Postmodernist Approaches Methods," 171. Also see Powell, *What Is Narrative Criticism? A New Approach to the Bible*, 23-34.

[91] Powell, *What Is Narrative Criticism? A New Approach to the Bible*, 23. Later Powell gives definitions for event, character, and setting: "events" are incidents or happenings that occur within a story; "characters" are the actors in the story, and "settings" are the spatial, temporal, and social locations for the events. Powell compares story elements with basic grammatical components of English sentences. "Events correspond roughly to verbs, for in them the story's action is expressed. Characters are like nouns, for they perform these actions or, perhaps, are acted upon. Character traits may be likened to adjectives since they describe the characters involved in the action. And settings? Settings are the adverbs of literary structure: they designate when, where, and how the action occurs." Ibid., 69.

[92] "Recognition of associations depends upon the degree to which the reader is familiar with the whole of the biblical text, the extent to which the parallels are thought to be explicit, and the willingness of the reader to consider certain narratives in conjunction with others." Gunn and Fewell, *Narrative in the Hebrew Bible*, 163.

[93] Bar-Efrat, *Narrative Art in the Bible*, 197.

[94] For an expanded discussion on narrative patterns categories found in biblical narrative see Powell, *What Is Narrative Criticism? A New Approach to the Bible*, 32-34.

[95] Narrative criticism, with the goal to determine the story's effect on the reader develops theories regarding a text's "implied reader" as well as its "implied author." Kingsbury

"the perspective from which the work appears to have been written, a perspective that must be reconstructed by readers on the basis of what they find in the narrative."[96]

To review, form criticism gives biblical scholarship structure through Gunkel's literary types of genre and form as well as Steck's foundational language elements. Conceptually, narrative criticism allows the scholar to examine an extraordinary event as an occurrence that is accepted as normative and rational within the linguistic world in which it exists. It also encourages the comparative study of narrative through conceptual and allusional links which, in turn, gives flexibility to form criticism's more rigid analysis. Mayfield stated that "it is not enough to lay out a tidy structure or to place each oracle or literary unit within its proper literary setting. The task of the interpreter, in the end, is to interpret, to provide meaning for an ancient text, to give clues as to its function and purpose."[97]

This thesis will attempt to gather disparate scriptures that at first may not seem to be connected. Utilizing the strengths of form and narrative criticism mentioned above it will be shown that these passages can be analyzed together. Moreover, in combination they not only define the formula of Divine/human relational dialogue within the biblical narrative but they also shed light on the Divine/human relationship. To that end, I invoke James Muilenburg's call to arms, "What I am interested in, above all, is in understanding the nature of Hebrew literary composition, in exhibiting the structural patterns that are employed for the fashioning of a literary unit, whether in poetry or in prose, and in discerning the many and various devices by which the predications are formulated and ordered into a unified whole."[98]

---

describes the implied reader as the "imaginary person whom the intention of the text is to be thought of as always reaching its fulfillment." Jack Dean Kingsbury, *Matthew as Story* (Philadelphia, Pa.: Fortress, 1986), 38. Focus on the implied reader often leads to more faith oriented investigation. "Whereas historical critics may be expected to suspend faith commitments temporarily in order to interpret texts from the perspective of objective, disinterested historians, narrative critics may be expected to adopt faith commitments temporarily in order to determine how texts are expected to affect their implied readers." Also see Powell, *What Is Narrative Criticism? A New Approach to the Bible*, 11-21. and Fokkelman, *Narrative Art in Genesis: Specimens of Stylistic and Structural Analysis*, 1-8.

[96] Powell, "Literary and Structuralist/Postmodernist Approaches Methods," 169.

[97] Tyler D. Mayfield, *Literary Structure and Setting in Ezekiel* (Tübingen: Mohr Siebeck, 2010), 16.

[98] Muilenburg, "Form Criticism and Beyond," 8.

C. Definitions

1. Dialogue vs. Conversation

From a biblical studies narrative analytical point of view the definition of *conversation* is a narrow formula (Gesprächs-) with elements of a vocative call to attention and the response constructed with the particle *hinnēh* plus a suffix.[99] *Speech* (Rede) is "a general term describing any oral communication enacted by one of the principals of a pericope."[100] Speech acts, however, "are simply things people do through language — for example, apologizing, complaining, instructing, agreeing and warning."[101] The term *dialogue*, as used in biblical studies, is more often employed in referring to structure instead of genre. It is defined as "a combination of speeches, each as in response to the other, with the pattern of response significant for special types of dialogue."[102] These structured speeches and types of dialogue are often interpreted intertextually through the use of structural repetition where the pattern of similarity is "based on the recurrence of at least one element — a sound, semantic feature, word, situation, theme, generic quality — that serves to link together the components of the pattern."[103] If dialogue is treated as an examination of separate speeches, intertextually compared or not, then the relational interaction of the dialogue can be lost.

In other avenues of biblical scholarship the Deity is often viewed as a divine patron of a household, clan, tribe and/or nation.[104] This scholarship examines the Divine/human relationship in terms of distinct levels of social organization and rarely as personal contacts. In the ancient Near East "the divine-human relationship may be described as mutually beneficial, for human beings [but, *added by ET*] it is one that is potentially hazardous and that requires caution"[105] due to the fact that these ancient gods were often as unpredictable as the human beings they oversaw. This concept of an anthropomorphic Deity still dominates "even though the inadequacy of this 'humanizing' of God is generally admitted."[106] Envisioning the

---

[99] Coats, *Genesis*, 320. For example: Gen 22:1; 1 Sam 22:12; Isaiah 58:9.
[100] Ibid., 320.
[101] David Nunan, *Introducing Discourse Analysis* (London: Penguin, 1993), 65.
[102] Coats, *Genesis*, 317.
[103] Meir Sternberg, *The Poetics of Biblical Narrative* (Bloomington, Ind.: Indiana University, 1987), 367.
[104] Joel S. Burnett, *Where Is God? Divine Absence in the Hebrew Bible* (Minneapolis, Minn.: Fortress, 2010), 25.
[105] Ibid., 11.
[106] Marjo C.A. Korpel and Johannes C. de Moor, *The Silent God* (Leiden: Brill, 2011), 60.

Divine as anthropomorphic does have the advantage of creating tension between Deity and human. "Being anthropomorphic, deities have interests of their own and thus want something in return from their human beneficiaries. Sometimes they want a great deal in return."[107] Wardhaugh, somewhat humorously, warns "involvement in conversation therefore requires the two (or various) parties to be conscious of each other's needs, particularly the need not to be offended."[108] Anthropomorphism has another advantage in that people of the ancient world lived with the expectation that their deities would speak and reply to prayers.[109]

Divine distance, or impediment analysis, seeks to break the bonds of dialogue to show that the Deity's absence or non-responsiveness is not simply a problem of unfulfilled expectation and interaction; it "expresses a crisis in the divine-human relationship."[110] To this end, much biblical scholarship attributes personal interaction with the Deity to only a few noteworthy individuals.[111] This belief is not limited to Israel:

> Stelae testify to the fact that ordinary people did not dare to address the deity directly themselves. Next to 'buffers' like stelae or images, they made use of professional intermediaries, such as priests, prophets, astrologers, diviners, magicians, spiritualistic mediums, or learned scribes. According to the Hebrew Bible the number of legitimate intermediaries between God and man was much smaller, though there is reason to suspect that in pre-exilic times more religious officials may have worked in Israelite sanctuaries too.[112]

Once an intermediary has been engaged it then becomes their duty to relay the divine message to the people or individual. Along similar lines,

---

[107] Burnett, *Where Is God? Divine Absence in the Hebrew Bible*, 10.

[108] Ronald Wardhaugh, *How Conversation Works* (Oxford: Basil Blackwell, 1985), 2.

[109] Korpel and de Moor, *The Silent God*, 77.

[110] Burnett, *Where Is God? Divine Absence in the Hebrew Bible*, 4. Wyatt describes a Deity's absence as "the most awful experience of exile." N. Wyatt, "The Meaning of El Roi and the Mythological Dimension in Genesis 16," *SJOT* 8 (1994): 150.

[111] Terrien points out that the stress is "put on the importance of outstanding moments of religious illumination or 'epiphany' within the lives of chieftains, poets, musicians, and other tribal leaders. Even when revelation is viewed as history, or rather when history is seen as the locus of revelation, the interpretation of events as media of divine self-disclosure depends upon the consciousness, reflection, and formulation of some gifted individuals." Samuel Terrien, *The Elusive Presence: Toward a New Biblical Theology*, Religious Perspectives 26 (New York: Harper and Row, 1978), 65. Korpel follows stating, "Direct communication between God and certain privileged people is confined mainly to descriptions of the early history of Israel. God addresses the first human beings directly in the Garden of Eden. He visits the patriarchs of Israel and engages in conversations with them." Korpel and de Moor, *The Silent God*, 111.

[112] Korpel and de Moor, *The Silent God*, 111.

societal boundary scholarship models the Divine/human relationship along the "servant-master" or patronage relationship lines.[113] The "superior to inferior" relationship paradigm then becomes the archetype for Divine/human relationships in ancient Israel and the Hebrew Bible.

In contrast to these rather engrained views on the Divine/human relationship, the scriptures also portray "a God who freely chooses relationships with humankind, a God whom human beings are free to seek, a God who responds."[114] While it is true that there are recorded incidences of human beings who do not address the Deity directly, it is also true that dialogue is a social and therefore public activity that requires the participants to exhibit trust in one another.[115] Dialogue is then a cooperative endeavor where communication between the Deity and human provides a medium for social interaction.

In order to facilitate the exchange of ideas as well as emotions, speeches, as defined by biblical scholarship, must be amalgamated into one dialogue. This then constructs a constantly created and recreated reality "which does not objectively exist beyond the consciousness of its individual [participants, *added by ET*]."[116] In cultural anthropology's discourse and conversation analysis, the term *dialogue* carries the connotation of all forms of communication, i.e., "to communicate in any of the ways that humans are capable of expressing meaning and for someone else to react to that communication."[117] Conversation analysis, however, aims "to describe, analyze and understand *talk* as a basic and constitutive feature of human social life."[118] In this form of analysis it becomes important to understand that positioning within dialogue "is based not only on what is said, but on the nuances of the words, the emotional and physical situation, and the reaction of the other participants in the

---

[113] Burnett states, "Knowing God in the Hebrew Bible entails further structural aspects of Israelite society that flowed from this emphasis on male superior-inferior relationships" and gives the examples of Exod 32:13; Num 14:24; Exod 14:24; Deut 34:5; Josh 24:29; Judg 2:8; 1 Kings 8:66, etc. to back up his claim. Burnett, *Where Is God? Divine Absence in the Hebrew Bible*, 15.

[114] Ibid., 178.

[115] Wardhaugh, *How Conversation Works*, 5.

[116] Nigel Rapport and Joanna Overing, *Social and Cultural Anthropology: The Key Concepts*, 2nd ed. (London: Routledge, 2007), 101-02.

[117] Victor H. Matthews, *More Than Meets the Ear: Discovering the Hidden Contexts of Old Testament Conversations* (Grand Rapids, Mich.: Eerdmans, 2008), 1.

[118] Jack Sidnell, *Conversation Analysis: An Introduction* (Chichester, West Sussex: Wiley-Blackwell, 2010), 1. Emphasis not original. In most of these cases it is the verbal form of communication that takes precedence.

conversation."[119] Even if the vision of scholarship defines Israel's special relationship to the Deity as a national event[120] that relationship still begins on the level of the individual or household.[121]

2. Discourse/Conversation Analysis

In cultural anthropology the term 'discourse' is "understood to mean ways of speaking which are commonly practiced and specifically situated in a social environment."[122] Scholars of discourse analysis are interested in the largest possible picture created by conversation. Nunan states that "discourse brings together language, the individuals producing the language, and the context within which the language is used." He defines discourse specifically as "the interpretation of the communicative event in context."[123] The methods associated with discourse analysis are very similar to that of form and narrative analysis within biblical studies, i.e., discourse analysis is described as requiring "a thorough study of the use of language forms, syntax, word order, and the context in which words are used in embedded dialogue or the surrounding narrative. It includes meanings related to the physical world, social understandings, as well as some knowledge of the time and place in which the statements are made."[124] This wide-swath approach, however, brings little to the table in the way of a new approach to biblical studies.

When examining Divine/human relational dialogue, conversation analysis is a more focused approach than discourse analysis. The difference stems, in part, "from the fact that [conversation analysis, *added by ET*] was developed within a sociological rather than linguistic tradition."[125]

---

[119] Matthews, *More Than Meets the Ear: Discovering the Hidden Contexts of Old Testament Conversations*, 53. Matthews later explains, "Positioning theory attempts to replace the fairly rigid social category of 'role' with the more flexible designation of 'position.' It recognizes the existence of the ever-changing kaleidoscope of possible positions within the social realm and in space." Ibid., 104.

[120] Both socially and politically.

[121] Burnett, *Where Is God? Divine Absence in the Hebrew Bible*, 13.

[122] Rapport and Overing, *Social and Cultural Anthropology: The Key Concepts*, 134.

[123] Nunan, *Introducing Discourse Analysis*, 6-7. Nunan defines context as referring to "to the situation giving rise to the discourse, and within which the discourse is embedded. There are two different types of context. The first of these is the linguistic context — the language that surrounds or accompanies the piece of discourse under analysis. The second is the non-linguistic or experiential context within which the discourse takes place." Ibid., 7-8.

[124] Matthews, *More Than Meets the Ear: Discovering the Hidden Contexts of Old Testament Conversations*, 18-19.

[125] Nunan, *Introducing Discourse Analysis*, 84.

For the cultural anthropologist conversation is defined as a naturally occurring interaction between two or more individuals. The analysis of these exchanges "aims to identify the principles enabling individuals to negotiate and exchange meanings."[126] Ordinary conversations, the kind we engage in on a daily basis, are the backbone of these studies.[127]

Moerman writes, "We all know that all talk is thoroughly and multifariously embedded in the historical, cultural, social, biographical, context of its occurrence. We make use of this in constructing and interpreting the sense, import, and meaning of every bit of talk we encounter."[128] The purpose of this thesis, however, is not to review the large contextual meaning of dialogue but to examine the dialogue itself to see what, if anything, can be gained regarding our knowledge of the Divine/human relationship through verbal dialogue. Dennis explains, "Each encounter with God is unique. Each leaves its own mark upon the one whom God meets."[129] If this is true then as we take a closer look at the individual encounters we will be able to build a better understanding of Divine/human relationship.

To review, these are the analytical definitions as they will be used in this thesis:

Dialogue or Conversation, as defined using cultural anthropology guidelines, is a verbal communication between two or more individuals with interaction carried out for social purposes rather than as an exchange of goods and services.[130] For ease of expression, the terms

---

[126] Ibid., 118. Johnstone argues that everything people say is the result of choice and therefore infuses meaningful exchange. Barbara Johnstone, *Discourse Analysis*, 2nd ed. (Malden, Mass.: Blackwell, 2008), 229.

[127] Conversation in scripture, according to Matthews, is "driven by the desire to draw the audience into a world that goes beyond their ordinary existence while at the same time playing off of ordinary events and expectations." Matthews, *More Than Meets the Ear: Discovering the Hidden Contexts of Old Testament Conversations*, 65. Conversation studies can also include spontaneously dialogue and the analysis of staged performances. See Matthews (165-166). Nunan maintains that, "ethnomethodologists insist that data should be derived from naturally occurring instances of everyday interaction. In particular, they reject the use of data obtained through formal experiments, interviews and other forms of elicitation." Nunan, *Introducing Discourse Analysis*, 85.

[128] Michael Moerman, *Talking Culture: Ethnography and Conversation Analysis* (Philadelphia, Pa.: University of Pennsylvania Press, 1988), 8.

[129] Trevor Dennis, *Sarah Laughed* (Nashville, Tenn.: Abingdon, 1994), 71.

[130] Here I follow Nunan. Nunan, *Introducing Discourse Analysis*, 118. To clarify, I will include examples of interior monologue as verbal communications which, according to Cotter, while rare are most often defined as "a record of what is going on in the

dialogue and *conversation* will be used interchangeably. Other forms of communication, those termed *non-verbal*, or narrative description elements will be considered where they play a definitive role within the verbal exchange.

Narrative or Narrative Elements are "plot, story, point of view, and character [descriptions... *added by ET*] These compositional techniques are integrated into the overall organizational structure of the narrative that the narrator supplies."[131]

Direct Discourse, also known as *speech* is when the narrator or author inserts a character's utterances into a narrative. This "usually occurs as part of a dialogue between two characters but occasionally appears as a monologue."[132] While technically, the biblical narrator is relating these non-live dialogues, instances of direct discourse will be treated as defined by dialogue and conversation above.

Embedded Dialogue, for biblical studies purposes, this is another term for Direct Discourse.

---

mind of the character[... *added by ET*] Whether or not a particular instance of reported speech is intended to reflect interior monologue, however, can require a judgment on the part of a translator. Since the Hebrew probably says simply 'he said' or 'she said,' the translator may have to decide from the context whether the character is speaking aloud." David W. Cotter, *Genesis*, Berit Olam (Collegeville, Minn.: Liturgical Press, 2003), xxxiii. Matthews explains, "In Biblical Hebrew narrative the verb *'mr* is used to signal direct speech when it is in its conjugated form, while when it appears in its infinitive form, *lē'mōr*, it signals 'free direct discourse' such as 'internal monologues or thoughts.'" Matthews, *More Than Meets the Ear: Discovering the Hidden Contexts of Old Testament Conversations*, 24. Alter argues, "It is not easy to determine in each instance why thought should be reported as speech. One is tempted to conclude that the biblical writers did not distinguish sharply between the two in their assumptions about how the mind relates to reality. Perhaps, with their strong sense of the primacy of language in the created order of things, they tended to feel that thought was not fully itself until it was articulate das speech. In any case, the repeated translation of thought into speech allows for a certain clarifying stylization, a dramatic vividness and symmetry of effect." Alter, *The Art of Biblical Narrative*, 68. Berlin adds that treating inner speech as direct speech, "besides adding to the scenic nature of the narrative, is the most dramatic way of conveying the characters' internal psychological and ideological points of view." Adele Berlin, *Poetics and Interpretation of Biblical Narrative*, BLS 9 (Sheffield: Almond Press, 1983), 64. The instances of internal monologue occurring within the examined texts will be addressed as direct speech where the internal utterance has a verbal corollary.

[131] Richard G. Bowman, "Narrative Criticism: Human Purpose in Conflict with Divine Presence," in *Judges and Method: New Approaches in Biblcial Studies*, ed. Gale A. Yee (Minneapolis, Minn: Fortress, 2007), 22.

[132] Ibid., 23.

Reported Dialogue is defined as instances where, within the confines of a conversation, one of the participants reiterates a previous dialogue. In conversation analysis this encapsulated dialogue would be analyzed separately from the overarching dialogue that contained it.

3. Initiation of Dialogue

Berlin contends that character is shown through words of an individual's speeches.[133] She states, "Biblical narrative makes extensive use of the speech and actions of characters to further the plot and to create characterization."[134] This is not only true for the human characters in scripture but also for the Divine and for our understanding of the kind of Deity encountered in the scriptures.[135] However, for a relationship to exist there must be communication in some form. The form we are exploring is dialogue.

In what will be examined here, we will see that the beginning of a dialogue with the Divine is often remarkable for its unremarkableness.[136] To begin a conversation, however, does require an interruption to something, even when that something is "only silence."[137] Often the opening verbal statement of dialogue suggests a preexisting relationship of some kind and "the possibility of mutual recognition."[138] Wardhaugh suggests that, "beginnings of conversations often involve a process of mutual 'feeling out'"[139] and yet the stress of opening a dialogue also involves "the organization of what gets talked about in the conversation and, where there are multiple topics to be broached, the order in which they get talked about."[140] From that point the process by which the dialogue develops is divided, not always equally, between the speakers.

---

[133] As opposed to actions which are considered narrator driven commentary.

[134] Berlin, *Poetics and Interpretation of Biblical Narrative*, 38.

[135] Terence E. Fretheim, *The Suffering of God: An Old Testament Perspective* (Philadelphia, Pa.: Fortress, 1984), 24.

[136] Sidnell asks the simple question, "How do conversations get started?" and answers that, for the most part, "the procedures that lie behind this accomplishment are hidden from view by their complete ordinariness; they are so much a part of us that we hardly notice them." Sidnell, *Conversation Analysis: An Introduction*, 197.

[137] Wardhaugh, *How Conversation Works*, 116. There are instances in the passages to be discussed where narrative elements do proceed and have some impact on the first verbal utterance. These will be addressed within the particular dialogue analysis.

[138] Sidnell, *Conversation Analysis: An Introduction*, 197.

[139] Wardhaugh, *How Conversation Works*, 120.

[140] Sidnell, *Conversation Analysis: An Introduction*, 199.

This, in conversation analysis, is called turn-taking.[141] Turn-taking influences the dialogue elements which build the conversation into the passages we will be investigating.

4. Dialogue Elements

For the purposes of this thesis dialogue has been defined as the verbal exchange between two or more individuals. In our case one of the participants is divine in nature.[142] These conversations will be studied "as normal happenings of daily existence, although they always succeed in preserving, by the use of some rhetorical or semantic device, the mystery of divine transcendence."[143] Using conversation analysis the dialogue becomes free to present an exchange suggestive of a "comfortable interaction, not dependent on social protocol such as hospitality, but merely the free exchange of information that occurs when no threat of danger is detected."[144]

Linguistically, a conversation consists of three main elements: initiation, response and evaluation with the final two steps often repeated until the termination of the exchange.[145] Within this structure, turn-taking provides coherence. Sidnell argues that turn-taking is "perhaps, the most fundamental feature of conversation[... *added by ET*] turns and turn-taking provide the underlying framework of conversation[... *added by ET*] they are distributed within an 'economy' of opportunities to speak."[146] Between dialogue participants, turn-taking allows for the achievement of

---

[141] Nunan, *Introducing Discourse Analysis*, 126.
[142] To clarify, we are not examining these conversations as theophanies or epiphanic visitations. Terrien states, "A 'theophany' insists on the visibility of the natural phenomena which accompany the divine appearances, but this visibility is subordinated to their *hieroi logoi*, the sacred words of revelation and command. A 'theophany' also concerns an individual, but this individual is a mediator, like Moses or Elijah. The theophanic intervention, as reenacted or proleptically acted in the cultus, addresses itself to a community at worship." He defines epiphanic events as "the sudden manifestation of a divine power or even a visual appearance of a deity... restricted to special individuals." Terrien, *The Elusive Presence: Toward a New Biblical Theology*, 70, 90n45.
[143] Ibid., 70.
[144] Matthews, *More Than Meets the Ear: Discovering the Hidden Contexts of Old Testament Conversations*, 7. A close examination of roles within society is labeled 'Positioning theory.' This approach "replaces the fairly rigid social category of 'roles' with the more flexible designation of 'position.' It recognizes the existence of the ever-changing range of possible positions within the social realm and in space." Ibid., 167-68.
[145] Nunan, *Introducing Discourse Analysis*, 36.
[146] Sidnell, *Conversation Analysis: An Introduction*, 36.

mutual understanding as they "negotiate meaning to ensure that they are being understood correctly, and that they are correctly interpreting the utterances of the other participants."[147] Turn-taking participants also differentiate themselves from each other and afford the listener/reader the opportunity to discover similarities and contrasts between the parties.[148] While turn-taking is an essential building block of conversation analysis it is not simply a "traffic management system."[149] The reader must be able to "interpret the sentences in relation to one another."[150]

In conversation analysis much of the turn-taking breakdown is rebuilt into paired utterances labeled "adjacency pairs", i.e., "question and answer, request and granting, offer and acceptance, greeting and greeting, complaint and remedy."[151] Questions establish a relationship between the dialogue partners.[152] They create a "slot" where an answer is expected and should be relevant.[153] In the instance where answers do not follow questions, however, "the conditional relevance that a question establishes ensures that participants will inspect any talk that follows a question to see if and how it answers that question. In other words, the relationship between paired utterance types such as question and answer is a norm to which participants themselves orient in finding and constructing orderly sequences of talk."[154] Adjacency pairs, therefore, compare and contrast participants and allow for the development and/or expansion of a relationship. These interactions within conversation can also be utilized to categorize individual identity.

One of the ways in which individual identity is established within dialogue is with the use of address.[155] Johnstone asserts that "every time

---

[147] Nunan, *Introducing Discourse Analysis*, 97.
[148] Wardhaugh, *How Conversation Works*, 18.
[149] Sidnell, *Conversation Analysis: An Introduction*, 56.
[150] Nunan, *Introducing Discourse Analysis*, 3.
[151] Sidnell, *Conversation Analysis: An Introduction*, 63-64. Also see Nunan, *Introducing Discourse Analysis*, 115.
[152] "Questions can also be seen to derive some of their effectiveness from being recipient-designed, which is to say they display a special attention to the details of the recipient's situation." Sidnell, *Conversation Analysis: An Introduction*, 198.
[153] Ibid., 63.
[154] Ibid., 63.
[155] Rapport and Overling state, "Individuality is tied inextricably to individual consciousness, to that unique awareness, and awareness of awareness, which is the mark of human embodiment." Rapport and Overing, *Social and Cultural Anthropology: The Key Concepts*, 216. For those who study identity within conversation the investigation is not a speculation of discourse, theory or power. Instead "they investigate how people display identity, in terms of ascribed membership of social categories, and the consequences of ascription or display for the interactional work being accomplished."

a form of address is used, it helps create, change, or reaffirm a social relationship, in addition to indexing a set of conventional expectations."[156] For the biblical storyteller "the goal [of dialogue, *added by ET*] is to create staged, reciprocal conversations that sound 'normal' or ordinary, but actually have a richer subtheme of meaning or dimension that exists side by side with the ordinary."[157] Johnstone also argues that the "choice of address form is always in some ways a strategic move as well as a response to a situation."[158]

Through the examination of Divine/human relational dialogue it is possible to raise awareness of the intensely personal characteristics of ancient scripture. As Terrien writes, "It is increasingly recognized that the traits of psychological subtlety that are displayed in the patriarchal stories of Divine-human encounter reflect the experiences of concrete individuals endowed with an exceptional stature."[159] As we will see, that stature comes, not from their social standing but from their personal interaction with the Divine.

5. Proper Names

In an attempt to determine if the use of a personal name as a form of address influences the Divine/human relationship, this thesis will be look at instances of dialogue that include the use of the human's proper name by the Deity.[160]

Biblical scholars are well aware that ancient Israel spent a great deal of time and thought on the origin and meaning of names.[161] But it is not

---

Bethan Benwell and Elizabeth Stoke, *Discourse and Identity* (Edinburgh: Edinburgh University Press, 2006), 69.

[156] Johnstone, *Discourse Analysis*, 140.

[157] Matthews, *More Than Meets the Ear: Discovering the Hidden Contexts of Old Testament Conversations*, 65.

[158] Johnstone, *Discourse Analysis*, 140. Sidnell explains that within conversations 'we select the name by which we presume our recipient knows the person to whom we want to refer. The name we use then is specifically designed for the particular recipient." Sidnell, *Conversation Analysis: An Introduction*, 5.

[159] Terrien, *The Elusive Presence: Toward a New Biblical Theology*, 64.

[160] The act of naming will be investigated only as a subset of the use of proper name within dialogues. For a detailed study of naming genre see Timothy D. Finlay, *The Birth Report Genre in the Hebrew Bible* (Tübingen: Mohr Siebeck, 2005), 35-36.

[161] Hermann Gunkel, *The Legends of Genesis: The Biblical Saga and Hisory* (New York: Schocken Books, 1964), 27-28. Matthews argues, "Putting a positive or negative name on something or someone that will then create a social identity for the person who is labeled. This in turn will influence his or her behavior and, unless the label is somehow removed or invalidated, will become the basis for or expectation of how that person

just wells, mountains, cities and sanctuaries that are distinguished by a
proper name. "Personal names in the Hebrew Bible often signal recognition of divine attention[... *added by ET*] As the biblical names and name-
giving suggests, before an individual is even old enough to know God, one
might be known by God."[162] Matthews further explains, "When people
talk, whether it is in a live conversation or in embedded dialogue in a
narrative, they are not only communicating their thoughts, bits of information, or accumulated knowledge. They are also communicating their
identities and their relative positions, and they are engaging in active social
interaction."[163]

In the opening chapters of Genesis the significance of creating and
naming the elements has been widely studied.[164] The Deity creates humankind in its own image[165] by interacting personally with elements already
created.[166] Brueggemann declares that this leaves the narrative with a
"sense that human persons are not isolated individuals, but are members
of a community of those authorized by the life-giving breath of Yahweh,
and so have humanity only in that membership."[167] Human membership
in a general community, however, does not recognize individuality. That
can only be done when elements of character can be isolated.

In his narrative study of Genesis Humphreys states:

> Naming or otherwise designating a particular character by a phrase
> ('the man in the white hat') or even a pronoun or general term ('the
> man'), concretizes and particularizes. The character becomes more

---

will act within society." Matthews, *More Than Meets the Ear: Discovering the Hidden
Contexts of Old Testament Conversations*, 167. For example: Abraham, Gen 17:5;
Isaac, Gen 17:17, 19; Jacob, Gen 25:26.

[162] Names also give direction to "the name givers' and name bearers' lives even before
birth. In the case of theophoric names, this notion is made all the more explicit in
the names themselves." Burnett, *Where Is God? Divine Absence in the Hebrew
Bible*, 29.

[163] Matthews, *More Than Meets the Ear: Discovering the Hidden Contexts of Old Testament Conversations*, 68.

[164] An excellent and detailed commentary is Westermann, *Genesis 1-11: A Commentary*,
74-278.

[165] Genesis 1:26, 27. Wenham states, "There is a special kind of creative activity involved
in making man that puts man in a unique relationship with his creator and hence able
to respond to him. But the 'image of God' is not part of the human constitution so
much as it is a description of the process of creation which made man different."
Gordon J. Wenham, *Genesis 1-15*, WBC 1 (Waco, Tex.: Word, 1987), 31. For a discussion regarding the use of "in the image" see Westermann (Westermann, *Genesis 1-11:
A Commentary*, 144-60.)

[166] Genesis 2:4-7.

[167] Walter Brueggemann, *Theology of the Old Testament: Testimony, Dispute, Advocacy*
(Minneapolis, Minn.: Fortress, 1997), 453.

than a type, a pronoun or general term ('your son'), especially with the addition of a descriptive word or phrase ('your only one, whom you love'), and when given a proper name ('Isaac'). The character is then experienced as a living individual, as not simply the particular set of traits or paradigm constructed in [the narrative. *added by ET*][168]

During the creation story it is only after humankind has truly "become as one of us" through procreation that the Deity identifies, in dialogue, a human by his proper name — Cain.[169] By contrast, the Deity has multiple titles.[170] These titles are the only terms available to define the Deity and, as Humphrey's states, they "seem to flow into and out of each other over the course of the narrative. The range of proper names Genesis uses for God reflects this fluidity in general modes of appearance."[171] The Deity may be indefinable but humankind can, with the use of a proper name,

---

[168] W. Lee Humphreys, *The Character of God in the Book of Genesis: A Narrative Appraisal* (Louisville, Ky.: Westminster John Knox, 2001), 20.

[169] Genesis 4:9. Prior to this point Adam is not considered a proper name. When the Deity calls human life into existence in Gen 1:26 the identifying marker assigned to humanity is האדם, interpreted as the species humankind. The Deity does speak to humankind in the garden but does not identify them with individual proper names. It is האדם who names both אשה "the woman" (Gen 2:23) and חוה "Eve" (Gen 3:20). It is not until after האדם has known Eve, who then bears a son identified by the narrator as Cain, that the direct article is dropped from humankind/mankind making it a proper name (Gen 4:25). אדם is then repeated six times in quick succession within four verses (Gen 5:1-4). There are three האדם exceptions: Gen 2:20, 3:17 and 21, all of which use the conjunction ל to introduce the humankind element. Westermann argues that these instances should be read with the article assumed. (Westermann, *Genesis 1-11: A Commentary*, 185-86, 229, 264, 338-339, 355.) Sarna's JPS Commentary counter-argues, "The Hebrew vocalization *le-'adam* (in 2:20) makes the word a proper name for the first time, probably because the narrative now speaks of the man as a personality rather than an archetypal human." Nahum M. Sarna, *Genesis*, JPS Torah Commentary (Philadelphia, Pa.: Jewish Publication Society, 1989), 22. It must be noted, however, that after each of these exceptions האדם is used again in the narrative.
As for the Woman in the Garden/Eve. She is named by האדם in Gen 3:20. She is not identified by a proper name by the Deity.

[170] Brown states, "The variety of ways God appears in the Hebrew Scriptures is nothing short of staggering." William P. Brown, "Manifest Diversity: The Presence of God in Genesis," in *Genesis and Christian Theology*, ed. Nathan MacDonald and Mark W. Elliott (Grand Rapids, Mich: Eerdmans, 2012), 3. Within our examination: In Gen 4 and 16 the Deity is identified by the narrator as YHWH. In Gen 17 the Deity is labeled Elohim. The narrative of Gen 18 recognizes three visitors to Abraham's tent prior to the relational dialogue. Within the conversation, however, the individual Deity is YHWH. Genesis 15, Abram's visionary dialogue, distinguishes the Deity as the Word of YHWH. Abram then addresses the Deity as Adoni YHWH and the Deity self-identifies as simply YHWH. In the final dialogue to be considered, Gen 32, Jacob wrestles with a man who may or may not self-identify as Elohim.

[171] Humphreys, *The Character of God in the Book of Genesis: A Narrative Appraisal*, 9.

be contained in a single word. The proper name becomes "the crucial factor in the construction of a character."[172] It is this character individuality that creates intimacy within dialogue.

Case in point: Hagar. While in the company of Abram/Abraham and Sarai/Sarah, Hagar is never spoken to directly.[173] She is only talked about and referred to as the Egyptian, a handmaid, a slave. Trible states this is because, "for Sarai, Hagar is an instrument, not a person."[174] The first individual to call Hagar by name is a messenger of the Deity in Gen 16:8. When Hagar is finally cast out in Gen 21 and faces the imminent death of Ishmael, she, in turn, refers to him, not by name or even "my son," but as "the child" (vv. 21:15-16a). With the use of language she has distanced herself both emotionally and figuratively from her son Ishmael.[175]

Within the conversations to be examined there are unique moments when humankind is identified by the Deity with the use of a proper name. It is here that the human then becomes a full and complete individual before the Deity.[176] The use of a proper name within a Divine/human relational dialogue then becomes an important element when determining identity and the relationship between participants.

D. DIALOGUE PARAMETERS

For the purposes of this thesis there are several parameters to be considered when identifying Divine/human relational dialogue within Genesis. The first consideration is the identification of elements to be examined. They are, as discussed above, setting in everyday life, dialogue including adjacency pairs, and the use of a proper name indicating an interpersonal relationship. The second consideration is then the parameters for the passage of scripture, i.e. where does the narrative with its included dialogue start and end.[177]

---

[172] Fred W. Burnett, "Characterization and Reader Construction of Characters in the Gospels," *Semeia* 63 (1993): 17.
[173] Tammi J. Schneider, *Mothers of Promise: Women in the Book of Genesis* (Grand Rapids, Mich.: Baker, 2008), 110.
[174] Phyllis Trible, *Texts of Terror: Literary-Feminist Readings of Biblical Narratives* (Philadelphia, Pa.: Fortress, 1984), 11.
[175] Ibid., 24.
[176] Humphreys, *The Character of God in the Book of Genesis: A Narrative Appraisal*, 20.
[177] Note that narrative parameters will be different from dialogue parameters since our dialogue analysis will only be looking at the conversational exchange.

In order to determine the parameters of each dialogue it will be necessary to take into account past scholarly analysis, grammatical and thematic
considerations as well as the passage's overall setting in literature and
narrative. The examination of these elements will take place within each
isolated dialogue chapter.

E. DIALOGUES INCLUDED

Using the methodology and definitions above this thesis will examine
six Divine/human relational dialogues in Genesis.[178] The first four conversations are classed as straight forward Divine/human dialogue in the
sense that human participants interact with the Deity as part of everyday
life. The fifth conversation is seen as "everyday life" but within the distinct circumstance of a nighttime vision. The final conversation is questionable on multiple levels and therefore will be examined separately. The
dialogues to be examined are: Gen 4:3-15 Dialogue with Cain; Gen 16:7-14
Dialogue with Hagar; Gen 17:15-22 Dialogue in which Sarai is renamed;
Gen 18:9-15 Dialogue between Abraham, the visitors and Sarah; Gen 15:1-17
Abram's visionary dialogue and finally Gen 32:25-31: Jacob's wrestling
dialogue.

There are four additional conversations that were considered for examination but rejected as not including enough of the required elements.
They are as follows:

– Within the Garden narrative there are several examples of communication between the Divine and humans. The first factor is the setting.
  The dialogues we will be examining are glimpses of moments in the
  everyday lives of the people of the Deity. The Garden setting, namely,
  living in the presence of the Deity, places these communications outside the narrative parameter of our examination. Second, for the most
  part these are speeches with commands but little or no verbal response
  by the human.[179] The third factor in rejecting the Garden narrative
  communications is the argument that no personal name is used by the
  Deity.[180]
– Genesis 17:1-14, containing the Abram/Abraham name change, was
  originally considered but rejected on the grounds that, while containing

---

[178] Note that the conversations will be examined out of chronological order.
[179] For example Gen 2:15-23.
[180] See the previous discussion in footnote 167 regarding proper name usage.

two proper names there is no verbal exchange. Abram reacts to the appearance and initial Divine utterance by falling on his face. He does not verbally respond until the conversation turns to Sarai and her name change in v. 17. As will be seen, an examination of the dialogue parameters does allow for a division of the communication in vv. 1-14 from the dialogue of vv. 15-22 which will be studied.

– Genesis 18:23-33, Abraham bargaining with the Deity regarding the destruction of Sodom and Gomorrah, was also considered. It is a proper dialogue in that both parties speak to each other and questions are directly addressed. There is, however, a lack of any proper name. The conversation is not about Abraham or his immediate family. The entire discussion revolves around haggling down the price of the cities' survival from fifty righteous souls to ten. While the dialogue is an interesting character study of Abraham it is not an interpersonal dialogue and therefore will not be considered here.

– The final Divine/human dialogue contained in Genesis that was considered and discarded was Gen 21:14-21, Hagar's second journey in the wilderness. The setting and divine inquiry is similar to the dialogue examined in Gen 16. This time, however, there is no recorded verbal response from Hagar or from Ishmael to the Deity's communication.[181] The dialogue is therefore not part of this thesis.

F. THESIS STRUCTURE

From the methodology and definitions of chapter 1 we have determined how to study Divine/human relational dialogue and the elements to be considered within the conversations of Genesis. Before an examination of these elements can be conducted, however, we must first justify the circumstances surrounding these conversations, extricate them from the adjacent narratives and then identify their narrative structure. For this purpose chapter 2 of this thesis will look at the situation of each dialogue in light of the following criteria. First will be the dialogue's setting within literature; where the conversation falls within the structure of the book as a whole. Following this will be observations of the dialogue's setting within the narrative; what comes immediately before and after the conversation. There will be a thorough discussion of the scholarly parameters

---

[181] The narrator states that the Divine heard the lad's voice but there is no indication as to what was said or to whom the utterance was directed.

of the narrative containing the dialogue along with an explanation of any differing determinations that might be made. Finally, each section will include a translation of the passage under discussion and a skeletal structure separating narrative from dialogue.

After dislodging the dialogue passage from its surrounding narrative, chapter 3 will employ three major elements to analyze the essence of the dialogue. First to be examined is the initiation of dialogue; who is the initiator and the form, if any, the verbal initiation takes. Second is the use of a proper name within the conversation. This discussion includes analysis of the name, its meaning and use. Another focus of this inquiry is to identify any bearing the name might have on the dialogue or the Divine/human relationship. The final investigation, titled Dialogue Analysis, will be an examination of adjacent pairs and turn taking as set within the dialogue. Using the tools of conversation analysis we will determine the structure, emphasis and character of the Divine/human relationship. This section will also include comments on traditional thematic analysis.

In chapter 4 the conclusions reached in chapters 2 and 3 will be brought together with the goal of identifying a Divine/human relational dialogue model that can then be applied to future study of scriptural passages beyond Genesis.

CHAPTER 2

THE CIRCUMSTANCES OF DIALOGUE

A. Genesis 4:3-15: Cain's dialogue

1. Setting in literature

For many scholars the patriarchal saga theme unifies the book of Genesis. However, within the book itself there are smaller units that must be considered. "In terms of subject matter, the book of Genesis breaks up into two distinct and unequal parts. The first contains chapters i-xi; it is restricted — if allowances are made for the Table of Nations — to what has come to be known as Primeval History. The second part, chapters xii-l, takes up the Story of the Patriarchs."[1]

For most scholars, the Primeval History has been considered an introduction to the remainder of Genesis and beyond.[2] Westermann suggests

---

[1] Speiser, *Genesis*, liii. Different commentators divide Genesis at different points: Speiser portions off Gen 1-11:32 and includes the genealogy. Coats breaks the first part of Gen at 1-11:9 by excluding the final genealogy. Von Rad divides Gen 1-12:3 including genealogy and closes with Abraham's call. While the dividing line between the Primeval History and the Patriarchal History has no bearing on this thesis I will be following Speiser's division of 1:1–11:32 and include the genealogy structure as part of the framework of Genesis.

[2] Von Rad states, as late as 1972, that chapters 1-11 are, "a broadly conceived preface, a prelude to the particular story with which the rest of the Pentateuch is concerned. The difference is underscored by the scope of the two subdivisions of Genesis. The patriarchal narratives take up four-fifths of the entire book, yet they cover only four generations of a single family. Primeval History, on the other hand, has the whole world as its stage, and its time span reaches back all the way to Creation." Ibid., liii. Westermann challenges this notion by charging that, "the approach to the problem of Gen 1-11 as a whole had been frustrated and shackled by two presuppositions which had been passed on uncritically from one generation to another. The first was the presumption that the two decisive passages which colored the whole of the primeval story were Gen 1 and 3. A tradition of more than a thousand years had imposed itself; under this influence, and for the most part quite unconsciously, one summed up the basic content of the primeval story under the heading 'Creation and Fall' ... The second presupposition is connected closely with the first. The one-sided emphasis on Gen 1-3 has already decided that the genealogies of chs. 1-11 can have no particular significance, in any case, no determining theological significance. The commentaries deal very thoroughly with the names listed in these genealogies; but there is scarcely ever any discussion of the meaning of the genealogies for the whole. To devalue implicitly the genealogies or to leave

that the unique character of Gen 1-11 is due to the fact that the genealogies create the framework upon which the narration hangs.[3] "Gen 1 has run its course with the creation of humans; it halts, while Gen 2-3 takes up the story. A succession of generations begins with Gen 4 and progresses from the first created pair to Abraham, who introduces the second part of Genesis, the patriarchal cycle."[4] The Divine dialogue with Cain is our only relational conversation contained in the Primeval History.

2. Setting in narrative

Coats states that "the first major unit of the OT contains a narrative description of events from long ago and far away."[5] While this quote may, at first, bring to mind the opening scene of a famous science fiction movie it is accurate for the discussion of the primal events in Genesis. In Gen 1 "the center of the stage was heaven, and man was but an item in a cosmic sequence of majestic acts. Here [in Gen 2, *added by ET*] the earth is paramount and man the center of interest."[6] Unlike the created elements (humankind included) in Gen 1 where all were declared 'good' there is imperfection in Gen 2. The world is now limited and less divine. Gen 1 set forth the facts of creation, separating the Hebrew doctrine from that of its neighbors. Genesis 2 then turns to focus on humankind and the tendencies toward sin. The narrative has set the stage for the hubris of humankind — the desire to become like God.[7] Out of chaos the Deity created order and out of order, due to humankind's imperfections comes the chaos of the life that must be lived. It is the combination that completes the narrative.[8]

---

them aside must have far-reaching effects on one's final understanding of and judgment on the primeval story." Westermann, *Genesis 1-11: A Commentary*, 2-3.

[3] Westermann also adds "The family trees or genealogies in Gen 1-11 belong to a many-faceted genre that runs through the whole of the Old Testament. This genre is found in a highly developed form in the patriarchal cycle, Gen 12-50, and occurs again only with the kings, the priests and priestly circle, and with the chronicler. It continues into the New Testament in the family tree of Jesus." Westermann, *Genesis 1-11: A Commentary*, 7.

[4] Ibid., 6.

[5] Coats, *Genesis*, 35.

[6] Speiser, *Genesis*, 18.

[7] Von Rad, *Genesis: A Commentary*, 57.

[8] According to von Rad, the doctrine and theology has, through narrative, "gained breadth of vision from the fact that everything is not fitted together quite so compactly. And precisely because here and there things do not fit and are not drawn together at the end, the narrative gains its unfathomable and inexhaustible character." Ibid., 100.

As Gen 4 opens, humankind while resistant is still very much dependent on the Deity for spiritual survival. With the continuation of the genealogy and the introduction of the first birth narrative, humankind becomes individual in the persons of Cain and Abel. The text now turns to examine how humans stand "in opposition to each other, the created world and to the Deity."[9]

For a brief moment we will consider the thematic discussions that have historically taken place throughout the Gen 4 dialogue. The reason behind this short assessment is to put exegetical comments used in the dialogue analysis in context.

A number of commentaries examine the theme of guilt and punishment in Gen 4 with special attention paid to the introduction of murder into human civilization.[10] These scholars often see mirror images of the paradise tales expanded into human society and comment that "human creatures live in strife and instability, a style of life that brings about violence and dissolution of relationships."[11] There are three relationships most often examined. They focus on the occupational theme, the conundrum of freewill before the Deity and fraternal relationship between the brothers. The fraternal theme will be examined as we investigate the proper names used in this passage.

   With regards to the occupational theme, some commentators see echoes of historic tensions in the descriptions of herdsman versus farmer.[12] Gunkel theorized that the original legend did not comment on the piety of the participants for a reason. That reason was to explain that the Deity "loves

---

[9] Ibid., 59.

[10] See Coats, *Genesis*, 64-65. Umberto Cassuto, *A Commentary on the Book of Genesis*, trans. Israel Abrahams (Jerusalem: Magnes, 1961), 213-27. Soggin and Bowden, *Introduction to the Old Testament: From Its Origins to the Closing of the Alexandrian Canon*, 169-70. Von Rad, *Genesis: A Commentary*, 106-09. Westermann examines guilt and punishment passages (Gen 3: 4:2-16; 6:1-4; 9:20-27; 11:1-9). Claus Westermann, *Elements of Old Testament Theology*, trans. Douglas W. Scott (Atlanta, Ga.: John Knox, 1978), 88.

[11] Coats, *Genesis*, 66.

[12] Cotter, *Genesis*, 42-43. Also see Thomas L. Brodie, *Genesis as Dialogue: A Literary, Historical, and Theological Commentary* (Oxford: Oxford University Press, 2001), 153. Kenneth M. Jr. Craig, "Questions Outside Eden (Genesis 4.1-16): Yahweh, Cain and Their Rhetorical Interchange," *JSOT* 86 (1999): 110. Gary A. Herion, "Why God Rejected Cain's Offering: The Obvious Answer," in *Fortunate the Eyes That See*, ed. Astrid B. Beck and Andrew H. Bartelt (Grand Rapids, Mich: Eerdmans, 1995).

the shepherd and animal sacrifice, but wants nothing to do with the farmer and fruit offerings."[13] There are two problems with this theory. First, for the theory to withstand examination it must be proved that the nomadic herdsman is the ideal prototype for Israel. This is not possible as "the evidence for such an ideal in biblical literature is extremely flimsy. Further, there is not the slightest suggestion in the text of any comparative evaluation of the vocations of Cain and Abel, nor is there the slightest disparagement of the tiller of the soil."[14] The second argument that undermines this theory is that the primary tension, and therefore the underlying reason for the narrative, is "not between people of diverse occupations; it is between siblings."[15]

La Sor states that "the author of Gen 1-11 was not interested in satisfying biological and geological curiosity. Rather, he wanted to tell who and what human beings are by virtue of where they came from: they are of divine origin, made in the image of the Creator, yet marred materially by the sin that so soon disfigured God's good work."[16] The thrust of this theme then becomes the examination of free will, both human and Divine.[17]

Cotter suggests that "the reasons the story gives for Cain's rejection is that Abel exercised his free will and brought the best, with the implications that Cain did not choose but simply took what was at hand."[18] Sarna takes this pursuit a step further. He looks to the Deity's reactions to each offering to explain human free will. Abel's offering is characterized as being "first of the flock" and "the fat" also interpreted as "the best parts." Cain's offering is simply identified as "from the land" without any additional details. "Abel appears to have demonstrated a quality of heart and mind that Cain did not possess. Cain's purpose was noble, but his act was not without a begrudging attitude. Thus the narrative conveys the fundamental principle of Judaism that the act of worship must be informed by genuine devotion of the heart."[19] When this argument is exhausted scholars also turn to the "disturbing development: God is unfair, and,

---

[13] Gunkel, *Genesis*, 43.
[14] Sarna, *Genesis*, 31.
[15] Brodie, *Genesis as Dialogue: A Literary, Historical, and Theological Commentary*, 153.
[16] William Sanford La Sor, David Allan Hubbard, and Frederic William Bush, *Old Testament Survey: The Message, Form, and Background of the Old Testament* (Grand Rapids, Mich.: Eerdmans, 1982), 75.
[17] T. Anthony Perry, "Cain's Sin in Gen. 4:1-7: Oracular Ambiguity and How to Avoid It," *Prooftexts* 25 (2005): 261.
[18] Cotter, *Genesis*, 42.
[19] Sarna, *Genesis*, 32.

more generally, life is unfair."[20] The last ditch theme to be developed is that the cause for all strife in life is the unexplainable nature of the Deity and that the Deity's motive is arbitrary and disconcerting to mere humans.[21]

3. Parameters

In 1979 Childs acknowledged that the genealogical superstructure of Genesis had been recognized by scholars for a long time.[22] To this day, however, commentators disagree on the exact semantic range of the term *toledot*.[23] While this thesis is not specifically interested in the overall genealogical structure of Genesis the *toledot* are important in that they serve as superscription to the dialogue contained within.[24]

The Primeval History is especially dependent on the *toledot* structure to supply continuity as history jumps forward quickly as opposed to the Patriarchal History which lingers on family stories. The strength of the

---

[20] Brodie, *Genesis as Dialogue: A Literary, Historical, and Theological Commentary*, 153.

[21] Humphreys, *The Character of God in the Book of Genesis: A Narrative Appraisal*, 56.

[22] Brevard S. Childs, *Introduction to the Old Testament as Scripture* (London: SCM, 1979), 145.

[23] Childs explains that the slight variation of the *toledot* formula "these are the generations of…" as it appears in Genesis leads commentators to wonder "whether exactly the same meaning is conveyed throughout the book." He goes on to reassure that "it is certain from the Hebrew syntax that the formula is always followed by the genitive of the progenitor and never the progeny. The immediate significance of this observation is that the first occurrence of the formula in 2.4: 'these are the generations of the heavens and the earth…' serves as a superscription to the account which follows and can, under no circumstances, either be shifted to a position preceding 1.1, or treated as a subscription to 1.1-2.4a." Childs, *Introduction to the Old Testament as Scripture*, 145.

[24] Von Rad and Speiser do not argue for a genealogical superstructure. They focus on explaining the structure of Genesis using source criticism and the links between major story arcs. La Sor and Blenkinsopp divide the Primeval Prologue into 5 *toledot* and the Patriarchal History into 3 *toledot*. (For a quick reference chart see La Sor, Hubbard, and Bush, *Old Testament Survey: The Message, Form, and Background of the Old Testament*, 69.) Defined by this structure the "natural divisions" mean the story of Cain and Abel is not separated out but is part of the greater "Eden and the Fall" story of Gen 2:4b-4:26. Ibid., 68-70. Also see Joseph Blenkinsopp, *The Pentateuch: An Introduction to the First Five Books of the Bible*, 1st ed. (New York: Doubleday, 1992), 58-97. Soggin sees a disjointed source structure in that he attributes the story of Cain and Abel to a non-Israelite source which was then usurped by the J source and leaves it at that. Soggin and Bowden, *Introduction to the Old Testament: From Its Origins to the Closing of the Alexandrian Canon*, 114-21. However, when discussing apodeictic forms of Israelite Law he includes Gen 4:10 and the shedding of innocent blood to the Israelite priestly source. Ibid., 164-77. His final comment on Gen 4 in the same book states that Gen 4:23, the "Song of Lemech" "has no characteristics which suggest that it should be related to any of the sources of the Pentateuch." Ibid., 178.

structure allows for the exploration of the internal divisions without threatening the connectivity of the history as a whole.[25] The Primeval story is built on, or grows out of, the genealogies surrounding it. Finley's close examination of birth narratives revealed the following for Gen 4, "Even if sections of the genealogy in Genesis 4 were originally separate, this threefold use of a birth report (4:1-2 Cain; 4:17 Enoch; 4:25 Seth) whose setting consists solely of the knowledge formula serves as a superstructure to bind them together."[26] Genesis 4 as a whole then, is a tightly integrated passage. Westermann saw the non-genealogical elements in chapter 4 as "an elaboration of a genealogical table."[27] Following the observation that the Primeval story is built on genealogies "the consequence of this for the structure of Gen 4 is that vv. 1-2 and vv. 17-26 belong together and form the genealogy which follows the creation."[28] Coats defined the structure of Gen 4 as including "an exposition, vv. 1-2, and a conclusion, v. 16, framing the major body of the narrative in vv. 3-15."[29]

Following Coates, the beginning of v. 3 serves as a link from the genealogy to the narrative elements of the dialogue. "And it came to pass from the extremity of days" is a formula used with particular emphasis throughout the Hebrew Bible. "In all places without exception the sentence describes a continuation of the event, never a beginning. At the beginning of v. 3 the sentence indicates clearly how closely genealogy and narrative are related."[30] The sequence of events that follow also depends on elements of structure. This time, however, it is not a record of birth but speeches connected by narrative that hold the story together.[31]

The initial part of the narrative contains mostly action, the exception being vv. 6-7. Westermann suggests that these verses could be omitted without damaging the progress of the action arguing that the "address by

---

[25] Childs, *Introduction to the Old Testament as Scripture*, 146.

[26] Finlay, *The Birth Report Genre in the Hebrew Bible*, 79.

[27] Westermann, *Genesis 1-11: A Commentary*, 285.

[28] Ibid., 285.

[29] Coats, *Genesis*, 63. Westermann argues that v. 2 served a dual purpose as the conclusion of the initial genealogical information and as the "*exposé*" of the narrative. Westermann, *Genesis 1-11: A Commentary*, 285.

[30] Westermann, *Genesis 1-11: A Commentary*, 294. Westermann expands other examples "The phrase מקץ ויהי usually indicated a passage of time, and so we read in Gen 8:6 'and it happened after the course of 40 days...'; also 18:3; 41:1; Ex 12:41; Num 13:25; Deut 9:11; 15:1; 31:10; Judg 11:39; 2 Sam 15:7; 1 Kings 2:39; Is 23:15, 17; Jer 34:14; 42:7; or with an indefinite indication of time, 2 Sam 14:28. The sentence ימים מקץ ויהי of Gen 4:3 occurs elsewhere only in 1 Kings 17:7, 'it happened after some time.'"

[31] Coats, *Genesis*, 64.

Yahweh to Cain, 6-7, is inserted into the narrative; it is a warning in the text as we have it and acts as a brake on the movement of the narrative itself."[32] The action of the narrative may not need the speech but this first speech by the Deity must be given in order to strengthen the crime-punishment cycle of the second section of dialogue which contains Cain's objections, his trial, penalty and his mark.[33] When vv. 6-7 and vv. 9-15 are examined as integral parts of a whole, the downward spiral of Cain's existence is explained.

The termination of the Cain and Abel narrative excludes v. 16. This verse is struck from the dialogue for its parallels to the introduction in vv. 1-2. Genesis 4:1-2 gives a detailed account of how Cain arrived in the world and takes pains to establish a relationship between YHWH and the man who has been 'gotten from YHWH.' Coats states, "The mother's birth saying in v. 1b, a play on the name and the verb *qānîtî 'îš* (I have gotten a man"), also notes the presence of the Lord. Verse 16, however, emphasizes Cain's loss of the presence: 'Cain went away from the presence of the Lord.'"[34] From this point on Cain dwells in the land of Nod, east of Eden. Westermann explains that the narrative "then moves back into the genealogical details out of which it had grown. And so we have a smooth transition to the genealogy that follows."[35] The structure of the genealogies in Genesis allows division within not only the book but within chapters. In Gen 4 there are three divisions signaled by the births of Cain, Seth and Enoch. It is only within vv. 3-15, however, that we have a Divine/human dialogue.

4. Translation

3. And it came to pass after many[36] days Cain brought fruit of the land as an offering to YHWH.

---

[32] Westermann, *Genesis 1-11: A Commentary*, 287.

[33] Westermann explains, "In the second part the pronouncement of the penalty, 11-12, follows the trial, 9-10. The conclusion, v. 16, could well follow immediately. The narrative would then be complete. However Cain's objection, 13-14, and God's reply, 15, are a necessary part of the narrative as a whole because they include the mitigation of the penalty which is characteristic of the crime-punishment narratives of the primeval story." Ibid., 287.

[34] Coats, *Genesis*, 64.

[35] Westermann, *Genesis 1-11: A Commentary*, 314-15.

[36] The word קץ can indicate the end of a definite or indefinite period of time. Francis Brown, S. R. Driver, and Charles A. Briggs, *The Broun-Driver-Briggs Hebrew and English Lexicon* (Peabody, Mass.: Hendrickson, 2005), 893.

4. And Abel[37] also brought the first born of his flock[38] and the fat parts. And YHWH favored[39] Abel and his offering.

5. But Cain and his offering he did not favor. And Cain was exceedingly angry[40] and his countenance fell.

6. And YHWH said unto Cain, Why do you burn with anger and why has your countenance fallen?

7. If[41] you do right is there not praise and if you do not do right sin will lie down[42] at the door and unto you will be his longing but you shall have dominion over him.

8. And Cain talked to Abel his brother and it came to pass as they were in the field Cain rose up against Abel his brother and killed him.

9. And YHWH said unto Cain, Where is Abel your brother? And he said, I know not. Do I have charge of my brother?

10. And he said, What have you done? A voice, the blood of thy brother, is calling out[43] to me from the ground.

11. And now, cursed are you from the ground which opened her mouth to receive the blood of your brother from your hand.

12. When you till the ground she will not give her strength to you. Quivering and wandering[44] you will be on the land.

13. And Cain said unto YHWH, My iniquity[45] is too great to bear.

14. Behold![46] You drove me out this day from the face of the ground and from your face I will be hidden and I will be quivering and wandering on the land. And it will be that all those who find me will kill me.

---

[37] The sentence begins with an inverted subject-verb word order.

[38] Colloquial for "small cattle usually of sheep and goats in one flock." BDB, 838.

[39] The verb שעה is defined as 'to gaze steadily, with interest or to regard with favor.' ibid., 1043.

[40] Craig states, "Given the Bible's economy of detail, the description of 'great' anger stands out. Cain is infuriated." Craig, "Questions Outside Eden (Genesis 4.1-16): Yahweh, Cain and Their Rhetorical Interchange," 113.

[41] The sentence begins with an indirect interrogation which, disjunctively, indicates an upcoming clause or clauses that will describe alternative or differing ideas. Also note that the difficulties of translation for this verse will be dealt with in the dialogue analysis section of this chapter.

[42] For a discussion of the range of meaning of רבץ see Ellen Van Wolde, "The Story of Cain and Abel: A Narrative Study," *JSOT* 52 (1991): 31.

[43] The verb צעק translates as to cry, cry out or call, usually for help as in Gen 18:13; Exod 3:7; Exod 22:21-24. BDB, 858.

[44] The translation of נוד as "to move to and fro, wander, flutter, show grief" includes the essence of aimlessness and as a fugitive in this case. Ibid., 626.

[45] "The Hebrew word 'awon conveys a semantic field that forces translators again into unfortunately limiting decisions. The meanings of 'awon range from 'misdeed or sin' through 'guilt' to 'punishment.' Most opt for 'punishment.'" Examples in Gen 4:3:22; 11:6; 15:3; 19:34; 27:11; 29:7 and 30:34. Humphreys, *The Character of God in the Book of Genesis: A Narrative Appraisal*, 59.

[46] The use of the demonstrative adverb הן is "less widely used than הנה, and in prose mostly confined to calling attention to some fact upon which action is to be taken, or a conclusion based." BDB, 243.

15. And YHWH said to him, No, all those who attempt to kill Cain I will punish seventy times. And YHWH placed on[47] Cain a sign so that all those who
find him will not kill[48] him.

5. Structure

Divine Dialogue with Cain	Gen 4:3-15
I. Narrative elements part 1	Gen 4:3-5
II. Dialogue part 1	Gen 4:6-7
III. Narrative elements part 2	Gen 4:8
IV. Dialogue part 2	Gen 4:9-15a
V. Narrative element part 3	Gen 4:15b

B. GENESIS 16:7-14: HAGAR IN THE WILDERNESS

1. Setting in literature

The first dialogue to be examined within the Patriarchal saga is Gen 16:7-14,
Hagar's initial Divine encounter in the wilderness.[49] Within this saga the
Terah *toledot*[50] deals with the succession of generations and the start of the
promise motif.[51] Focused chapters within the story (15:1-17:17) revolve
around family relations and desires.

While the above mentioned family chapters focus on Abram/Abraham,
it is the underlying theme of conflict between the women that caused Coats
to title sections of this drama the 'Sarah-Hagar Novella.'[52] When centered

---

[47] Note that "*to set a sign* IN *someone* means to bring an affliction on a person, intended
to serve as an example to others [Exod 10:2; Isa lxvi:19; Ps lxxviii:43, *added by ET*].
To set a sign FOR *someone* signifies to appoint a token for a person's good and benefit
(compare Exod 15:25)." Cassuto, *A Commentary on the Book of Genesis*, 227. Emphasis
original.

[48] For a discussion of the verb נכה see: J. Conrad, "נכה," *TDOT* IX:415-23.

[49] Narratively Abraham's dialogue with YHWH in Gen 15 comes first. However, due to
its visionary setting it will be examined in a later chapter.

[50] Generally defined as Gen 12-25. Blenkinsopp examines the common practice of dividing
Gen 12-50 into three sections: 12-25; 25-36 and 37-50. Blenkinsopp, *The Pentateuch:
An Introduction to the First Five Books of the Bible*, 98-99. Speiser is more specific when
he states that "the patriarchal narratives in Genesis comprise three major subdivisions:
A. The Story of Abraham (xii 1-xxv 18); B. The Story of Jacob (xxv 19-xxxvii 2a);
C. Joseph and His Brothers (xxxvii 2b-1 26)." Speiser, *Genesis*, LVIII.

[51] Claus Westermann, *Genesis: A Practical Commentary*, trans. David Green (Grand
Rapids, Mich.: Eerdmans, 1987), 95.

[52] Coats includes the following verses under the title (16:1-16; 17:1-27; 18:1-15, 18:16-
19:38; 20:1-18 and 21:1-21). Coats, *Genesis*, 127-55. Brueggemann agrees with
these divisions but does not include passages beyond 18:15. Walter Brueggemann,
Genesis (Atlanta, Ga.: John Knox, 1982), 150-62. See also Lai Ling Elizabeth Ngan,

on Abram, chapter 16 is often tied to the preceding chapters through references to Egypt,[53] the promise of a son and the blessing of nations. The
degree to which the women play a role is often negated. Brueggemann
went so far as to declare the Hagar centered narrative of Gen 16 a 'playful
anecdote.'[54] Humphreys said:

> It is striking that in an episode that could prove critical to Abram's
> story, the episode in which the issue of seed is apparently resolved,
> Yahweh engages not Abram or Sarai, but a foreign, female slave of a
> barren wife. Hagar's place in this regard is unique. She is at once the
> center of Yahweh's attention but she will also prove to be another
> byway on the narrative path toward the seed Abram needs to possess
> the land of Canaan and become a great nation.[55]

Hagar's first encounter with the Deity, and the first full dialogue between
the Divine and a woman, can then be seen as profound on several levels.

2. Setting in narrative

From narrative analysis we can see that the Hagar dialogue is a departure from the main story of Abram/Sarai. As early as Gen 11:29, 30 the
reader is well aware that Abram has married Sarai and that she is barren,
specifically noting that she is without a child. Throughout subsequent
chapters Sarai is identified as Abram's wife and sometimes called his
sister. She is not, however, identified as barren again until Gen 15:2, 3.[56]
This is the setting for the dialogue in Gen 15[57] which reveals the covenant between Abram and the Deity and the promise of numerous descendants (v. 5) and land (v. 18).[58]

"Neither Here nor There: Boundary and Identity in the Hagar Story," in *Ways of Being,
Ways of Reading*, ed. Mary F. Foshett and Jeffrey Kah-Jim Kuan (Saint Louis: Chalice,
2006), 73.

[53] Genesis 12:10-20; 13:1, 10; 15:18.

[54] Brueggemann, *Genesis*, 153. Finlay advocates that this view is mistaken. He proposes
that "the role of the Genesis 16 episode within this larger narrative is not limited to
delaying the birth of Isaac; it marks a stage where although Sarai's plans to be 'built
up' through giving Hagar to Abram have failed, Abram believes he has obtained the
son of promise." Finlay, *The Birth Report Genre in the Hebrew Bible*, 102.

[55] Humphreys, *The Character of God in the Book of Genesis: A Narrative Appraisal*, 101.
Also see S. Nikaido, "Hagar and Ishmael as Literary Figures: An Intertextual Study,"
VT 51 (2001): 221.

[56] In a vision dialogue with the Deity Abram describes himself as "going childless"
implying that his wife has not borne him any children.

[57] Which will be examined in a following chapter.

[58] It should be noted that the womb from which the initial descendant will come is not
specifically identified by the Deity or the narrator at this time.

Within this context the opening sentence of Gen 16 is important. "And Sarai, wife of Abram did not bare to him."[59] This choice of words seems to indicate that the focus of the following narrative and subsequent dialogue will return to the fulfillment of the promise of seed.[60] The narrative does not play out as expected however. Brichto noted that the story of Gen 16 "points to the realization of that promise – its first realization – in the heir who will spring from Abram's loins, but not from Sarai's."[61]

Just as Sarai was previously identified by her status as Abram's wife Hagar is now identified in the narrative as Sarai's Egyptian handmaid.

> In addition to foregrounding Sarai by naming her at the narrative's very beginning and immediately thereafter underlining that the Egyptian slave-girl is hers, not Abrams', the narrator will continue to stress the distances (and proximities) of the characters from (and to) one another as also from (and to) the God who personally presides over the destiny of this family he has chosen for his purposes.[62]

The interrelation between the three main characters in the narrative is a tangle of emotions.[63] Hagar becomes the victim of Sarai's scheming and Abram does nothing to protect or prevent the ensuing abuse. From this point "the attention of the narrative does not return to issues faced by Abraham and Sarah, but remains with Hagar. Indeed, God's attention is focused on Hagar. Sarai and Abraham have sent Hagar away, not God."[64] Indeed, it is only the Deity who steps in to rescue Hagar.[65] Von Rad states that the "primary point in [this, *added by ET*] narrative is that God follows the one who goes forth from Abraham's house too; and it is a great wonder that his eyes are also open to mankind, that he includes it in his plans for history and that he established oases in the desert for Hagar and Ishmael too."[66] While some scholars interpret Abram's ensuing actions as

---

[59] Genesis 16:1
[60] Westermann states that "Chapter 16 consists of a single narrative made up of two: the rise to its climax is a quarrel narrative, the descent to its resolution describes an encounter with a messenger of God." Westermann, *Genesis: A Practical Commentary*, 127.
[61] Herbert Chanan Brichto, *The Names of God: Poetic Readings in Biblical Beginnings* (Oxford: Oxford University Press, 1998), 213.
[62] Ibid., 213.
[63] Speiser, *Genesis*, 120.
[64] Terence E. Fretheim, *Abraham: Trials of Family and Faith* (Columbia: University of South Carolina Press, 2007), 96.
[65] David Noel Freedman, *Genesis*, in *Eerdmans Commentary on the Bible*, ed. James D. G. Dunn and J. W. Rogerson (Grand Rapids, Mich.: Eerdmans, 2003), 51.
[66] Von Rad, *Genesis: A Commentary*, 196-97.

evidence of Abram's belief that Ishmael is the promised son,[67] von Rad
will not concede to the idea that Hagar's promised child is the fulfillment
of Abram's divine covenant. "The narrator seems to be most sympathetic
toward Hagar, although she offended most obviously against right and
custom. But the reader understands that a child so conceived in defiance
or in little faith cannot be the heir of promise."[68]

Between the individuals Sarai and Abram, and the statements made
regarding them, is the seemingly isolated narrative of an ancestress in
danger.[69] "Moving the story [of Gen 16, *added by ET*] from a sad beginning to a happy ending is Hagar,"[70] a woman who is nominally described
as an unchosen handmaid. Yet through narrative analysis we will see that
the Hagar focused dialogue runs counter to the Abram/Sarai narrative
surrounding it on almost every level.

Within the structural parameters under discussion there are several narrative themes to be examined. For scholars these narrative thematic considerations fall into three prominent categories. The first is social in nature
and includes discussions of power, social structure and the idea of chosen
versus unchosen. The second theme most often discussed is that of the
heir of promise. The final theme frequently commented upon is an awareness of unique elements within the passage. However, the significance of
the total uniqueness is rarely addressed. We will take a quick look at each
of these topics.

First, in terms of the story of Hagar coupled with that of Sarai/Sarah,
the connecting narrative theme is often described as a power struggle
between the women.[71] Within this overarching theme, however, is the
odd presentation of the singular Hagar narrative in Gen 16. Humphreys

---

[67] Finlay writes, "The role of Genesis 16 episode within this larger narrative is not limited
to delaying the birth of Isaac; it marks a stage where although Sarai's plans to be 'built
up' through giving Hagar to Abram have failed, Abram believes he has obtained the
son of promise." Finlay, *The Birth Report Genre in the Hebrew Bible*, 102.

[68] Von Rad, *Genesis: A Commentary*, 196. Turner comments that, in regards to the
possible fulfillment of the promise in Ishmael, it is interesting to note that chapter 16
begins with the word Sarai and ends with the word Abram. Sarai is barren in direct
opposition to the "concluding statement [that, *added by ET*] goes out of its way to stress
Abram's paternity at the expense of Sarai's maternity." Laurence A. Turner, *Genesis*
(Sheffield: Sheffield Academic Press, 2000), 80.

[69] Coats, *Genesis*, 127.

[70] Trible, *Texts of Terror: Literary-Feminist Readings of Biblical Narratives*, 19.

[71] Often labeled a "conflict narrative." See Claus Westermann, *Genesis 12-36: A Commentary*, trans. John J. Scullion (Minneapolis, Minn.: Augsburg, 1985), 235. Also see
Alan Cooper, "Hagar in and out of Context," *USQR* 55 (2001): 37.

examined the theme of authority and power between the women and Abram in chapter 16 and labeled it "muddied." He went on to state:

> It is striking that the women, who are at the lower levels of authority, exercise the most controlling power, both over the situation and, more problematically, the one over the other. The male Abram consents to the authority exercised by Sarai and then gives assent to her reassertion of authority over Hagar even when it leads to abuse of the handmaid. And Yahweh, through his messenger, in asserting his authority, undercuts the structure by engaging directly the one person with the least authority. But he does so only to tell her to go back and submit to the abuse of the woman with authority over her.[72]

The text goes to great lengths to emphasize the social structure within the family by labeling Hagar a woman, handmaid and Egyptian.[73] Trible noted that in the initial dialogue between the messenger and Hagar that "matching the messenger's designation, 'maid of Sarai,' the phrase, 'Sarai my mistress,' indicates the continuing power of the social structure."[74] Humphreys maintains that v. 9 continues "to underscore the motif of authority/power/control in this unit"[75] when the messenger's commandment to submit sends her back to her abusive past. Mirroring Hagar's strife and the current 'muddied' social structure within which she must live is that of Ishmael's predicted future.

> While Ishmael's future strife (16:12) might seem to perpetuate the disharmony within Abram's household, it actually shows a role change. This is emphasized by the motif of "hand" (*yād*). Abraham told Sarai that Hagar "is in your hand" (*yād*) (16:6); the angel told Hagar to return to Sarai and "submit under her hand" (*yād*) (16:9). Of Ishmael the angel predicted, "with his hand (*yād*) against everyone and everyone's hand (*yād*) against him" (16:12). Ishmael's destiny shows that Hagar's present position — under another's hand — will not be perpetuated in her son.[76]

---

[72] Humphreys, *The Character of God in the Book of Genesis: A Narrative Appraisal*, 101-02.

[73] Ibid., 101.

[74] Trible, *Texts of Terror: Literary-Feminist Readings of Biblical Narratives*, 15.

[75] Humphreys, *The Character of God in the Book of Genesis: A Narrative Appraisal*, 101. Ngan states, "To take notice of someone's ethnic identity is to distinguish a person from others, identify a person by her or his features, or prejudge a person's abilities or worth.[... added by ET] In an environment in which ethnic identity determines not only group membership and the right to land and livelihood, but also community solidarity and mutual support, to identify someone as belonging to a different ethnic group has significant implications. Not only does it label that person as 'not one of us,' but her or his 'otherness' invokes fear and suspicion." Ngan, "Neither Here nor There: Boundary and Identity in the Hagar Story," 72, 76.

[76] Turner, *Genesis*, 79.

The change in socially accepted roles is evident when Hagar receives
a birth narrative nearly parallel to that of Abram. The narrative theme of
chosen versus unchosen is highlighted when the messenger of YHWH
participates in direct dialogue with a female individual who has been
socially described as nothing but an outsider.[77] Within the greater conflict
narrative is the underscoring theme that the Deity plays an important role
in the lives of the unchosen.

The second most common narrative theme of Gen 16 is an examination
of the possible fulfillment of the promise of seed to Abram in Gen 15.
Von Rad states that "Ishmael is not the heir of promise but a secondary
descendant who retires from the line of promise. The reader, therefore, has
experienced a very strange incident which contains a special significance."[78]
The significance of the incident is twofold. "God has not exclusively
committed himself to Abraham-Sarah. [And, *added by ET*] God's concern
is not confined to the elect line."[79] Brueggemann suggests that, "theologically, [the, *added by ET*] narrative asserts that Abraham and Sarah did
not believe the promise."[80] Discussions of whether or not Abram and
Sarai believed the promise was fulfilled in Ishmael are problematic as the
text can be interpreted in almost any direction with equal weight. However, the declaration in v. 12 that Ishmael would live 'against all men (or
brethren) and they against him' suggests, to Hagar at least, that there is a
distinct possibility that Abram will have more progeny.

The third frequently discussed theme is that of uniqueness but the
approach is often fragmented. With the introduction of the covenantal
promise we have the first indication of Hagar's uniqueness in the patriarchal narratives.

> So far in the ancestral narratives Abram has been the only person
> to hear such talk. God will repeat [the promise to Isaac (26:2-6, 24)
> and Jacob (28:13-15; 35:9-12; 46:3-4) Joseph gets it second hand
> from his father (48:3-4), *added by ET*] but to no one else[... *added
> by ET*] Hagar, then, is one of just four people in Genesis to hear the
> language of promise from God's own lips, and she a woman, a slave,
> an Egyptian.[81]

---

[77] This stresses the theological implications "that God is turned toward the outsider."
Brueggemann, *Genesis*, 152.
[78] Von Rad, *Genesis: A Commentary*, 196. Brueggemann sees Ishmael's birth narrative
as a kind of detour, only a second tier theme whose primary function is to supply an
alternative to the original promise. Brueggemann, *Genesis*, 152.
[79] Brueggemann, *Genesis*, 153.
[80] Ibid., 151.
[81] Dennis, *Sarah Laughed*, 67.

Hagar is only one of four (and the only woman) to receive the promise yet "this promise to her lacks the covenant context that is so crucial to the founding fathers"[82] making her unique even within this elite group.

As we proceed through the pericope there is a continual stream of exceptional attributes afforded to Hagar in chapter 16. Verse 6 finds her fleeing from Sarai making Hagar "the first person in the Bible to flee oppression, indeed the first runaway slave."[83] Verse 7 contains "the first appearance of the angel of the Lord in the Bible."[84] In v. 8 Hagar is addressed by the messenger of YHWH using her proper name. In the entire Hagar story Abram/Abraham and Sarai/Sarah never address her in this manner. To them she is woman/handmaid/the Egyptian but never Hagar. Only after this personal address does she speak for first time. Fretheim describes the event in this manner, "God presents the divine self to her in such a way that she is drawn out rather than reduced to self-effacement and silence."[85] Verses 9 and 10 contain a command and the promise of innumerable descendants which, in turn, contain two more unique statements. The Divine's "demand here that she should return to Sarai sounds harsh, but it is coupled with the first statement of the promises of this kind directly to a woman. This is also the first birth oracle, 'you have conceived and shall bear a son and shall call his name,' a formula that regularly announces the birth of saviors within the Bible (cf. Judg 13:3; Isa 7:14; Luke 1:31)."[86] The result of all these unique elements is Hagar's response "an astonishing act undertaken by no other person in the Hebrew Bible."[87] She names the Deity and does so using the term *El-Roi* which occurs nowhere else in the Hebrew Bible. "It is Hagar's name for God, and Hagar's alone. It arises out of, and speaks eloquently of, her own private encounter with him."[88] The closing statement in v. 14 is a singular

---

[82] Trible, *Texts of Terror: Literary-Feminist Readings of Biblical Narratives*, 16. Drey claims the reason Hagar receives the promise is not because of her standing before the Deity or her connection to Sarai/Sarah but because she is the wife of Abram. Philip R. Drey, "The Role of Hagar in Genesis 16," *Andrews University Seminary Studies* 40, no. 2 (2002): 193.

[83] Phyllis Trible and Letty M. Russell, *Hagar, Sarah, and Their Children: Jewish, Christian, and Muslim Perspectives*, 1st ed. (Louisville, Ky.: Westminster John Knox, 2006), 40.

[84] Freedman, *Genesis*, 51.

[85] Fretheim, *Abraham: Trials of Family and Faith*, 97.

[86] Freedman, *Genesis*, 51. Also see Trible and Russell, *Hagar, Sarah, and Their Children: Jewish, Christian, and Muslim Perspectives*, 41.

[87] Katheryn Pfisterer Darr, *Far More Precious Than Jewels: Perspectives on Biblical Women*, 1st ed. (Louisville, Ky.: Westminster John Knox, 1991), 141.

[88] Dennis, *Sarah Laughed*, 71.

event in which the interaction between a woman and the Deity results in the etymology of a place.[89] The story of Hagar in vv. 7-14, considered "strange" and "odd" by many scholars for a variety of reasons, might be better served to be termed unique due to its overwhelming singularity on so many different levels.

3. Parameters

Moberly stated that "as the narrative of Genesis 12-50 now stands, there are five major characters: Abraham, Isaac, Jacob, Joseph — and God. The most important of these is God, and it is he who provides the unity within Genesis 12-50 as a whole."[90] Within this division Brueggemann designates Gen 16:1-18:15 a distinct portion of the Abraham cycle within the Patriarchal saga.[91] He did not divide his commentary, as most scholars do, with the direct line of the individual patriarch. He grouped three passages together, 16:1-16, 17:1-27 and 18:1-15, because he felt the text revolved around the issue of faith in a Deity whose promise tarried too long.[92] Structurally the themes of faith in the Deity and the character of the Deity are too fluid to sustain a structural parameter argument.

For other scholars it is the individual who takes center stage.[93] Coats determined that the discord inherent in the "Sarah-Hagar Novella" is a structural theme within the Abraham cycle.[94] He groups passages containing either each woman or both which give him the pericope Gen 16:1-21:21. Most commentaries respect but do not follow Coats' overarching structural thematic approach. Instead, the most common first division is to hold Gen 16:1-16 as a unit.[95] After this first examination, most scholars break down Gen 16 into three sections vv. 1-6; 7-14; 15-16.[96] The

---

[89] Humphreys, *The Character of God in the Book of Genesis: A Narrative Appraisal*, 105.
[90] Walter Moberly, *Genesis 12-50* (Sheffield: JSOT Press, 1992), 19.
[91] Brueggemann, *Genesis*, 150-62.
[92] Brueggemann also stated "While the three units focus on the same theme, they have no natural connection with each other. They are of difference sources and reflect the varied ways in which Israel responded to this troublesome delayed promise." Ibid., 151.
[93] Eissfeldt wisely stated, "at the centre of the tribal and national sagas there are always individuals." Otto Eissfeldt, *The Old Testament: An Introduction*, trans. Peter R. Ackroyd (New York: Harper and Row, 1965), 40.
[94] Coats, *Genesis*, 127-55.127-155
[95] Speiser, *Genesis*, 116-21. See also Fretheim, *Abraham: Trials of Family and Faith*, 95-99.
[96] The second portion of the division is defined as vv. 7-14. For division arguments see: Westermann 16:1-16 (1-6; 7-14; 15-16), Westermann, *Genesis: A Practical Commentary*, 123. Wenham 16:1-16 (1-6; 7-14; 15-16), Gordon J. Wenham, *Genesis 16-50*,

isolation of vv. 7-14 marks a structurally distinct narrative. "From the perspective of the faith of Abraham and Sarah, the story is oddly presented. It is structured as a Hagar story... Only by inference is this story concerned with Abraham and Sarah."[97] It is this second portion of the division (16:7-14) that is under examination in this thesis. This structural division of chapter is understandable if the exegete is using the following three structural themes as parameters.

The first structural theme is location. Eissfeldt suggested dividing sagas along the lines of their localities or surrounding natural phenomena and by the leading characters mentioned within.[98] Coats commented that the introduction of a new character in the form of a messenger of YHWH and narrative description of Hagar's position "near a spring of water in the wilderness" (v. 7) "typically represent major structural divisions in the OT narrative."[99] Finlay's analysis of the setting follows Coats. "The different locations mark the main divisions of this unit: scene one (Gen 16:1-6) and scene three (vv. 15-16) take place in Abram's household but scene two (vv. 7-14) is set in the wilderness."[100] Using this criteria the passage begins in v. 7 and concludes in v. 14 due to the fact that "the scene opens with the angel finding Hagar by a well and closes with the well being named, enhancing the scene's concentric symmetry."[101]

The second structural theme is etymological. Eissfeldt threw his net wide when stating that sagas which "are often concerned with the explanation of a name may be readily understood from the belief in the intimate connection between object and name which is common to ancient Israel and to many ancient and primitive peoples. Thus a whole series

---

WBC 2 (Dallas, Tex.: Word, 1994), 3-4. Trible 16:1-16 (1; 2-6; 7-14; 15-16), Trible, *Texts of Terror: Literary-Feminist Readings of Biblical Narratives*, 9-19. Note that Trible sees the chapter in terms of episodes separating out v. 1 as an introduction to the first episode. Coats follows the separation of v. 1 but divides vv. 7-16 after v. 12 making vv. 13-16 the conclusion. Coats, *Genesis*, 129. Von Rad goes so far as to divide the chapter into five sections vv. 1-3; 4-6; 7-8; 9-14 and 15-16. Von Rad, *Genesis: A Commentary*, 190-97.

[97] Brueggemann, *Genesis*, 152.

[98] "If we divide the sagas into those which are connected with localities or other natural phenomena and those which center around a human group or a single individual — in other words into place sagas or nature sagas, and tribal or leader sagas — we may get a general picture of the wealth of the material." Eissfeldt, *The Old Testament: An Introduction*, 38.

[99] Coats, *Genesis*, 131.

[100] Finlay, *The Birth Report Genre in the Hebrew Bible*, 98.

[101] Wenham, *Genesis 16-50*, 9. Verses 15 and 16 are not, therefore, considered part of this division because they are not tied back to the previous verses by geographical location.

of sagas are simply etymological sagas."[102] The intervening dialogue of
vv. 7 and 14 explains the naming of the well *Beer-lahai-roi*.[103] The etymological interest is not, however, just in the naming of the well. It also
exists very explicitly within Ishmael's birth announcement.

The final structural theme, and the theme most often mentioned in
commentaries, is that of Ishmael's birth announcement. This, however, is
the weakest of the structural arguments. Eissfeldt stated that "The really
characteristic sagas for Israel are those of the tribe and people. These rest
upon the view that all human communities have an ancestor or — more
rarely — an ancestress, whose life and actions are decisive for the fortunes of their descendants."[104] Chapter 16 goes to great length and detail
in foretelling the birth and life of Ishmael. The disadvantage of this structural theme is the climax in v. 11 with the "traditional formula for the
announcement of the birth and future destiny of an important child" and
"the proud, fierce character of the Ishmaelite desert tribesmen"[105] as
delineated in v. 12. Verses 13 and 14 are only tangentially connected to
this structural thematic choice.

Combining these structural themes allows us to determine specific
parameters for analysis. According to Coats vv. 7 and 8 function "as a
bridge between the story developed in vv. 1-6 and the narratives to follow.
The story in effect shifts its structural line of development from the
contention between Sarai and Hagar to an annunciation to Hagar that she
would give birth to a son."[106] Included in v. 7 is the narrative description
of Hagar's location in the wilderness. This location becomes important and
symmetry demands a follow up. By concluding our parameter with v. 14
the structure of the narrative unites the God who sees with the God who is
seen. The etymology of *Beer-lahai-roi* becomes the final consequence of
Hagar's dialogue with the Divine.[107] The well's location "between Kadesh

---

[102] Eissfeldt, *The Old Testament: An Introduction*, 38.
[103] Literally translated as "'the Well of the Living One of Vision' or as most of the versions
and English translations take it 'the Well of the Living One who sees me' [... *added
by ET*] The name is said to derive from the way in which Hagar addressed the Lord as
El-Roi, 'God of Vision' or 'God who sees me'." Robert Davidson, *Genesis 12-50*,
(Cambridge Bible Commentary: Cambridge: Cambridge University Press, 1979), 53.
[104] Eissfeldt, *The Old Testament: An Introduction*, 40. Also see Nikaido, "Hagar and
Ishmael as Literary Figures: An Intertextual Study," 219.
[105] Davidson, *Genesis 12-50*, 52, 50.
[106] Coats, *Genesis*, 131.
[107] Van Seters disagrees with the etymological theme for v. 14. He states, "There is no
indication in the story itself that the encounter was considered extraordinary or created
a holiness at that place. The encounter functions only to communicate to the slave girl

and Bered" confirms her original wilderness location in v. 7 and becomes a fitting conclusion to this Divine-human encounter.

4. Translation

7. And a messenger of YHWH found[108] her near a spring of water in the wilderness, near a spring on the road to Shur.[109]
8. And he said, Hagar Sarai's handmaid,[110] Where have you come from and where will you go? And she said,[111] I am fleeing from Sarai my mistress.
9. And the messenger of YHWH said to her, Return to your mistress and bow down[112] under her hands.
10. And the Messenger of YHWH said to her, I will cause your seed to multiply. And I will not count its abundance.
11. And the messenger of YHWH said to her, Behold, you are pregnant and you will bring forth a son and will call his name Ishmael[113] because YHWH has heard your afflictions.[114]

---

the destiny of her offspring." John Van Seters, *Abraham in History and Tradition* (New Haven, Conn.: Yale University Press, 1975), 193.

[108] Ngan argues that the verb implies an active seeking on YHWH's part. Ngan, "Neither Here nor There: Boundary and Identity in the Hagar Story," 81.

[109] Sarna notes that "in the Hebrew, the 'spring on the road to Shur' contains a play on words: *'ayin* may mean 'an eye' as well as 'a spring,' and *shur* can mean 'to see' and also 'a wall.' The verb *sh-u-r* is used together with *'ayin* in poetic texts. The place where Hagar takes refuge thus suggest 'a seeing eye.' She calls God *El-roi*, 'God of seeing,' and the well after the 'Living One Who sees me' (v. 13)." Sarna, *Genesis*, 120. Brodie comments "The road [Hagar, *added by ET*] is on, 'the way to Shur,' goes toward Egypt. The terrain is wilderness. The word *šûr*, 'Shur,' may also be read as a verb, 'to see,' a word that links with the rest of the Hagar story." Brodie, *Genesis as Dialogue: A Literary, Historical, and Theological Commentary*, 238.

[110] Schneider states that "Hagar is defined as a *shiphchah* because it shows her status in the context in which she is living, highlights some of the functions she is intended to perform, and establishes the legitimacy of those around her to use her in that way. It does not mean that it is nice, nor does it mean that Hagar is in a good situation, but the references are to situate her rather than to demean her." Schneider, *Mothers of Promise: Women in the Book of Genesis*, 105. For a thorough discussion on the translation of the Hebrew word *shiphchah* see Schneider's discussion of Hagar's description on pages 103-108.

[111] Hagar is "one of only three women in Genesis to engage in dialogue with God. The other two are the woman in the Garden and Sarah." Dennis, *Sarah Laughed*, 67.

[112] This is the only use of the Hithpael form of the verb עָנָה in the Torah and the only use of the Hithpael imperative 2fs in the entire canon. Wenham, *Genesis 16-50*, 10.

[113] Genesis 16:11-12 is the first annunciation scene in the Bible. Dennis, *Sarah Laughed*, 67. For a thorough discussion of annunciation type-scenes see Finlay, *The Birth Report Genre in the Hebrew Bible*, 85-161.

[114] Alter notes that "the noun derives from the same root as the verb of abuse (or, harassment, harsh handling, humiliation) used for Sarai's mistreatment of Hagar [in v. 6, *added by ET*]." Robert Alter, *The Five Books of Moses* (New York: W.W. Norton, 2004), 79.

12. And he will be a wild ass of a man. His hand will be against[115] all men and they will be against him. Amid all his brothers will he dwell.
13. And she called the name of YHWH who was speaking to her God who sees me[116], because she said, Also, have I not continued to see after he has seen me?[117]
14. And thus the well was called Beer-lahai-roi; Behold it is between Kadesh and Bared.

5. Structure

Divine Dialogue with Hagar	Gen 16:7-14
I. Narrative element part 1	Gen 16:7
II. Dialogue	Gen 16:8-13
III. Narrative element part 2	Gen 16:14

C. GENESIS 17:15-22: SARAI RENAMED

1. Setting in literature

The second Patriarchal saga dialogue to be examined within this thesis is Gen 17:15-22 in which the Deity informs Abraham of Sarai's new name and clarifies once and for all that the covenant son will be the forthcoming Isaac, not Ishmael. Working from the classic fivefold *toledot* arrangement of Genesis, the Patriarchal sagas are most often divided according to their principal characters.[118] These family sagas,[119] while connected

---

[115] Brodie states, "Hagar will learn to live with Sarah's antagonism. Her son, too, will live with antagonism. The angel announces that the son will have to deal with the face or presence of his brothers. The experiences of mother and son are related by verbal echoes." Brodie, *Genesis as Dialogue: A Literary, Historical, and Theological Commentary*, 238.

[116] With regards to the term *El-roi* Speiser argues, the "MT is pointed defectively, perhaps on purpose, to leave the reader a choice between this, i.e., 'God of seeing,' one whom it is permitted to see, and the *rō'i* of the last clause, 'one who sees me.' The explanatory gloss that follows is hopeless as it now stands." Speiser, *Genesis*, 118. Also see Wyatt, "The Meaning of El Roi and the Mythological Dimension in Genesis 16," 143.

[117] "Without emendation, the Hebrew is difficult, lit. 'Have I really seen hither after he has seen me?' BHS and many modern translations emend 'hither' to 'God' and insert 'and I lived,' so that the whole remark reads 'Have I really seen God and lived after my seeing (him)?'" Wenham, *Genesis 16-50*, 3.

[118] Genesis 12-25; 25-36 and 37-50. Blenkinsopp, *The Pentateuch: An Introduction to the First Five Books of the Bible*, 99.

[119] Coats defines family saga as presenting "the history of a family in such a manner that the qualifying principles of the family appear most sharply in the foreground." Coats, *Genesis*, 102.

through genealogy, have distinct elements within the structure and narrative that distinguish Gen 12-25 from those that surround it. While Gen 11 closes with the generations of Terah, "the function of this genealogy is not so much to connect Abraham with the preceding events, as the previous genealogies have done, but to provide the reader with the necessary background for understanding the events in the life of Abraham which follow."[120]

Genesis 12 then begins the story of Abram and his quest for progeny. "Starting out from this point, and covering a period of 100 years, the following narrative moves through a series of crises to a partial resolution."[121] Throughout the Abraham saga[122] a central theme emerges — the concern over the promise of a covenant son.[123] Coats states that this saga as a whole "begins with the exposition, moves to a center focused on the covenant between Abraham and God, then returns to a theological conclusion designed to confirm the character of Abraham as it was set forth in the exposition."[124]

The central focus of Gen 17 then becomes the defined promise to Abraham. Coats states, "The oath is originally given to the childless family as a promise for the birth of a son, then subsequently expanded to include the birth of a great nation, the gift of land, and a blessing." Humphreys comments that the Deity "may have flirted with alternatives to a hierarchy based in gender and ethnicity in his encounter with Hagar, but in Genesis 17 he reinscribes patriarchal structures to which he subscribes."[125]

As for Abram's change of name in Gen 17:5, scholars debate its unequivocal meaning and purpose.[126] When understood within the context

---

[120] John Sailhamer, *The Pentateuch as Narrative: A Biblical-Theological Commentary* (Grand Rapids, Mich.: Zondervan, 1992), 137.

[121] Blenkinsopp, *The Pentateuch: An Introduction to the First Five Books of the Bible*, 100.

[122] Defined by Coats as Gen 11:10-25:26. Coats, *Genesis*, 97-102.

[123] Sailhamer calls it a 'central event.' Sailhamer, *The Pentateuch as Narrative: A Biblical-Theological Commentary*, 137.

[124] Coats, *Genesis*, 98.

[125] Humphreys, *The Character of God in the Book of Genesis: A Narrative Appraisal*, 110.

[126] Von Rad stated, "The name 'Abraham' is linguistically nothing else than a 'lengthening' of the simpler 'Abram,' which means 'my father (the god) is exalted.'" Von Rad, *Genesis: A Commentary*, 199. Sarna simplifies the argument by stating that to make a name great "your name Abram will be enlarged by the addition of a syllable." Sarna, *Genesis*, 124. Cotter, expanding the explanation, states that "The change in name here is intended to convey a real change in Abram's identity. So, just as his people [are, *added by ET*] to be made great, his name is 'made great,' i.e., lengthened." Cotter, *Genesis*, 109. Coats brings in elements of etiology, "The act itself indicates lordship and suggests a shift in the understanding of covenant for this text. To give a name is

of the covenantal focus "this new name, incorporating the nuances of agglomeration or conglomeration, is then explicated not only in terms of nations but of kings; hence the element of royal dynasties points not to changing dynastic lines in one nation but to many dynasties in many nations."[127] Within the literary structure of the Patriarchal saga this covenant then becomes "the primary metaphor for understanding Israel's life with God. It is the covenant which offers to Israel the gift of hope, the reality of identity, the possibility of belonging, the certitude of vocation."[128] The understanding of this covenant is also key to the dialogue discussed in this chapter.

2. Setting in narrative

Narrative analysis often describes Gen 17 as a collection of divine speeches.[129] The first speech (vv. 1-8) deepens the original covenant made in chapter 15[130] and changes Abram's name to Abraham.[131] The second speech (vv. 9-14) delivers the "Covenant of Circumcision," which is prescribed for Abraham and his household[132] and fulfilled in the final verses of chapter 17.[133] The third and final speech (vv. 15-22) changes

---

to express suzerainty. The name change does not control the development of the oracle, however. There is no law, no stipulation of relationship. To the contrary, here the name change is rooted in the divine promise: 'Your name shall be Abraham, for I have made you father of a multitude.' The sentence has elements of a name etiology but it is not spelled out in full." Coats, *Genesis*, 134.

[127] Brichto, *The Names of God: Poetic Readings in Biblical Beginnings*, 226.

[128] Brueggemann, *Genesis*, 154.

[129] Humphreys notes that "taken together these three extensive speeches by God in this episode constitute his longest utterance since he spoke into the chaotic void and created a cosmos in Genesis 1 and reconstituted it in Genesis 8." Humphreys, *The Character of God in the Book of Genesis: A Narrative Appraisal*, 108. Also see Sailhamer, *The Pentateuch as Narrative: A Biblical-Theological Commentary*, 156-60. and Turner, *Genesis*, 80.

[130] Brodie, *Genesis as Dialogue: A Literary, Historical, & Theological Commentary*, 240.

[131] Westermann argues that "Abraham, the father of a family in the early narratives, here becomes the father of nations. This expansion finds expression in a change of name: Abram becomes Abraham. The word *hāmôn*, 'multitude' (represented in the translation by 'many'), plays on the final syllable. The new name is analogous to the throne name given a king at his enthronement. Abraham is thus elevated to a new status: he is father of Israel and father of nations." Westermann, *Genesis: A Practical Commentary*, 130.

[132] Turner observes that "The only human action of any note in the chapter is Abram's circumcision of his household. Yahweh's lengthy speech does more than provide a break in the narrative action. It also gives a summary reminder of the covenant promises while developing them further in significant ways." Turner, *Genesis*, 80.

[133] Fretheim makes an interesting observation when he notes, "it is striking that Abraham never explicitly agrees with God's plans in 17:20-21, though his move to circumcise

Sarai's name to Sarah, foretells the birth of Isaac and clarifies that Ishmael is not the covenant son. Within this final speech, however, Abraham responds and questions, making this third division a dialogue, not a speech.

In the opening verses of the chapter (vv. 3-6) Abraham made no verbal response to the Deity's statements regarding his name change or the reiteration of the covenant through circumcision. His submission to the Deity goes uncontested. The announcement that Sarai, now Sarah, will conceive and give birth to the covenant son, however, brings a retort of laughter and bewilderment.[134] "Abraham appears to take exception to what his God offers him. He seems confused by all this."[135] The declaration by the Deity has opened the floodgates that wash away any notion that Hagar is the mother of promise within the covenant.[136] The Deity's response to Abraham's statement, "Oh that Ishmael might live before thee" brings divine comfort in the understanding that Ishmael too shall be the father of a great nation but Isaac is to be the chosen son.

Commenting on v. 19 Dennis laments that "at last [Sarah, *added by ET*] belongs to the world of those promises. She is no longer an outsider. How tragic, then, that at this, her great moment, she is not on stage! Such fine words have been spoken, such momentous words have issued from the mouth of God, and she is not there to hear them!"[137] The point of the Divine assertion that Sarah is the mother of promise, from a narrative point of view, is not that Sarah is off stage but that the covenant has finally been defined in more exacting terms. Humphreys states:

> God's covenant with Isaac seems more focal and restricted than that announced as marked by circumcision above. For it included Ishmael among other male members of Abraham's household. This one is

his household (17:23-27) would be a general sign of trust and obedience." Fretheim, *Abraham: Trials of Family and Faith*, 110.

[134] Phillips suggests that in both cases (vv. 3, 17) "Abraham's physical response may be indicative of consternation which accompanied his incredulity" Elaine A. Phillips, "Incredulity, Faith, and Textual Purposes: Post-Biblical Responses to the Laughter of Abraham and Sarah," in The Function of Scripture in Early Jewish and Christian Tradition, ed. by Craig A. Evans and James A. Sanders, JSNTSup 154 (Sheffield: Sheffield Academic Press, 1988), 23.

[135] Humphreys, *The Character of God in the Book of Genesis: A Narrative Appraisal*, 110. Von Rad states that "Abraham's laugh brings us in any case to the outer limits of what is psychologically possible. Combined with the pathetic gesture of reverence is an almost horrible laugh, deadly earnest, not in fun, bringing belief and unbelief close together." Von Rad, *Genesis: A Commentary*, 203.

[136] Fretheim argues that "while Genesis 16:15-16 gives readers the impression that Ishmael is the promised son, God's promise is refined to specify that Sarah is to be the mother of this son (17:15-20)." Fretheim, *Abraham: Trials of Family and Faith*, 94.

[137] Dennis, *Sarah Laughed*, 46.

established with the still to be born son Isaac, whose announcement triggered laughter and whose appearance will upset the natural biology of birth.[138]

Through this general narrative analysis we then see that vv. 15-22, while contained within the general concept of divine speech, can be separated out into divine dialogue due to the interactions between the Deity and the humans involved in the discussion.

Within the structural parameters under discussion in Gen 17 there are three narrative thematic considerations which fall into sub-categories of the overarching concept of Abraham's covenant with the Deity.[139] Under the covenantal umbrella is first, the theme of the promises that have previously been given to Abram and their expansion here in chapter 17; second the covenant of circumcision; and third, the name changes given to Abram/Abraham and Sarai/Sarah. We will take a quick look at each of these topics.

The overall narrative theme of chapter 17 is the discussion of covenant. Brueggemann calls it "binding Abraham to God in radical faith."[140] Within this theme is first, the expansion of the Abrahamic covenant. Wenham states, "This chapter is a watershed in the Abraham story. The promises to him have been unfolded bit by bit, gradually building up and becoming more detailed and precise, until here they are repeated and filled out in a glorious crescendo in a long and elaborate divine speech."[141] This sub-categorical theme includes comparisons with alternate versions of the same covenant as stated in chapter 15. For some scholars the changes made to the covenant in chapter 17 are more revisional than a restating of the promise in chapter 15.[142]

The second narrative sub-theme is the covenant of circumcision. It follows and corresponds well with the first theme. After summarizing the aforementioned promise, the Deity instructs Abraham on the new

---

[138] Humphreys, *The Character of God in the Book of Genesis: A Narrative Appraisal*, 111.

[139] Warning observed that "In no other chapter of the Hebrew Bible does the noun ברית occur as often as in Genesis 17." Almost half of the occurrences in Genesis are found in this chapter. Wilfried Warning, "Termiinological Patterns and Genesis 17," *HUCA* 70-71(1999-2000): 97.

[140] Brueggemann, *Genesis*, 154.

[141] Wenham, *Genesis 16-50*, 16.

[142] Trible and Russell, *Hagar, Sarah, and Their Children: Jewish, Christian, and Muslim Perspectives*, 42.

requirement of circumcision. Verses 9–14 detail the commandment and instruction on how the act is to be carried out.[143] Westermann observes that the promise is primary because "the command is based on the promise."[144]

The third narrative theme primarily associated with discussions of Gen 17 is that regarding the name changes of Abram and Sarai.[145] For this discussion, however, there are a multitude of explanations for the change which, in turn, take up volumes. For some, the expanded name form "carries with it an intimation of [Abram's, *added by ET*] God-given destiny."[146] For others the form is insignificant "but this story invests the change with great significance."[147] Most, however, do agree that the new names and new promises for both Abraham and Sarah shape a somewhat different future for the characters discussed.

3. Parameters

Brueggemann groups Gen 16, 17 and 18 together due to their specific focus on Abraham. He does, however, describe Gen 16:1-18:15 as having three distinct pieces.[148] Extending from this point many scholars delineate chapter 17 as a distinct unit including all 27 verses.[149] Brueggemann describes chapter 17 as "ponderous, disciplined, and symmetrical."[150] Internal divisions of the chapter, however, vary according to the interest of the scholar.

Coats declares Gen 17 to be "a series of speeches providing promises, instructions for circumcision, and a formal annunciation of the birth of Isaac."[151] If the chapter is divided using divine speeches as a collective unit scholars break the final verse elements between vv. 21 and 22, describing vv. 22-27 as a 'conclusion.' When using circumcision as

---

[143] Verses 23-27 conclude the chapter by reporting the narrative of how the command was carried out.

[144] Westermann, *Genesis: A Practical Commentary*, 129.

[145] A detailed discussion of the impact of the name change for Abram and Sarai will be discussed in another section of this chapter.

[146] For example: Sarna, *Genesis*, 124.

[147] Cotter, *Genesis*, 108.

[148] Brueggemann, *Genesis*, 150-62.

[149] For example: Speiser, *Genesis*, 122. See also Wenham, *Genesis 16-50*, 13-19.

[150] Brueggemann, *Genesis*, 153. In comparison, from a source critical point of view, von Rad characterizes the same chapter as without "a unified structure [or, *added by ET*] continuity." Von Rad, *Genesis: A Commentary*, 197.

[151] Coats, *Genesis*, 136. Later Coats defines dialogue as "a combination of speeches, each in response to the other, with the pattern of response significant for special types of dialogue." (317). Ibid., 317.

a unit divider scholars tend to separate vv. 1-14 as the institution of circumcision and vv. 15-27 as the promise of a son and the act of circumcision.[152]

The most common partition of the chapter is four sections. Sarna states, "The [chapter, *added by ET*] divides into four parts, artistically set forth in a carefully designed arrangement."[153] The breakdown is as follows: vv. 1-8 Abram is to be progenitor of numerous nations and kings and his name is changed to Abraham; vv. 9-14 the law of circumcision is set forth; vv. 15-22: Sarai's name is changed to Sarah and the Deity declares her to be the progenitrix of numerous nations and of kings; vv. 23-27 the law of circumcision is carried out by Abraham on his household.[154] The pattern of a name change and promise of nations and kings is included in vv. 1-8 and again in vv. 15-22. The second time the emphasis is on Sarai/Sarah and the promise is more complete.

What makes vv. 15-22 a dialogue unit? First, according to Coats, is the evidence of a renewed speech formula which combines "the subject of the promise for great posterity with a promise for a son. The speech, addressed to Abraham, opens with a name change for Sarai, and on the heels of the change comes a promise for blessing for her."[155] Wenham adds that this fourth divine speech contained within chapter 17 "does not build on the third; it takes an entirely new turn" and specifically addresses Sarah.[156] Second, in the introductory verses of the chapter Abraham remained a "dumb recipient of the promise"[157] when the Deity appeared. In vv. 17 and 18 Abraham again falls on his face but this time we have his questions and comment[158] followed by the Deity's

---

[152] For example: von Rad, *Genesis: A Commentary*, 197-203.

[153] Sarna, *Genesis*, 122.

[154] Cotter states that this division results in a story whose second two units are in parallel with the first two. Cotter, *Genesis*, 107. Westermann has a distinct and detailed division which still singles out vv. 15-21 as a separate dialogue. His breakdown for chapter 17 is vv. 1-3a; 3b-21 [further delineated as: 3b-8, 9-14, 15-21, *added by ET*]; 23-27. He states, "The discourse in 17:3b-21 has three parts: promise (vv. 3b-8), command (vv.9-14), and promise (vv.15-21). This shows that the promise is primary; the command is based on the promise." Westermann, *Genesis: A Practical Commentary*, 129.

[155] Coats, *Genesis*, 135.

[156] Wenham, *Genesis 16-50*, 25.

[157] In that no verbal reaction or response is recorded. Von Rad, *Genesis: A Commentary*, 199.

[158] Coats declares one speech, that of "v. 17, is a complaint; the other, v. 18, an appeal for Ishmael." Coats, *Genesis*, 133.

responsive answers and promises. Third, v. 22 is included in this unit parameter because it draws attention to the Deity's dramatic exit from the dialogue. "The end of his speech is described much more fully than usual. Usually nothing is said about God ceasing to speak or going away: he just stops and the next event is described." Finally, as the dialogue ends, what follows in vv. 23-27 reflects back to vv. 9-14 serving as a conclusion to the institution of the law of circumcision. Because this theme of circumcision is not mentioned within the dialogue of vv. 15-22, it can therefore also be used to define our parameters.

4. Translation

15. And Elohim said unto Abraham, Your wife Sarai, you will not call her Sarai because her name is Sarah.
16. And I will bless her and also you will have a son from her and I will bless her and she will be to nations; kings of peoples will come from her.
17. And Abraham fell upon his face and laughed[159] and he said in his heart, Will a son be born to[160] one who is one hundred years old and will[161] Sarah who is ninety bear?
18. And Abraham said unto Elohim,[162] O that Ishmael might live before you.[163]
19. And Elohim said, Indeed,[164] Sarah your wife will bear you a son and you will call his name Isaac and I will set my covenant with him, a covenant forever and with his seed after him.

---

[159] "All three biblical traditions relating to the birth of Isaac (cf. 17:19; 18:12; 21:6) emphatically connect the name with human laughter." Sarna, *Genesis*, 127.

[160] In comparing this use with Isaiah 66:8 Wenham argues that the intent of the use of the imperfect is to express potential or surprise. Wenham, *Genesis 16-50*, 16.

[161] Wenham states "שרה-ואם or the following ה are often deleted, because double-barreled questions usually take the form ואם ... ה, not here, ואם ה ... ה. This unusual construction underlines Abraham's disbelief." Ibid., 16.

[162] Cotter argues that with the use of the definite article (*hā*) before the word *'ĕlōhîm* "the narrator indicates that Abraham is not really attending to God of the covenant[... *added by ET*] when used without the definite article, [*'ĕlōhîm*, *added by ET*] is a proper name for God in Hebrew just as in English. However when the definite article is used it becomes simply a generic word for any deity or divinity[... *added by ET*] So whomever Abraham thinks he is talking to, the narrator tells us readers, it is not the covenant God but simply Abraham's mistaken notion of who *the* god he relates to might be." Cotter, *Genesis*, 111.

[163] Sarna argues for a translation of "your favor" over "before thee." "Hebrew *lifnei* seems to have this meaning in other texts (cf. Gen 10:9; 27:7; Hos 6:2). Abraham fears for the life of Ishmael because God's words appear wholly to exclude the boy from the benefits of the covenant." Sarna, *Genesis*, 126.

[164] Unlike v. 3 where Abraham receives no rebuke from the Deity, here "God rebukes Abraham very firmly. His doubt is emphatically contradicted by the opening אבל 'indeed' instead of הנה 'behold,' which is more usual in an announcement scene." Wenham, *Genesis 16-50*, 26.

20. As for Ishmael, I have heard you.[165] Behold I will bless him and cause him to be fruitful and he will become many. Twelve princes[166] will he father and I will give to him a great nation.
21. I will set my covenant with Isaac whom Sarah will bear to you at the appointed season in the following year.
22. And he finished speaking with him and Elohim went up from Abraham.

5. Structure

	Divine Dialogue with Abraham	Gen 17:15-22
I.	Dialogue part 1	Gen 17:15-16
II.	Narrative element part 1	Gen 17:17a
III.	Dialogue part 2	Gen 17:17b-21
IV.	Narrative element part 2	Gen 17:22

D. GENESIS 18:9-15: ABRAHAM, VISITORS AND SARAH

1. Setting in literature

The third Patriarchal dialogue to be examined is that of Gen 18:9-15. Here, in the middle of the Terah *toledot*, the promise of a covenant son is finally heard by both parents. Sarna explains that within the overarching *toledot* "the divine promise has been unfolding in stages. First, in 15:4, Abraham was assured that his heir would be a natural-born son; then, in 17:16-21, he was assured that Sarah would bear this child; now a time limit is set for the fulfillment of the promise."[167] Whereas chapter 15 first uses the word covenant, it is chapter 17 where the divine promise becomes physical covenant with the application of the Law of Circumcision. Along with their name changes "Abraham and Sarah are set to become the father and mother of many nations."[168] They are primed but Sarah is, as yet, an unknowing participant.

In Chapter 18:1-8 Abraham, as patriarch, is the primary figure but in vv. 9-15 everything changes. "The pace is slowed to allow for the

---

[165] Noting the play on Ishmael's name, שמעתיך "I have heard you."
[166] Genesis 25:12-16 lists the twelve chieftains.
[167] Sarna, *Genesis*, 130. Brueggemann considers these chapters as having "three distinct pieces" to the overall covenant puzzle, i.e., 16:1-16; 17:1-27; 18:1-15. Brueggemann, *Genesis*, 150-62.
[168] Mark G. Brett, *Genesis: Procreation and the Politics of Identity* (London: Routledge, 2000), 63.

weightiness and drama of the transaction."[169] The spectacle then becomes the revelation of the promise to Sarah and of her reaction regarding its startling consequences. For these verses Abraham is muted, again, to a secondary role in the dialogue. It is not until after the dialogue closes that Abraham once more takes center stage.[170] Sarah is not mentioned again until chapter 20 as the family sojourns in Gerar and then when she bears Isaac in chapter 21 finally fulfilling the covenant promise begun in chapter 15.

2. Setting in narrative

In order to discuss the narrative setting of divine dialogue in chapter 18 we must first analyze Abraham's understanding of the identity of his visitors.[171] In Gen 17:3 Abraham's reaction to the Deity's appearance is to "fall on his face." In chapter 18, while the reader is aware that YHWH has appeared, "from Abraham's perspective it is three men (18:2). This explains Abraham's actions[... *added by ET*] So it is not likely that he knowingly scrambles about his encampment hastily putting together a meal."[172] Contrary to this theory Brichto argues, "Abraham had from the moment he espied them recognized that these 'three men' were stand-ins for YHWH. This recognition is expressed in his immediate run to greet them and his prostration before them."[173] Brichto's supposition, however,

---

[169] Brueggemann, *Genesis*, 158.

[170] For some scholars chapters 18 and 19 are more tightly intertwined than chapters 17 and 18. Van Seters claims that chapter 17 is a "freely composed doublet of" chapter 18. Van Seters, *Abraham in History and Tradition*, 284. Westermann and Wenham, however, see the complex embracing chapters 18 and 19. Wenham explains, "The unity of these stories (18&19) is shown by the same actors appearing in most of the scenes, most obviously the angels in 18:1-19:23, Lot throughout chap. 19 and by implication in 18:20-32, and Abraham throughout chap. 18 and in 19:29. Furthermore, the storyline in 19:1-22 closely parallels that in 18:1-30, encouraging a comparison to be made between the righteous heroes of these chapters, Abraham and Lot." Wenham, *Genesis 16-50*, 40. Also see Westermann, *Genesis: A Practical Commentary*, 134-36. The difference in interpretation of the literary divisions depends on the choice of narrative elements compared.

[171] Brueggemann states that clarification concerning the identity of the visitor(s) is the "primary critical question." Brueggemann, *Genesis*, 157.

[172] Turner, *Genesis*, 84. Fretheim agrees with this perspective. Fretheim, *Abraham: Trials of Family and Faith*, 111. As does Wenham, who states that v. 2 "makes clear, he at first thought they were simply men." Wenham, *Genesis 16-50*, 45. Dennis argues that not only does Abraham not recognize his visitors "what is more he never penetrates the disguise." Dennis, *Sarah Laughed*, 48.

[173] Brichto, *The Names of God: Poetic Readings in Biblical Beginnings*, 231.

is not well supported as Speiser explains Abraham's address of "my Lord" in v. 3. Speiser argues:

> At this stage Abraham is as yet unaware of the true identity of his visitors, so that he would not address any of them as God; and he cannot mean all three, because the rest of the verse contains three unambiguous singulars. What the text indicates, therefore, is that Abraham has turned to one of the strangers whom he somehow recognized as the leader. In vv. 4-5 he includes the other two as a matter of courtesy.[174]

The difficulty in deciphering this text is the fact that this particular divine appearance is unique in its configuration in the Hebrew Bible.[175]

Is it three visitors or one visitor with a retinue? Westermann returns to source criticism to explain the alternating narrative identification of the visitors.[176] For von Rad the lack of clarity regarding the visitor's identity is "the relationship of the 'three men' to Yahweh."[177] He solves the dilemma by clarifying that "the most obvious answer seems to be that Yahweh is one of the three men. This assumption would become certainty when in chs. 18:22 and 19:1, after Yahweh's departure, the 'two messengers' come to Sodom."[178] For many scholars the exact moment of recognition of the Deity by both Abraham and Sarah is uncertain.[179] What is certain from these arguments, however, is that the Deity is present even if the representation and recognition cannot readily be defined.[180]

---

[174] Speiser, *Genesis*, 129.

[175] See pages 205-206 for von Rad's examples of multiple Divine visitors from extra-biblical traditions. Von Rad, *Genesis: A Commentary*, 204-05.

[176] Westermann's explanation joins two narratives, "one dealing with three visitors, the other dealing with one visitor who promises a son." Westermann, *Genesis: A Practical Commentary*, 135.

[177] Von Rad, *Genesis: A Commentary*, 204.

[178] Ibid., 204. Von Rad goes so far as to suggest the reader consider two of the visitors a "guards of honor" for the Divine third personage. Humphreys follows the argument that YHWH is one of the three visitors. Humphreys, *The Character of God in the Book of Genesis: A Narrative Appraisal*, 115.

[179] For example see Humphreys, *The Character of God in the Book of Genesis: A Narrative Appraisal*, 116. See also Fretheim, *Abraham: Trials of Family and Faith*, 111.

[180] Humphreys states, "Readers to this point have met God in various guises and under diverse names, and have perhaps come to expect the unexpected in the mode of God's appearing in the story-world of the text. The effect for us is a certain tentativeness, an inability to pin down in concrete and graphic terms how God is present." Humphreys, *The Character of God in the Book of Genesis: A Narrative Appraisal*, 115-16. Fretheim states that "While God conveys no self-identification, this text is similar to other theophanic narratives." Fretheim, *Abraham: Trials of Family and Faith*, 110. See also Gen 16:7-14; 26:24. Speiser makes an interesting observation. He states that the reader is well aware of the Deity's presence but "not how to distinguish him from

The opening lines of chapter 18 indicate that interaction with the Deity in this chapter is not a "chance encounter."[181] Abraham, seated in the door of his tent, raises his eyes to see three visitors standing before him. He is solicitous to them and eager to please. A meal is prepared and shared. The dialogue that follows the meal, however, seems to make Abraham superfluous. Focusing on Sarah and her reactions, Abraham is only mentioned as a type of mediator between the Divine and Sarah. The narrative then returns to Abraham, the visitors, and specifically the Deity, as the relative righteousness of Sodom is debated.

The fact that the narration is unclear as to exactly when Abraham and Sarah recognize their visitors as Divine only increases the overall tension and irony of the story. There is tension in that once again disbelief, awe or possibly doubt are expressed when Sarah laughs[182] and then directly challenges the Deity. Irony because the overall Abraham/Sarah narrative is a "story about a call embraced. But in this central narrative, the call is not embraced. It is rejected as nonsensical."[183] The discussion in the presence of Sarah, however, makes this account different from chapter 17.[184] This change of focus is not crucial to the narrative through line, but it is vital to the dialogue.

The conclusion of the dialogue in v. 15 is abrupt and seemingly incomplete. Fretheim suggests that "the narrator's intent may well be to leave the reader (as well as Sarah and Abraham) in a state of some uncertainty as to how God's future will work itself out."[185] Consider the following verses where Abraham takes on the role of intercessor for the city of Sodom.[186] The dialogue of Gen 18, however, focuses on the individual Sarah and her ability to procreate at her advanced age. Verses 16-23 then focus on a larger issue, that of "God's treatment of any righteous one (not merely Lot) in his judgment of the wicked."[187] Instead of focusing

---

the other two. To that extent, therefore, we are made to share Abraham's uncertainty and thus re-enact the patriarch's experience." Speiser, *Genesis*, 131.

[181] Turner, *Genesis*, 84.

[182] Abraham's response in 17:16-17 and Sarah's reaction and question in 18:12 are essentially the same. Fretheim argues that "this exchange keeps both Sarah and Abraham on the same level regarding the reception of the promise and will link up with her response to the naming of Isaac." Fretheim, *Abraham: Trials of Family and Faith*, 114.

[183] Brueggemann, *Genesis*, 159.

[184] Wenham, *Genesis 16-50*, 47.

[185] Fretheim, *Abraham: Trials of Family and Faith*, 116.

[186] It is interesting to note that this intercession follows a dialogue in which Abraham made no response to the Deity's questions and accusations regarding Sarah. Victor P. Hamilton, *The Book of Genesis: Chapters 18-50* (Grand Rapids, Mich.: Eerdmans, 1995), 14-26.

[187] Sailhamer, *The Pentateuch as Narrative: A Biblical-Theological Commentary*, 170.

on the relationship of the individual to the Divine, the narrative now explores the theme of individual and society in relation to their Deity's declarations of righteousness.[188] Throughout the chapter the narrative shows "great interest in the human frame of mind and the temptation into which men were lead precisely in their capacity as recipients of promise"[189] all of which is linked by the Divine visitors.

With the structural parameters of chapter 18 defined most often as vv. 1-8, 9-15 and 16-23 what remains is to discuss the narrative thematic discussions contained within our divine dialogue. The most common overarching theme for this chapter is that of hospitality.[190] Contained within this theme is the birth announcement to Sarah which can be considered a subset of hospitality as a good portion of the dialogue is directly engaged with her hospitable or inhospitable reception of the divine declaration.

The opening verses of chapter 18 describe Abraham's hospitality in detail. "While Abraham is generous and just, God is even more so."[191] This divine generosity takes the narrative form of the blessed birth announcement which has been crafted in such a way as to emphasize the miraculousness of the promise.[192] Brueggemann observes that "the story is constructed to present the tension between this inscrutable speech of God (that comes as promise) and the resistance and mockery of Abraham and Sarah who doubt the word and cannot believe the promise."[193]

Sarah's reaction to this birth announcement is somewhat understandable.[194] "In a world in which children were a woman's status and in which childlessness was regarded as a virtual sign of divine disfavor"[195]

---

[188] Speiser, *Genesis*, 135.

[189] Von Rad, *Genesis: A Commentary*, 208.

[190] Fretheim categorically states that vv. 1-8 are about hospitality. Verses 9-15, he argues, "retain some interest in hospitality, with their focus on Sarah's reception of the announcement" and that "in 18:16-33, issues of divine hospitality are raised, especially regarding God's reception of the human word. God receives the 'outcry' from those affected by the conduct of the people of Sodom and Gomorrah and moves to deal with it." Fretheim, *Abraham: Trials of Family and Faith*, 110-11.

[191] Brodie, *Genesis as Dialogue: A Literary, Historical, and Theological Commentary*, 243.

[192] Ibid., 244.

[193] Brueggemann, *Genesis*, 158.

[194] Wenham states, "These remarks of Sarah's show us the basis of her doubts. She laughed not out of cocky arrogance but because a lifelong disappointment had taught her not to clutch at straws. Hopelessness, not pride, underlay her belief." Wenham, *Genesis 16-50*, 48.

[195] Susan Niditch, "Genesis", in *Women's Bible Commentary*, ed. Carol A. Newsom and Sharon H. Ringe (Louisville, Ky.: Westminster John Knox, 1998), 20.

Sarah now learns firsthand, although somewhat surreptitiously, that she is to be the only mother of the covenant son. While Abraham had a similar reaction to the promise in chapter 17 here "the form of the announcement with its dramatic sense of amazement matches its substance. The surprise is yet another speech-event in which the world of Abraham and Sarah is decisively changed. Their world of barrenness is shattered by a new possibility that lies outside the reasonable expectation of their perceptual field."[196] The hospitality of the Deity in the form of the birth announcement is given directly to Abraham. It is, however, intended for Sarah specifically.[197]

3. Parameters

The parameters for chapter 18 are relatively straight forward.[198] On a large scale, linking the appearances of Abraham and Lot, some scholars consider Gen 18:1-19:38 to be a unit.[199] Sarna treats Gen 18:1-33 as a whole unit separate from the report of Lot in Sodom in Gen 19.[200] Within chapter 18 most scholars create two or three individual sections with the most common breaks being vv. 1-15 and vv. 16-33 or vv. 1-8, 9-15 and vv. 16-33.[201] For scholars choosing to separate vv. 1-8 from 9-15, vv. 1-8 are often described as the "hospitality" verses.[202] Brueggemann, however, sees vv. 1-8 as only setting the stage for the birth announcement given in v. 10.[203]

---

[196] Brueggemann, *Genesis*, 158.
[197] Darr argues this because Abraham has already received the promise in chapter 17. Darr, *Far More Precious Than Jewels: Perspectives on Biblical Women*, 102.
[198] A minor disagreement comes up in the division of topic or theme with regard to Gen 18:15 and 16. Most scholarship ends the narrative section at the end of v. 15. Von Rad and Westermann include v. 16 before the division. Von Rad's states, "every reader feels that v. 16 is to some extent a conclusion." His argument however is diachronic. Von Rad, *Genesis: A Commentary*, 208. Westermann includes the verse because Abraham "scarcely appears" in vv. 9-16. Westermann, *Genesis: A Practical Commentary*.
[199] Wenham, *Genesis 16-50*, 40. Von Rad argues that the narrative complex begins in chapter 18 and ends with 19:38 but he is again using diachronic argumentation. Von Rad, *Genesis: A Commentary*, 204.
[200] Sarna, *Genesis*, 128-34.
[201] For a two section breakdown see: Speiser, *Genesis*, 128. Van Seters, *Abraham in History and Tradition*, 203. Coats, *Genesis*, 136. Turner, *Genesis*, 83-86. Brueggemann divides the passage into two sections: Gen 18:1-15 and 18:16-19:38. Brueggemann, *Genesis*, 157-67. For a three section breakdown see: Wenham, *Genesis 16-50*, 44. Gunkel, *Genesis*, 192.
[202] Wenham, *Genesis 16-50*, 44. Dennis, *Sarah Laughed*, 48. Westermann goes so far as to call these introductory verses "a masterful description of a visit — arrival, invitation, hospitality." Westermann, *Genesis: A Practical Commentary*, 134.
[203] Brueggemann, *Genesis*, 158.

Now that the meal has concluded, Gunkel sees vv. 9-15 as a reward given to Abraham for passing a test of hospitality "admirably."[204] For Wenham, however, the true purpose of the visit becomes evident[205] as the discussion turns toward Sarah and her reception of the birth announcement. For the purposes of our analysis of the dialogue in Gen 18 it is simple enough to define our narrative dialogue parameters as vv. 9-15. Within these verses it is also interesting to note that the theme of hospitality can be stretched to include not only receiving guests but the words they speak as well.

4. Translation

9. And they[206] said to him, Where is Sarah your wife? And he said, Behold, in the tent.
10. And he said, I will return to you in the living season and behold Sarah, your wife, will bear a son. And Sarah heard in the doorway of the tent behind him.[207]
11. And Abraham and Sarah were old. It had ceased to be with Sarah after the manner of women.[208]

---

[204] Gunkel, *Genesis*, 197.

[205] Wenham, *Genesis 16-50*, 47.

[206] In support of evidence of a Divine element Fretheim explains, "Yahweh has assumed human form and is included among the three men[... *added by ET*] The separation between Yahweh and two of the messengers in 18:22 and 19:1, 13 supports this interpretation, as does the shift between singular (18:3, 10-15) and plural (18:9)." Fretheim, *Abraham: Trials of Family and Faith*, 111. While discussing a diachronic argument for the difficulties of this passage Coats stated another theory that "perhaps the plural company of messengers can speak in the singular for Yahweh, or Yahweh was himself one of the visitors." While the diachronic argument is not part of this thesis I find the theory interesting. Coats, *Genesis*, 137.

[207] Von Rad explains, "The question whether in v. 10b the door of the tent was 'behind him' (i.e., Yahweh) or Sarah was 'behind it' (i.e., the door of the tent) is answered according to the former by the LXX, according to the latter by the Masoretes." Von Rad, *Genesis: A Commentary*, 207. Speiser agrees that in the MT the statement "behind him" is "far from clear. Sam. and LXX read the first pronoun as feminine this would mean that Sarah was not far from the speaker; in Heb., however, the pronominal suffix at the end is more likely to refer either to the tent of the entrance, so that the received version is to be preferred." Speiser, *Genesis*, 130.

[208] In other words, Sarah has entered menopause. "The placement of this verse is particularly important. Someone definitely considered it relevant for the reader to know and remember the age and status of Abraham and the status of Sarah's fertility before letting the reader know her response. If the onset of menopause for Sarah was not relevant for understanding the following comments, then this information would not have been included. But it is here to help readers understand Sarah's reaction." Tammi J. Schneider, *Sarah: Mother of Nations* (New York: Continuum, 2004), 69.

12. And Sarah laughed within herself saying,[209] I am worn out of pleasure[210] and my lord is old?[211]
13. And YHWH said unto Abraham, Why did Sarah laugh? saying, Really? Will I bear when I am old?[212]
14. Is a thing difficult[213] for YHWH? At the appointed time I will return to you, at that time of life[214] Sarah will have a son.
15. And Sarah deceived[215] saying, I did not laugh because she feared and he[216] said, Yes,[217] you laughed.

---

[209] Regarding internal speech, see the in-depth discussions on styles of discourse (direct, indirect and free indirect) in biblical Hebrew see Galia Hatav, "(Free) Direct Discourse in Biblical Hebrew," *HS* 41 (2000). Also see C. L. Miller, *The Representation of Speech in Biblical Hebrew Narrative: A Linguistic Analysis*, HSM 55 (Atlanta, Ga.: Scholars Press, 1996).

[210] Sarna notes the "Hebrew *'ednah* is now known to mean 'abundant moisture' as in an exact antonym of 'withered.'" Sarna, *Genesis*, 130. Turner stated that "the term used, while unique to this verse, is thought to convey the sense of sexual pleasure. If Abraham and Sarah are experiencing no sexual pleasure, then they are no longer having sexual relations. What better way to demonstrate disbelief in the hope of a child?" Turner, *Genesis*, 84.

[211] Wenham sees the double question put forth by Sarah to be a "circumstantial clause turning question into virtual negation" which allows for a translation of "Am I not worn out and is not my lord old?" Wenham, *Genesis 16-50*, 37. Brichto observes "The formulation of this internal dialogue, starting with a prepositional phrase and continuing with a perfect tense — expressive of completed action in a future time — is a masterful touch by the narrator[... *added by ET*] for it points to an act that must take place preliminary to the fulfillment of the prophecy." Brichto, *The Names of God: Poetic Readings in Biblical Beginnings*, 233.

[212] Note the grammatical differences between Sarah's utterance and the Deity's response; "Sarah's reflection is unexpectedly stripped of its bluntness when repeated by God; the expression *bālā*, for the 'decay' of old clothes, and *'edna*, 'sensual pleasure,' are not repeated." Von Rad, *Genesis: A Commentary*, 207.

[213] Fretheim argues that the exact meaning of the Deity's question is "difficult to discern. The difficulty is in part due to uncertainties regarding the precise meaning of the word *pele'*, translated 'wonderful' or 'hard/difficult.'" Fretheim, *Abraham: Trials of Family and Faith*, 115.

[214] Sarna explains, "The phrase *ka-'et hayyah* recurs only in 2 Kings 4:16f and in a similar context. Its exact meaning is uncertain. The first element is 'at the/this time.' The second is taken by Rashbam, Bekhor Shor, and Radak to be the postbiblical *hay(y)ah*, 'a pregnant woman.' The phrase would then refer to the nine months of pregnancy. Alternately, *hayyah* could also simply mean 'life,' as in Ezekiel 7:13 and Job 33:18, 20." Sarna, *Genesis*, 130.

[215] "The stem *khs* denotes subservience or deceit." Speiser, *Genesis*, 130.

[216] Humphreys notes "the 'he' who has the last word could be either Yahweh or Abraham." Humphreys, *The Character of God in the Book of Genesis: A Narrative Appraisal*, 119.

[217] "In Heb. a reply often repeats the wording of the pertinent question or statement[... *added by ET*] The verbal form is preceded by *lo' ki*. The particle *ki* is, among many other things, an adversative. When it follows a positive or rhetorical statement, its sense is often 'no,' in conjunction with the negation *lo*', it conveys the opposite meaning, hence here 'Yes.'" Speiser, *Genesis*, 130.

5. Structure

Divine Dialogue with Abraham	Gen 18:9-15
I. Dialogue part 1	Gen 18:9-10a
II. Narrative element	Gen 18:10b-11
III. Dialogue part 2	Gen 18:12-15

E. Genesis 15:1-17: Abram's visionary dialogue

1. Setting in literature

As previously explained, Genesis is most often divided into two main parts:
The Primeval History (Gen 1-11) and the Patriarchal Sagas (Gen 12-50).
Within the Patriarchal Sagas the Abrahamic narrative comprises chapters 12:1-25:18. From a literary standpoint Gen 15 is considered pivotal.[218]
Overall the focus of the larger arc is the covenant promise as given to
the Patriarch and its eventual fruition. Within this arc, chapter 15 plays
a crucial role in that it ties the promise of land and seed to the promise
of a "great reward" and lays "the foundation of Israel's entire history."[219]

For Coats, Gen 15 is isolated from other chapters by its structure. He
explains that it "does not develop the stages of a tale; it reveals no plot
of a story; it is not narrative." He continues, seeing the chapter as highly
formulaic, "composed entirely of speeches[... *added by ET*] arranged in
a rather loose order."[220] These speeches include the dialogue which we
are examining. The conversation, the first between Abram and YHWH,
"allows Abram to express his views on the development of the nationhood
promise. Previously his actions and words have given indirect indicators
of his perceptions."[221] It is interesting to note that the promise will not

---

[218] Brueggemann states that, "Theologically, it is probably the most important chapter
of this entire collection." Brueggemann, *Genesis*, 140. Also see Laurence A. Turner,
Announcements of Plot in Genesis, JSOTSup 96 (Sheffield: JSOT Press, 1990), 70. See
also Westermann, *Genesis 12-36: A Commentary*, 230.

[219] John Ha, *Genesis 15: A Theological Compendium of Pentateuchal History* (Berlin:
W. De Gruyter, 1989), 221.

[220] Coats, *Genesis*, 123. Coats is relatively unique in his view of this "loose" structure.
Williamson disagrees arguing, "without 'seed,' the prospect of land was worthless...
without land the promise of seed was meaningless." Paul R. Williamson, *Abraham,
Israel and the Nations: The Patriarchal Promise and Its Covenantal Development in
Genesis*, JSOTSup 315 (Sheffield: Sheffield Academic Press, 2000), 133-34. For a
more in-depth examination of the sections considered to be part of the chapter please
see the parameters section of this chapter.

[221] Turner, *Genesis*, 73.

benefit Abraham directly. It is his descendants who will, in fact, inherit the land of Canaan.

As Fretheim shows it is clear from the extensive listing of divine promises within the Abrahamic arc that "God's promises play a central role in the story."[222] Here, within the literary confines of chapter 15, however, the promise of land and seed are inextricably bound. Williamson explains, "The effect of [the, *added by ET*] symmetry between the two distinct units of the chapter is to bind the promise of seed and the promise of land together in such a way that the fulfillment of the latter is absolutely dependent on the fulfillment of the former."[223] For this reason the promise of a single son is extended to the promise of descendants becoming as numerous as the physical stars through multiple generations.[224]

Genesis 15 also includes the first Abrahamic covenant ceremony. "For the first time in the history of religions, God becomes the contracting party, promising a national territory to a people yet unborn. This pledge constitutes the main historic title of the Jewish people to its land, a title that is unconditional and irrevocable, secured by a divine covenant whose validity transcends space and time."[225] The promises made in previous chapters are here, in chapter 15, solidified. Literarily, the chapter as a whole constitutes "the 'great reward' promised to the patriarch."[226]

2. Setting in narrative

The narrative setting for Gen 15 is intricately woven into the fabric of the Abraham Saga. Coats describes chapters 12 to 16 as narratives that "develop family relationships."[227] For Cotter it is chapters 15 and 17 that combine to form "the heart of the stories about the first generation of the family God has chosen."[228] Throughout all of these chapters, and

---

[222] Fretheim, *Abraham: Trials of Family and Faith*, 30.
[223] Williamson defines the distinct units as vv. 1-6 and 7-21. Williamson, *Abraham, Israel and the Nations: The Patriarchal Promise and Its Covenantal Development in Genesis*, 123.
[224] See von Rad, *Genesis: A Commentary*, 21-33. Also see Coats, *Genesis*, 125.
[225] Sarna, *Genesis*, 115.
[226] Williamson, *Abraham, Israel and the Nations: The Patriarchal Promise and Its Covenantal Development in Genesis*, 135.
[227] Coats, *Genesis*, 123.
[228] Cotter explains, "Genesis 15 [has, *added by ET*] God committing himself in the covenant between the pieces, and Genesis 17, Abraham committing himself and his

well into the remainder of Abraham Saga, the twin themes of the promise of land and seed are distinct, creating a fundamental structural element within the patriarchal promises.[229] But it is not only the patriarch who benefits from the thematic emphasis. Fretheim observed, "The promises are spoken about several people, including chosen as well as unchosen (Ishmael). The promises focus on several themes (descendants, name, nation[s, *added by ET*], kings, blessing) and the promises for chosen and nonchosen are remarkably similar."[230]

Within these chapters, for those chosen, unchosen or marginalized, the theme of seed or lack thereof is most prominent. Davidson argues that Gen 15 harkens back to the "concluding section of chapter 13 (vv. 14-18)" where the promise of Abram's future multitude of seed is compared to the dust of the earth and the breadth of his land is described.[231] The slight expansion of the promise in Gen 12:1-3, 7 sets up the narratives of chapters 15 to 18 where human insight stresses the fact that the promise has yet to be fulfilled. Gunkel stated, "The legends in chaps. 15, 16, and 18 relate to one another in the use of this ['no descendant', *added by ET*] motif. Abraham does not articulate a request for children. Reverence hinders him from requesting explicitly. He can only complain."[232] Brueggemann, however, argues that barrenness is the issue at the center of chapter 15.[233]

The concern over the lack of an heir is underlined in light of the narrative of chapter 14. Focusing on Lot's captivity and rescue, Gen 14:16, describes Abram returning home after successfully liberating Lot 'his brother.' From this incident Turner observed,

> Abram's concern for Lot in ch. 14 had once again illustrated how important to Abram his nephew was for the establishment of the promised great nation. Therefore, the rendering of 15:2-3 in modern translations take us by surprise. In response to Yahweh's announcement that his 'reward shall be very great' (15:1b), Abram counters that he

male descendants in the covenant of circumcision [which, *added by ET*] bracket Genesis 16." Cotter, *Genesis*, 97.

[229] Westermann, *Genesis: A Practical Commentary*, 118.

[230] Fretheim also recognizes that "the promises are unilaterally declared by God, with no prior conditions stipulated (for example, the character or moral statue of the recipient)." Fretheim, *Abraham: Trials of Family and Faith*, 30.

[231] Davidson, *Genesis 12-50*, 41.

[232] Gunkel, *Genesis*, 179. Humphreys adds, "Talk about being a shield and of a great reward are fine, but the lack of heirs is foremost for Abram, all the more so it would seem in light of the earlier promises in Genesis 12:1-3, 7; 13:14-17." Humphreys, *The Character of God in the Book of Genesis: A Narrative Appraisal*, 94.

[233] Brueggemann, *Genesis*, 140.

still has no offspring and that 'the heir of my house is Eliezer of Damascus' (15:2b), adding 'a slave born in my house is to be my heir' (15:3b). Such translations seem to leave Lot entirely out of the picture by introducing an unknown character, Eliezer.[234]

The Deity's detailed response in Gen 15:4 effectively "unchooses" both Eliezer and Lot from the line of inheritance. Therefore, while the exclusion is specifically stated, the fulfillment is not. Chapters 16 and 18 must come to pass before the concern is addressed directly.

Returning again to the initial promises of Gen 12, it must be remembered that "God has promised 'seed,' not simply 'heir.'"[235] Coats defines the promise of a son as an oracle of salvation and the promise for land, introduced in Gen 12:7, as the first in a series of oaths to Abram.[236] These land oaths include a command to look and walk the land from north to south, east to west "for I will give it unto thee" (Gen 13:14, 17), the land from "the river of Egypt unto the great river, the river Euphrates" (Gen 15:18), and "all the land of Canaan" (Gen 17:8). There is a difference, however, in chapter 15. The promise is accompanied by a "solemn assurance" in vv. 13-16.[237] This assurance, if it can be called such, includes a description of suffering, alienation, enslavement and considerable delay in the fulfillment of the promise of land. The one receiving the promise will not live to obtain it. Abram's relationship with the land will not be personal. The land and its occupation by Abram's descendants are tied to a much larger divine purpose.

Within the narrative arc of Gen 12-18 chapter 15 is detached to a certain extent by its theological emphasis. Von Rad calls vv. 13-16, "a cabinet piece of Old Testament theology of history."[238] Davidson observed that these same verses "are designed to answer questions that must have troubled readers of the Abram stories. If God promises the land to Abram, why was there such a long delay in the land coming into the possession of Abram's descendants?"[239] For Sarna the inclusion of the three stages of suffering and redemption, i.e. alienation, enslavement,

---

[234] Turner, *Genesis*, 73.

[235] Fretheim, *Abraham: Trials of Family and Faith*, 36.

[236] Coats, *Genesis*, 125-26.

[237] Westermann, *Genesis 12-36: A Commentary*, 223.

[238] Von Rad, *Genesis: A Commentary*, 188. Brueggemann agrees explaining that Gen 15:12-16 "contain a historical reflection on the course of the promise in the history of Israel." Brueggemann, *Genesis*, 148.

[239] Davidson, *Genesis 12-50*, 46. Davidson follows von Rad who states that these verses are aetiological, "designed to clarify a riddle: Abraham had received the promise, but it was not fulfilled for many generations." Von Rad, *Genesis: A Commentary*, 187.

and oppression followed by judgment of the oppressor, the Exodus, and settlement in Promised Land has a true purpose. "It is obvious that the biblical conception of the origins and growth of the people of Israel — the idea of nationhood resulting from a process of natural proliferation rather than through the amalgamation or confederacy of existing tribes — means that the realization of the divine promises can be envisaged as taking place only after the passage of many years."[240]

Throughout the narrative of Gen 12-18 the promise of land and seed is prominent. The fact that each reiteration seems to build on the previous announcement is obvious. However, within this narrative framework, chapter 15 and the Divine/human relational dialogue it contains, addresses details undeclared in other passages. These features highlight the Deity's plan and purpose for the humans involved but does not yet specify through whom or when the fulfillment will take place. That is left for future chapters.[241]

Within the parameters of chapter 15 there are three common narrative thematic discussions that occupy scholars: the double covenant promise of land and seed, the parallel structure of the two chapter sections and the possible significance of the described ritual. We have already examined, to a certain extent, the twin covenant promises so it will only be touched on briefly here. The parallel structure as well as the covenant ritual and its significance will be looked at in more depth.

For most scholars the prominent theme within chapter 15 is the reiteration and expansion of the covenant promise for an heir and land.[242] While many scholars divide the chapter into two distinct parts (vv. 1-6 and 7-21) and examine each promise separately it must be noted that the promises of land and seed are in concert with each other in both sections.

[240] Sarna, *Genesis*, 115.
[241] Sailhamer suggests that the fulfillment is actually contained in the covenant at Sinai. He argues that the Deity's response in Gen 15:9-17 recounts "the establishment of a covenant between the Lord and Abraham. Thus it is fitting that in many respects the account should foreshadow the making of the covenant at Sinai[... *added by ET*] In the Lord's words to Abraham (15:13-16) the connection between Abraham's covenant and the Sinai covenant is explicitly made by means of the reference to the four hundred years of bondage of Abraham's seed and their subsequent 'exodus'[... *added by ET*] Such considerations lead to the conclusion that the author intends to draw the reader's attention to the events at Sinai in his depiction of the covenant with Abraham." Sailhamer, *The Pentateuch as Narrative: A Biblical-Theological Commentary*, 152.
[242] For example: Speiser, *Genesis*, 115. Westermann, *Genesis: A Practical Commentary*, 117. Cotter, *Genesis*, 98. Arvid S. Kapelrud, "The Covenant as Agreement," *SJOT* 1 (1988): 32-33.

"Neither of these two aspects of the patriarchal promise stands on its own."[243] Because these two divine expressions are so intimately intertwined the result has led scholars to a second prominent narrative thematic discussion: the parallel structure of the chapter.

Westermann considers the chapter's two sections as distinct, independent and self-contained narratives.[244] Williamson concurs but admits that while the promises are separate segments they are "broadly parallel."[245] Coats argues that "one can recognize two segments of speeches that hang together, each as a dialogue between Yahweh and Abram. The two segments develop parallel lines and, though embracing quite diverse traditions, qualify as complements."[246] These complementary parallels tie the segments together for a reason. Brueggemann suggests that "in their present form verses 1-6 and 7-21 may be considered as the relation between an *act of commitment* and *dramatic affirmation* of that commitment."[247]

There are numerous investigations into this parallel structure and most describe the structure as: divine promise (vv. 1, 7), Abram's questions or concerns (vv. 2-3, 8), the Deity's response containing reassurance and promises (vv. 4-5, 9-17 or through to v. 21).[248] The Deity's initiation of dialogue in both vv. 1 and 7 includes a form of self-identification.[249] Abram's questions and concerns, first for an heir and then for his promised land, are followed by the Deity's detailed response. Scholarship, however, often sees these detailed responses as referencing the Exodus.[250]

> Abraham's exodus from his homeland to a foreign land (v. 7) finds a chiastic parallel in his descendants' exodus from a foreign land (v. 13) to their homeland. The double blessing for Abraham's descendants alluded to in v. 14 and v. 16 mirrors the double "curse" anticipated in vv. 2-3. The repetitions in vv. 13-16 are not superfluous; rather,

---

[243] Williamson, *Abraham, Israel and the Nations: The Patriarchal Promise and Its Covenantal Development in Genesis*, 133.

[244] Westermann, *Genesis: A Practical Commentary*, 117.

[245] Williamson, *Abraham, Israel and the Nations: The Patriarchal Promise and Its Covenantal Development in Genesis*, 122.

[246] Coats, *Genesis*, 123.

[247] Brueggemann, *Genesis*, 148. Emphasis original.

[248] For example see Williamson, *Abraham, Israel and the Nations: The Patriarchal Promise and Its Covenantal Development in Genesis*, 123-24. Interestingly enough, this pattern is found elsewhere in the Hebrew Bible. In most cases, however, it is directly linked to the call experiences of the prophets. Davidson, *Genesis 12-50*, 42.

[249] See the Initiation of Dialogue section of this chapter for more details.

[250] Brueggemann states, "The verses survey in prospect the history of Israel with special reference to the oppression in Egypt and the Exodus from Egypt." Brueggemann, *Genesis*, 148.

the information about Abraham's descendants being "strangers in
a land which is not their own" (v. 13) serves as a subtle reaffir-
mation of the two different aspects which unite the chapter as a
whole.[251]

The reference to the Exodus is not without merit. In v. 7 the Deity self-
identifies and then states, "I brought thee out from Ur of Chaldees." The
phrase "I brought you out" "occurs twenty-two times in the Pentateuch.
In every case except this one the reference is to God bringing Israel out
of Egypt."[252] There are arguments against a direct correlation however.

Westermann agrees that the self-presentation formula resembles "Exodus 20:2; Deuteronomy 5:6; and especially Leviticus 25:38."[253] Von
Rad, however, states that any similitude between the passages ends there.
Any relation between Gen 15:16 and Exod 12:40 is unclear, especially
in light of the translation difficulties of the word *generation* (*dōr*).[254]
Genesis 15:14 also triggers disagreement. Sarna states that the divine
judgments received by the nation whom the Hebrews will serve is a reference "to the plagues, which are so referred to in Exodus 6:6, 7:4, and
12:12."[255] Westermann, on the other hand, categorically states that v. 14
"can scarcely be a reference to the plagues, because they occur in the
context of the liberation of Israel. The sentence is to be understood in
the same sense as v. 16b; it concerns God's just action in the history of
the nations."[256] A significant justification can be effectively built for either
argument depending on the view of the scholar.

The third narrative theme often discussed by scholars is that of the
covenant ritual or ceremony that is contained in Gen 15:9-11, 17. Brueggemann states that these verses "present a curious ritual act that is probably
very old. While the specific details of the action are obscure, the act suggests a solemn and weighty binding of the two parties to each other."[257]
From the very beginning of this discussion there are differing opinions

---

[251] Williamson, *Abraham, Israel and the Nations: The Patriarchal Promise and Its Covenantal Development in Genesis*, 128.

[252] Gordon J Wenham, "The Religion of the Patriarchs," in *Essays on the Patriarchal
Narratives*, ed. A.J. Millard and D.J. Wiseman (Leicester: Inter-Varsity, 1980),
182. Sarna reiterates that the predominant reference to the Exodus equates "the
two pivotal, formative events in the history of the Jewish people." Sarna, *Genesis*,
114.

[253] Westermann, *Genesis: A Practical Commentary*, 120.

[254] Von Rad, *Genesis: A Commentary*, 187.

[255] Sarna, *Genesis*, 116.

[256] Westermann, *Genesis 12-36: A Commentary*, 227.

[257] Brueggemann, *Genesis*, 148.

which originate with the definition of ritual and ceremony.[258] The difficulty lies in the request for identifiable sacrificial animals[259] when no
clear sacrifice is described.[260] What is clear is that the Deity's response
to Abram's question in v. 8 involves a rite of some kind for which Abram
must prepare.

The strange interlude of v. 11 also causes many problems for scholars.
Van Seters states that "since there is such great economy of presentation,
it is hardly possible that this is simply meant as a picturesque detail."[261]
Both Van Seters and Sarna see the "birds of prey as a reference to Egypt."[262]
Regardless of the merits of the ritual/sacrifice arguments or the Egyptian
association, some scholars recognize the rite, however they define it, as
constituting some kind of an answer from the Deity to Abram.[263] Ha,
however, explains that within the context of the narrative, the rite which

[258] Von Rad labels the passage a "ritual of covenant-making." Von Rad, *Genesis: A Commentary*, 186. Gunkel calls it a "solemn covenant ceremony." Gunkel, *Genesis*, 176.
Coats follows von Rad stating that the promise "is presented in the context of an oath
ritual." Coats, *Genesis*, 125.

[259] Westermann explains "in verses 9-10, the action associated with the oath has been
confused with a sacrificial ceremony: all sacrificial animals are named, where as only
a single animal is necessary for the oath ceremony. The thrice-repeated 'three-year-
old' also reflects sacrificial practice." Westermann, *Genesis: A Practical Commentary*,
121.

[260] Sarna states, "Clearly no sacrifice is involved, for there is no altar, no mention of the
sprinkling of blood as in Exodus 24:8, and no suggestion that the animals are either
eaten or burnt. The meaning of the ceremonials is to be sought elsewhere." Sarna,
Genesis, 114. Also see von Rad, *Genesis: A Commentary*, 186.

[261] Brueggemann states, "The verses survey in prospect the history of Israel with special
reference to the oppression in Egypt and the Exodus from Egypt." Brueggemann,
Genesis, 148.

[262] Van Seters argues that the "birds of prey were primary symbols for the Egyptian
monarch, so we may well have a reference here to the omen contained in vv. 13-16."
Van Seters, *Abraham in History and Tradition*, 258. Sarna's examination goes a bit
further. "The otherwise terse and austere style of the narrative makes it certain that
the incident here recorded has special significance[... *added by ET*] In Egyptian art
this bird [most likely a falcon, *added by ET*] represents the important god Horus with
whom the living king was identified. It is possible, therefore, that the sudden appearance of the birds of prey, and of Abram successfully warding them off, symbolically
portends the sharp and menacing change that is to take place in the fortunes of the
Israelites at the hands of the Egyptians while it also prefigures their rescue through the
merit of the patriarch." Sarna, *Genesis*, 115.

[263] Williamson explains that, as presented, the rite is a "formal ratification of a covenant
between God and Abraham; of this there can be no doubt." Williamson, *Abraham,
Israel and the Nations: The Patriarchal Promise and Its Covenantal Development in
Genesis*, 135. Also see Turner notes, "Yahweh's 'proof' to Abram that he would have
a son of his own had amounted to an inspection of the heavens (15:5). Confirmation
of the land promise to Abram's descendants through that child is achieved by the
ceremonial slaughter of assorted animals. While formally sealing the covenant promise

Abram prepares in vv. 9 and 10 is accomplished in v. 17.[264] This covenant then becomes, according to Speiser, "the charter on which Israel's
national position was founded."[265]

To reiterate, the most prominent narrative thematic discussion usually
associated with Gen 15 are the double covenant promise of land and
seed, the parallel structure of the two chapter sections and the possible
significance of the described ritual. These scholarly approaches do have
merit and are valid but often overshadow the dialogue contained within.

3. Parameters

There is an obstacle in defining the parameters of dialogue in Gen 15.
The difficulty lies in extricating the dialogue elements from the overwhelming scholarship regarding the chapter's introduction of covenant,
its nature and impact. Nearly all scholarship sees the chapter as a whole
with a subdivision of vv. 1-6 and 7-21.[266] This twofold division is most
often described in terms of "Promise and Covenant."[267] One stand out
among these scholars is Sarna who, while describing vv. 1-6 as a dialogue regarding the promise of offspring and vv. 7-21 as a dialogue

---

between the two parties, the act provides no more hard evidence to Abram than had
the celestial bodies previously." Turner, *Genesis*, 75.

[264] Ha, *Genesis 15: A Theological Compendium of Pentateuchal History*, 50.

[265] Speiser, *Genesis*, 113. While outside the scope of this discussion there are numerous
treatises on the equating of this rite and examples of extra-biblical covenant making
rites. Sarna explains, "It would seem that the form of this covenant is modeled after
the royal land-grant treaty common in the ancient Near East. By this instrument a king
bestows a gift of land on an individual or vassal as a reward for loyal service." Sarna,
Genesis, 114.

[266] See Speiser, *Genesis*, 110. Von Rad, *Genesis: A Commentary*, 181-90. Van Seters,
Abraham in History and Tradition, 249. Coats, *Genesis*, 122-23. Westermann, *Genesis: A Practical Commentary*, 117. Wenham, *Genesis 1-15*, 325. Turner, *Genesis*,
73-76. Fretheim, *Abraham: Trials of Family and Faith*, 35. Gunkel bifurcates the
chapter after v. 7. Gunkel, *Genesis*, 178-93. Moshe Anbar, *Genesis 15: A Conflation
of Two Deuteronomic Narratives*, JBL 101 (1982): 40. Very occasionally a scholar
will single out v. 6 dividing the chapter as vv. 1-5, 6, 7-21.

[267] See Speiser, *Genesis*, 110. Von Rad, *Genesis: A Commentary*, 181-90. Brueggemann,
Genesis, 140-50. Brodie entitles his sections "The promise of progeny: crisis and
faith" and "The promise of land: covenant, death, and knowing." Brodie, *Genesis as
Dialogue: A Literary, Historical, & Theological Commentary*, 227-30.
This division is strengthened by scholarly comparison of elements contained in both
sections: Divine self-identification and promise (vv. 1, 7), Abram's apprehension
(vv. 2-3, 8), and reassurance by word and symbolic action (vv. 4-5, 9-21). Cotter,
Genesis, 98. Also see Wenham for a detailed chart comparing the subdivisions.
Wenham, *Genesis 1-15*, 325.

regarding the promise of national territory, actually divides the chapter into three distinct parts: 1-6, 7-17 and 18-21.[268] From this division there is room for discussion regarding the exclusion of vv. 18-21.

I acknowledge that vv. 18-21 are included in most research involving the Abram covenant as presented in chapter 15.[269] However, there is an interesting absence of a connecting *waw* at the beginning of v. 18. While it is clear that the verses are connected with the preceding promise,[270] there is some discussion that the verses in this section are more a concluding description of the geographical boundaries of the covenant land than a continuation of the covenant ceremony.[271] Von Rad states, "The narrator explains the event in v. 18, not with a reference to a deeper 'meaning,' but rather by stating the fact of the concluded covenant with almost juristical objectivity and then by paraphrasing the substance of the guarantee given by Yahweh."[272]

The missing *waw* is certainly not compelling enough on its own to categorically support the exclusion of vv. 18-21 from our discussion.[273] In order to pronounce the conclusion of Divine/human relational dialogue in Gen 15 as v. 17 we must look at the components of dialogue in vv. 7-17. Verse 7, with the repeated Divine self-identification, introduces a new theme to the conversation.[274] Abram's response is to pose a question (v. 8). He specifically asks "to know" how the promise of the gift of land will be fulfilled. The Deity's response is a commandment to take animals of various kinds to the Deity (v. 9). The following verse describes Abram

---

[268] Sarna, *Genesis*, 112-18. Brichto follows Sarna's tri-part division entitling the segments as Episode A, B and Coda. Brichto, *The Names of God: Poetic Readings in Biblical Beginnings*, 203.

[269] Brueggemann states that "The promise and question of verses 7-8 at the beginning and the promise of verses 18-21 at the end provide an envelope for this unit." Brueggemann, *Genesis*, 150.

[270] Williamson, *Abraham, Israel and the Nations: The Patriarchal Promise and Its Covenantal Development in Genesis*, 129.

[271] Sailhamer, *The Pentateuch as Narrative: A Biblical-Theological Commentary*, 152.

[272] Von Rad, *Genesis: A Commentary*, 188. Westermann claims that "verses 12-16 and 19-21 are secondary additions." This argument, however, is mostly supported by source analysis which is not being employed by this thesis. Westermann, *Genesis: A Practical Commentary*, 120.

[273] Williamson notes variant uses of *waw* throughout the passage. He states, "The narrative thread is 'broken' in a number of places by the non-use of the *waw*-consecutive: the conjunctive hiphil perfect והאמן at the start of v. 6; the avoidance of *waw*-perfects in vv. 14-16; and the complete absence of *waw* in the opening temporal phrase, ביום ההוא (v. 18)." Williamson, *Abraham, Israel and the Nations: The Patriarchal Promise and Its Covenantal Development in Genesis*, 126.

[274] Ha, *Genesis 15: A Theological Compendium of Pentateuchal History*, 48.

fulfilling this request (v. 10). The Deity then continues in v. 13 stating that through this action Abram will "surely know."[275] The answer is in direct response to Abram's v. 8 query. There are several signs given to Abram in vv. 13-16 to emphasize his ability "to know." The Deity then, in v. 17, completes the ceremony which was begun with Abram's initial concern in v. 8. If dialogue elements are detached from the solidified covenant discussion it can be seen that all that passes for discussion between the Divine and Abram begins in v. 1 and concludes with v. 17. Verses 18-21 then become, as expressed by Van Seters, a description of "a divine grant of land with its boundaries specified."[276]

4. Translation

1. After these words the word of the Lord was with Abram[277] in a vision[278] saying, Fear not[279] Abram, I am your shield and your very great reward.
2. And Abram said, Adoni YHWH[280], what will you give to me since I am childless and the heir of my house[281] is Eliezer of Damascus.

---

[275] Using the infinitive absolute for emphasis, Sarna states that this is "the response to the query of verse 8." Sarna, *Genesis*, 115.

[276] Van Seters, *Abraham in History and Tradition*, 259.

[277] Westermann also observed that "the word of God that comes to Abraham has the form of an oracle of salvation, consisting of a reassurance formula 'Do not be afraid' and its motivation. This form is especially common in Deutero-Isaiah. It is reminiscent of royal oracles such as appear often in Babylonian texts." Westermann, *Genesis: A Practical Commentary*, 118. According to Van Seters, "This phrase or the variant nominal form in v. 4, is a *terminus technicus* for the report of a divine speech to a prophet. It first occurs in prophetic works in Jeremiah and becomes very frequent in Ezekiel. It also occurs frequently throughout the Deuteronomistic history in narrative having to do with prophets and was undoubtedly a convention for reporting prophetic revelation." Van Seters, *Abraham in History and Tradition*, 253.

[278] Wenham explains, "'Vision,' מחזה, is rare in Hebrew and used only of Balaam (Num 24:4, 16) and contemporaries of Ezekiel (13:7). Second- and third-millennium Akkadian texts show that visions were a recognized and very ancient mode of revelation."

[279] Lipton observed, "The reassuring 'fear not' frequently accompanies divine revelation, although the context in which it occurs here suggests that the reassurance was intended to exceed the duration of the vision." Diana Lipton, *Revisions of the Night: Politics and Promises in the Patriarchal Dreams of Genesis*, JSOTSup 288 (Sheffield: Sheffield Academic Press, 1999), 187.

[280] The term is only used here, in v. 8 and Deut 3:34; 9:26 as the beginning of direct speech. Anbar, *Genesis 15: A Conflation of Two Deuteronomic Narratives*, 42.

[281] Turner notes that "the phrase 'the heir of my house' is an attempt to render *ben mešeq bêtî*. Nobody has a clue what *mešeq* means and all attempts to translate are shots in the dark." Turner, *Genesis*, 73. Anbar notes "The term is found again only in Eccl 2:7, but is used in Mishnaic Hebrew." Anbar, *Genesis 15: A Conflation of Two Deuteronomic Narratives*, 42.

3. And Abram said, Behold you have given me no seed and behold a son of my house[282] will inherit.
4. And Behold the word of YHWH came to him saying, This one will not inherit because he who comes from your bowels will inherit.
5. And he brought him outside and said, Look to the heavens and count the stars if you are able to count them and he said to him, Thus your seed will be.
6. And he believed[283] in YHWH and he counted it to him as righteousness.[284]
7. And he said to him, I am YHWH[285] who brought you out from Ur of Chaldees and gave you this land as an inheritance.
8. And he said, Adoni YHWH, how will I know that I will inherit it?
9. And he said to him, Take[286] to me a heifer three years old[287] and a she-goat three years old and a ram three years old and a turtle dove and a young pigeon.
10. And he took all of these and he cut[288] them in two in the middle and he laid each part side by side but the bird he did not divide.

---

[282] Turner notes that the literal reading "son of my house" "does not allow us to be any more specific than seeing *ben-bêtî* as referring to a member of Abraham's household." Turner, *Announcements of Plot in Genesis*, 71. See also Westermann, *Genesis 12-36: A Commentary*, 220. John Skinner, *A Critical and Exegetical Commentary on Genesis*, 2nd ed. ICC 1 (Edinburgh: T. & T. Clark, 1930), 279.

[283] It is interesting to note the varied comments on this particular verb. Speiser states that "'believed' does not always do justice to the original. The basic sense of the form is 'to affirm, recognize as valid.' In other words, the result is not so much a matter of objective faith as of absolute fact." Speiser, *Genesis*, 112. Wenham, identifying the technicality of the translation, states the "*waw* consec + 3 masc sg pf hiph אמן. It is unusual for single events in past time to use pf + *waw*; impf + *waw* is usual. It may indicate repeated action in the past, 'He kept on believing.'" Wenham, *Genesis 1-15*, 324.

[284] Sarna argues that the Deity is subject of the verb. "Hebrew *tsedakah*, usually 'righteousness,' sometimes bears the sense of 'merit.' The idea is that Abram's act of faith made him worthy of God's reward, which is secured through a covenant. This interpretation is supported by Nehemiah 9:7-8 and by similar phraseology in Psalms 106:30f." Sarna, *Genesis*, 113.

[285] "Yahweh's self-identification not only recalls that of v. 1, but also provides a theological continuum through its use of the hiphil of the verb יצא." Williamson, *Abraham, Israel and the Nations: The Patriarchal Promise and Its Covenantal Development in Genesis*, 128.

[286] Regarding the use of the word "to take" and its description of a possible ritual Wenham observed, "This very common word often introduces a ritual such as a sacrifice. The list of animals that follows covers all those species that could be offered in sacrifice." Wenham, *Genesis 1-15*, 331.

[287] Following Speiser, Sarna notes that the translation "three years old" most likely means "the unique Hebrew *meshullash*. A beast of three years was considered to be full grown and was broken for service. A less likely translation is 'threefold,' meaning three of each species." Sarna, *Genesis*, 115. Speiser notes that "the choice of the animals used for the purpose was governed by ritual custom and economic conditions." Speiser, *Genesis*, 112.

[288] Westermann remarked that, "the verb used for cutting, בתר, occurs only here, the noun בתר here and in Jer. 34:18 where the same rite is described." Westermann, *Genesis 12-36: A Commentary*, 225-26.

11. And the birds of prey descended upon the carcasses and Abram drove them away.
12. And it came to pass the sun went down and a deep sleep fell upon Abram and behold a terror of great darkness fell upon him.
13. And he said to Abram, Surely you will know that your seed will be a stranger in a land which is not theirs and they will serve them[289] and they will oppress them four hundred years.
14. And the nation which they will serve I will judge and afterwards they will leave with great possessions.
15. And you will die in peace[290] and will be buried at a good old age
16. And the fourth generation will return here because the iniquity of the Amorites is not complete as of now.
17. And it came to pass the sun went down and there was a thick darkness and behold, a fire pot of smoke and a torch of fire passed through the parts.

5. Structure

Divine Visionary Dialogue with Abram	Gen 15:1-17
I. Narrative element part 1	Gen 15:1a
II. Dialogue part 1	Gen 15:1b-4
III. Narrative element part 2	Gen 15:5a
IV. Dialogue part 2	Gen 15:5a, b
V. Narrative element part 3	Gen 15:6
VI. Dialogue part 3	Gen 15:7-9
VII. Narrative element part 4	Gen 15:10-12
VIII. Dialogue part 4	Gen 15:13-16
IX. Narrative element part 5	Gen 15:17

F. GENESIS 32:25-31: JACOB'S WRESTLE

1. Setting in literature

The final Divine/human relational dialogue to be examined sits outside the Abrahamic cycle yet is firmly rooted in the Patriarchal Sagas of Genesis. The conversation, as contained in Gen 32:25-31,[291] reveals Jacob's

---

[289] Sarna explains the translation, "Literally 'they shall serve them,' the subject being 'your offspring,' and the object understood to be the rulers of the foreign land." Sarna, *Genesis*, 116.

[290] This is the first occurrence of שלום in the scriptures. Westermann, *Genesis 12-36: A Commentary*, 227. Speiser noted that the word "seldom means 'peace' in the usual sense of the term; the emphasis is rather on security, satisfaction, or fulfillment; in other words, here 'in peace of mind, untroubled.'" Speiser, *Genesis*, 113.

[291] Note that in English translations the corresponding verse number is one digit lower than the Hebrew text. The MT verse numbers will be used throughout this chapter and changed within quotes to avoid confusion.

nocturnal struggle with a man or Divine representative in which names are changed, names are withheld and blessings are given. Whether or not the man is the Deity will be discussed in the thematic section. Until that time, the fact that the conversation reveals several divine elements within a relational dialogue means that it must at least be included in our examinations.

Within the stories of the Patriarchs Jacob's overall story is played out against that of his brother Esau and the desire for the birthright. Chapter 32 recounts a moment just prior to the brothers being reunited after years of estrangement. Speiser stated that in "biblical history in general, and patriarchal history in particular, [the story, *added by ET*] unfolds on two planes. At the one level, man is entangled in his ephemeral personal affairs; at the other level, there can be glimpsed a master plan wherein man is used as the unwitting tool of destiny."[292] Jacob's experience in Gen 32 is an encapsulation of this theory. Personally Jacob is facing a reunion with a brother who may or may not be willing or welcoming. The nighttime wrestle can be taken as a foreshadowing of this reunion. On another level the wrestling takes on an emotional and spiritual intensity with Jacob's demands for a blessing and the bestowal of a new name with its references to the Deity and mankind.

Within the Jacob narrative the experience at Penuel does not seem to leave any lasting impression on the patriarch other than a wounded thigh and the etymological reasoning behind the prohibition to eat sinew from the shank.[293] Jacob settles in Canaan and the strife continues; his sons destroy Shechem, his beloved wife Rachel dies in childbirth while Reuben defiles another wife's bed.[294] The contention between Joseph and his brothers is fueled by Jacob's love for the former over the latter, resulting in a divided family. The final discord for Jacob comes not in life, but in death. He dies in Egypt but requests burial in Canaan.[295] The request is not without distress as Joseph and his brothers must ask for permission to leave Egypt to allow their father his final peace and rest.[296] The dialogue of Gen 32 is unique in the narrative but not out of place. It is indicative of Jacob, his life and even his death.

---

[292] Speiser, *Genesis*, 256.
[293] Gen 32:32.
[294] Gen 34:25-31; 35:16-20; 22.
[295] Gen 49:29.
[296] Gen 50:4-6.

2. Setting in narrative

The completely unique[297] dialogue in Gen 32 is at the forefront of a new
beginning; one where the only thing literally standing between Jacob and
the Promised Land is a potentially Divine being. For Coats, however,
the wrestling narrative is a not just an individual unit, but "an element
in a larger story (32:4-33:17). It functions [here, *added by ET*] as a part
of the description of Jacob's confrontation experience, an intensification of
the crisis that gives plot to the story." The following narrative and dialogue, he continues, "appears as a story within a story in order to heighten
the tension of the larger narrative context. Jacob must confront Esau. As
a foreshadowing of that central confrontation, he confronts the mysterious
man, wrestles with him, and wins."[298]

In Gen 32:6, 7 and 11 Jacob expresses fear and doubt in the face of
almost sure hostility from his brother. Jacob's reaction to the fear of the
upcoming meeting is to separate his family from their surroundings and
then himself from everyone. For some this setting apart is a mark of divine
affinity for Jacob.[299] Others see it as a careful orchestration of the forthcoming meeting.[300] Regardless of the interpretation, what is not debated
is the fact that Jacob is alone when the mythical episode begins.[301] This
point, Coats claims, is "intrinsic for the story. It names the protagonist as
Jacob and places him in isolation, appropriate for the mysterious character of the following struggle."[302] Having prepared for a meeting with his
brother, Jacob must first survive this strange encounter.

Narrative themes and interpretive difficulties regarding this passage are
almost without number.[303] The theme of most interest to this thesis is the

---

[297] Gunkel, *Genesis*, 349.
[298] Coats, *Genesis*, 229.
[299] Barthes sees the narrative as pointing to "the familiar *setting apart* of the one chosen
by God." Roland Barthes, *Image, Music, Text*, trans. Stephen Heath (New York: Hill
and Wang, 1977), 130. Emphasis original.
[300] Humphrey's observes, "Having invoked, petitioned, and reminded God of his past
pledges for a secure future, Jacob does not simply sit back and wait for events to unfold.
He stages the meeting with his brother in carefully choreographed waves of servants
and gifts of livestock (Gen 32:14-22; ET 32:13-21)." Humphreys, *The Character of
God in the Book of Genesis: A Narrative Appraisal*, 190.
[301] Barthes, *Image, Music, Text*, 126.
[302] Coats, *Genesis*, 229.
[303] Brueggemann explains that "the encounter of 32:22-32 [is, *added by ET*] perhaps the
most extensively interpreted text in the patriarchal materials." Brueggemann, *Genesis*,
266. Sarna lists the problems as involving "the imagery, the geographic locale, the
purpose of the assault, the identity of the assailant, the significance of the name change,

discussion regarding the identity of Jacob's assailant. Brueggemann argues that the opaque portrayal of Jacob's attacker is important to the narrative because "it is part of the power of the wrestling that we do not know the name or see the face of the antagonist. To be too certain would reduce the dread intended in the telling."[304] Gunkel blames the difficulty in understanding the natural state of Jacob's assailant on the lack of proper nouns and subject fluidity.[305] Davidson argues that scholars can only assume the story "has taken many centuries to reach its present form and which has assimilated material, some of it very primitive."[306] Alter goes so far as to give the narrative a "folkloric character." He states, "The notion of a night spirit that loses its power or is not permitted to go about in daylight is common to many folk traditions, as is the troll or guardian figure who blocks access to a ford or bridge."[307] From this folktale position the identification of Jacob's assailant sometimes wanders into a demonic explanation.

Davidson states that the identity of the man "may have its roots in stories, widespread in many cultures, of the river spirit who has to be placated or defeated before he will allow the traveler to cross."[308] Cotter counters this argument with what he sees as obvious; Jacob's experience with YHWH at Bethel endows the patriarch with the ability to discern between the Deity and a river demon.[309] Sarna describes this concept of a "river spirit" as a "demonic being whose power is restricted to the duration of the night and who is unable to abide the breaking of the dawn."[310] While he agrees that folk tales may have influenced the literary model for this narrative he also states that this interpretation is not compatible with Israelite monotheism.

> Nothing in the text connects the mysterious assailant with a river-spirit. The stranger does not interfere with the passage of personnel, livestock, and baggage. It is only after these have already crossed the river that

the cohesion of the diverse elements, and the place of the story within the larger narrative unit." Sarna, *Genesis*, 403.

[304] Brueggemann, *Genesis*, 267.

[305] Gunkel, *Genesis*, 349. Gunkel, however, claims an ancient origin for the story which influences the identity of the attacker.

[306] Davidson, *Genesis 12-50*, 184.

[307] Alter, *The Five Books of Moses*, 180.

[308] Davidson, *Genesis 12-50*, 185. He goes on to compare the attacker to spirits and ghosts who haunt the night and disappear with the dawn and uses the example of Hamlet's father *Hamlet*, I. i. 157.

[309] Cotter, *Genesis*, 245.

[310] Sarna, *Genesis*, 403.

> he becomes active... The usual pattern requires the spirit to assume
> the form of animals, serpents, and monsters in a constant shift from
> one guise to another in the course of the struggle... The fact that the
> assailant blesses Jacob proves that it cannot be a demon, for the notion
> of eliciting and receiving a blessing from a demon is unexampled and
> inconceivable in a biblical context.[311]

For Sarna, the identity of the antagonist rests with Esau. He does not
claim the assailant to *be* Esau. He identifies him as Esau's alter ego or a
celestial patron of Esau.[312] This concept of a personal or local deity
seems to solve the issue of the demand for a blessing but it is not an easy
alliance. Von Rad agrees the attacker is Divine but admits:

> The enigmatic word about Jacob's prevailing is one of those roomy,
> strangely floating statements, so characteristic for this story. It once
> referred quite realistically to the struggle with the demon whom Jacob
> took on and from whom he wrestled a victory. This astonishment at
> such suicidal courage was certainly not diminished when this nocturnal
> assailant was later considered to be Yahweh himself.[313]

On the opposite end of the argument spectrum Coats staunchly defends
the assailant's identity to be that of a man. With regards to the statement
"ye persisted with Elohim and with men and ye prevailed" and the naming
of Peniel, he states, "The name suggests that the story should be interpreted as a struggle between Jacob and God, but that point alone does not
do justice to the explanation."[314] Jacob, now known as Israel, has and will
struggle with both the Deity and with mankind. At the conclusion of the
narrative Jacob claims to have seen the Deity face to face and thus names
the location Peniel. Coats argues that "the story makes no reference to the
'face-to-face motif" and therefore there is no connection to the etiology
or foreshadowing of the name Peniel."[315]

Landing somewhere in the middle of all these attempted explanations,
Alter eloquently combines the concepts of a metaphoric spirit and human
identity. He states:

> Appearing to Jacob in the dark of the night, before the morning when
> Esau will be reconciled with Jacob, [the assailant, *added by ET*] is
> the embodiment of portentous antagonism in Jacob's dark night of the
> soul. He[, the assailant, *added by ET*] is obviously in some sense a

---

[311] Ibid., 403.
[312] Ibid., 404. Sarna supports this decision with midrashic examples.
[313] Von Rad, *Genesis: A Commentary*, 322.
[314] Coats, *Genesis*, 230.
[315] Ibid., 230.

doubling of Esau as adversary, but his is also a doubling of all with whom Jacob has had to contend, and he may equally well be an externalization of all that Jacob has to wrestle with within himself.[316]

The only seemingly concrete argument for a divine identity to the attacker is shrouded in the night time setting. Within the Jacob cycle it is only during the night that the Deity is revealed to Jacob.[317]

And still the argument continues. Fokkelman suggests that the only path to the attacker's identity is "by judging him by his words and actions."[318] In the same vein, Speiser follows Gunkel and states that Jacob only recognizes the true identity of his attacker when "the physical darkness [has, *added by ET*] begun to lift."[319] Von Rad claims a divine identity due to the fact that "this clutching at God and his power of blessing is perhaps the most elemental reaction of man to the divine."[320] Davidson describes the relationship between the Divine and Israel, both the man and people, as "a costly, turbulent struggle in the darkness of tragedy, exile and persecution, but an authentic experience in which they came face to face with God."[321] It is beyond the bounds of this thesis to attempt a definitive description of the identity of Jacob's attacker. It is, however, my intent to describe this turbulent relationship through the examination of dialogue. For that purpose we will concede the identity of the assailant to be, at least, divine in nature and therefore included in this examination.

3. Parameters

In his examination of the Jacob narrative in Gen 32 and 33, Sarna states, "The action divides itself into two main parts: 32:4-22 describe Jacob's preparations for his encounter with Esau; 33:1-17 relate the story of the actual meeting of the two brothers. In between is the strange narrative of the struggle between Jacob and a powerful assailant (Gen 32:23-33)."[322] Most commentaries agree with this division assessment.[323]

---

[316] Alter, *The Five Books of Moses*, 180.
[317] Genesis 28.
[318] Fokkelman, *Narrative Art in Genesis: Specimens of Stylistic and Structural Analysis*, 213.
[319] Speiser, *Genesis*, 256. See also Gunkel, *Genesis*, 349.
[320] Von Rad, *Genesis: A Commentary*, 321.
[321] Davidson, *Genesis 12-50*, 186.
[322] Sarna, *Genesis*, 223.
[323] For example see: von Rad, *Genesis: A Commentary*, 319. Skinner, *A Critical and Exegetical Commentary on Genesis*, 407. Fokkelman, *Narrative Art in Genesis: Specimens of Stylistic and Structural Analysis*, 208. Hamilton, *The Book of Genesis: Chapters 18-50*, 326. Cotter, *Genesis*, 244.

For the sake of this thesis the parameters of the Gen 32 dialogue are vv. 25 to 31. This breakdown is at odds with most commentaries.[324] The argument for exclusion is as follows: Verses 22-24 are pure narrative describing Jacob settling his entourage on the south side of the Jabbok river.[325] The only bearing these verses have on the following dialogue is to emphasize that Jacob is alone when the wrestling encounter takes place. Verses 25 and 26 are included because they introduce the parties who are wrestling and the actions that influence the initiation of dialogue. Verse 32 describes Jacob passing over Penuel after the conclusion of the dialogue and the encounter. Verse 33, as Sarna describes it, is "a historical note tracing the origin of an Israelite dietary abstention to the previously described episode."[326] Therefore, vv. 32 and 33 are excluded from the dialogue as they hold a similar narrative emphasis as vv. 22-24.

4. Translation

25 And Jacob was left to himself and he wrestled[327] with a man until the rising of the dawn.
26 And he perceived that he had not prevailed over him and, as Jacob wrestled with him, he touched a hollow of his thigh and dislocated the hollow of his thigh.
27 And he said, Send me away because the dawn rises. And he said, I will not send you away unless you bless me.
28 And he said unto him, What is your name? And he said, Jacob.
29 And he said, Jacob, I will not say your name again for it is Israel because you persisted[328] with Elohim and with men and have prevailed.

Gunkel, Brueggemann, Coats and Wenham agree to an overall narrative theme in Gen 32:1-33:17. However each does identify Gen 32:22-32 as an "extended encounter" within this narrative. Brueggemann, *Genesis*, 260. Also see Gunkel, *Genesis*, 343. Coats terms the interlude "The Tale of Jacob's Strife at Jabbok." Coats, *Genesis*, 224. Wenham labels the passage as "Scene 4." Wenham, *Genesis 16-50*, 287.

[324] I found only one example of a "dialogue only" delineation of verses. In his examination of the "Tale of Jacob's strife at Jabbok" Coats does distinguish the dialogue portion of the narrative from the surrounding verses. He defines the dialogue as being contained within vv. 27-30 only. This separation, however, is intricately woven into the overall tale as he defines vv. 25-33. Coats, *Genesis*, 228-29.

[325] Ibid., 227.

[326] Sarna, *Genesis*, 228.

[327] Here and in v. 26 the verb is ויאבק possibly a play on the name Yabbok (יבק) and Jacob (יעקב). Wenham, *Genesis 16-50*, 295.

[328] Westermann argues that the rare Hebrew word שרת "to persist or wrestle," is chosen in homage to Sarah because of the name Israel. Westermann, *Genesis: A Practical Commentary*, 230.

30   And Jacob asked and he said, Declare[329] your name and he said, Why do you ask this? And he blessed him there.

31   And Jacob called the place Peniel[330] because I saw Elohim face to face and my life was delivered.

5. Structure

	Divine Dialogue with Jacob	Gen 32:25-31
I.	Narrative element part 1	Gen 32:25-26
II.	Dialogue	Gen 32:27-30a
III.	Narrative element part 2	Gen 32:30b-31

G. THE CIRCUMSTANCES OF DIALOGUE: CONCLUSIONS

Our study so far has trod fairly familiar scholarly territory. The setting in literature and narrative for each passage have been examined and explained. The parameter discussions have varied slightly according to the individual passage. The combination of traditional form and narrative analysis has allowed for some small variations in parameters. In each case, however, it has been shown that the passage containing the dialogue can clearly be demarcated from the surrounding narrative. Isolation of the passage from the overall narrative is the first step in divorcing the Divine/human relational dialogue from the narrative. The structural analysis at the end of each section is the second step. By identifying what is considered strictly dialogue versus what is defined as narrative, we are able to isolate verses containing relational conversation. This allows a glimpse into the intimate "two shot" of Divine/human relational dialogue. The next chapter will consider the disengaged dialogue in three elemental blocks: initiation of dialogue, the use of proper names and dialogue analysis.

---

[329] Humphreys argues, "Rather than the direct 'What is your name?' (Gen. 32:28; ET 32:27), Jacob asks, 'Relate, please, your name' (Gen 32:30; ET 32:29)." Humphreys, *The Character of God in the Book of Genesis: A Narrative Appraisal*, 195.

[330] According to Sarna "Peniel is most plausibly identified with Tulul adh-Dhahab, which stands on the Jabbok a few miles from where it flows into the Jordan. It was a place of strategic importance." Sarna, *Genesis*, 228. Von Rad noted that there are two forms of the name, Peniel in v. 31 and Penuel in v. 32. They "differ in essentially only the archaic nominal ending; the latter is used in v. [31, *added by ET*] because it makes the pun on the word for face, which is used in the language of the narrator, clearer." Von Rad, *Genesis: A Commentary*, 323.

CHAPTER 3

THE ESSENCE OF DIALOGUE

Now that the narrative passages containing conversation have been identified and dislodged from the surrounding narrative sagas it is time to
examine the elements that make them Divine/human relational dialogues.
In this chapter we will look at the act of initiating dialogue, the use of a
proper name within conversation and analyze adjacency pairs within the
dialogue that allow for an expansion of the Divine/human relationship.

A. INITIATION OF DIALOGUE

Sidnell states that, "talk is at the heart of human social life. It is through
talk that we engage with one another in a distinctively human way."[1] The
dialogues under examination are not, however, between ordinary humans.
They are with the Deity yet they are distinctively human-esque. For each
of these conversations, it is the unremarkable-ness of their initiation
that makes them remarkable. "And YHWH said," "And Elohim said,"
"and they (or he) said."[2] There is no expression of surprise that such
an event can, will or should take place. The conversations that we are
about to examine are, at their inception, at least, expressed in such a way
as to be part of the everyday experience of both the human and Divine
participants.[3]

---

[1] Sidnell, *Conversation Analysis: An Introduction*, 1.

[2] Of the six dialogues examined five are termed direct speech. Genesis 15, while containing a relational conversation, is separated out as a prophetic vision deemed "free direct
discourse" due to the introductory infinitive *lē'mōr*. Matthews explains, "Direct speech
is shaped in the narrative as dialogue between characters, which perks up our ears to
listen more carefully and allows us to empathize with or identify with the speaker(s)
better. In Biblical Hebrew narrative the verb *'mr* is used to signal direct speech when it
is in its conjugated form, while when it appears in its infinitive form, *lē'mōr*, it signals
'free direct discourse' such as 'internal monologues or thoughts.'" Matthews, *More
Than Meets the Ear: Discovering the Hidden Contexts of Old Testament Conversations*,
24.

[3] G. David Schwartz, "God the Stranger," *Horizons in Biblical Theology* 20 (1998): 36.
Brown considers these conversations (in 16, 18, 15 & 32) to be "theophanies in minia-
ture" in comparison to the pyrotechnics as featured in Exodus and beyond. He notes that

Gen 4:6

ויאמר יהוה אל-קין למה חרה לך ולמה נפלו פניך

And YHWH said unto Cain, Why do you burn with anger and why has your countenance fallen?

Gen 16:8

ויאמר הגר שפחת שרי אי-מזה באת

And he said, Hagar, Sarai's handmaid, where have you come from and where will you go?

Gen 17:15

ויאמר אלהים אל-אברם שרי אשתך לא-תקרא את-שמה שרי כי שרה שמה

And Elohim said unto Abraham, Your wife Sarai, you will not call her Sarai because her name is Sarah.

Gen 18:9

ויאמרו אליו איה שרה אשתך

And they said unto him, Where is Sarah your wife?

Gen 15:1

אחר הדברים האלה היה דבר־יהוה אל־אברם במחזה לאמר אל־תירא אברם אנכי מגן לך שכרך הרבה מאד

After these words the word of YHWH was with Abram in a vision saying, Fear not Abram, I am your shield and your very great reward.

Gen 32:27

ויאמר שלחני כי עלה השחר

And he said, Send me away because the dawn rises.

The initiation of dialogue in Gen 4 is both ironic and bland:[4] Ironic in the sense that, after spending five verses setting the narrative stage, the Deity does not discuss Abel or his "regarded" offering. Instead the Divine

---

when God appears in Genesis "the focus is predominantly on the substance of what God says rather than on the substance of God's presence." Brown, "Manifest Diversity: The Presence of God in Genesis," 6.

[4] Westermann argues that vv. 6-7 are not even necessary to the progress of the events of Gen 4 and goes so far as to suggest that they could be omitted all together without affecting the overall structure of the narrative. His focus is on a two part narrative corresponding to genealogic information. For Westermann the dialogue in vv. 6-7 is disruptive to his analysis of vv. 3-5 and v. 8. Westermann, *Genesis 1-11: A Commentary*, 287.

chooses to speak to the human who is angry; bland in the sense that, within the first verbal utterance, there is no direct reprimand for the anger, a warning of danger or an expression of tragedy that will soon engulf the participants.

Genesis 16 has a somewhat similar introduction. Once again, the Deity is intervening in the life of an unlikely, even unregarded, person. And yet, in approaching the woman there is no fear on Hagar's part as the Divine speaks her name for the first time, something no other human has done or will do in the text.

The dialogues of Gen 17 and 18 are conversations where the majority of the discussion involves the patriarch but not the individuals who are spoken of. The opening statement of Gen 17 is than announcement or declaration of Sarai's proper name. A name, it seems, not known to those with whom she lives. In Gen 18 the verses just prior to the dialogue go to great length to stress the home setting in an effort to integrate Sarah into the conversation. The first query of chapter 18 is a straightforward question designed to ensure Sarah's proximity to the coming conversation.[5]

The dialogues of Gen 15 and 32 contain wording and structure that separate them from our first four conversations. Genesis 15, "couched in prophetic language,"[6] is set within a vision.[7] Genesis 32 has detached Jacob from his family. Moreover, within the dialogue of Gen 32 the identity of the initiator is not immediately clear due to the abundant use of the indeterminate 3ms.[8] In order to work out the identity of the original spokesperson one must work backwards from v. 28 where Jacob finally identifies himself by name. In both of these cases, however, the opening verbal statement

---

[5] Fretheim argues that the question in v. 9 "is designed to make sure Sarah is within earshot of what is about to be said." Fretheim, *Abraham: Trials of Family and Faith*, 112.

[6] Westermann, *Genesis: A Practical Commentary*, 118. The introductory information, "the word of YHWH came unto Abram," is not a standard formula in the Pentateuch. In fact, this is the only occurrence in the entire Pentateuch. Ha, *Genesis 15: A Theological Compendium of Pentateuchal History*, 65.

[7] Van Seters notes that this opening sequence "seems to be a rather strange combination of two different modes of prophetic reception of revelation that are usually kept quite distinct." Van Seters, *Abraham in History and Tradition*, 253. Sarna does not see any inconsistency. He does, however, treat the elements as distinct. "The present occasion language is employed that is elsewhere reserved for prophetic pronouncements, such as the formula, unique in the Torah, 'The word of the Lord came to[... *added by ET*]' Similarly, the word for 'vision' derives from the stem 'to see,' which is largely used in connection with the prophetic experience." Sarna, *Genesis*, 112.

[8] Barthes states this lack of identifying pronouns is "a style which a purist would describe as *muddled* but whose lack of sharpness doubtless posed no problem for Hebrew syntax." Barthes, *Image, Music, Text*, 132.

is a command[9] which is different from our other conversations and yet the verbs are still in the Qal form. The statements are not made to punish or crush the human. They are formulated to get the attention of the addressee.

Matthews remarks that "within narrative, the reader is guided by verbal forms (tense, person) and discourse markers that indicate to the audience when a quoted statement is about to be made or to signal the beginning of narrative frames that section off exchanges of direct speech."[10] Through the participation of two or more individuals these "direct speeches" develop into conversation. The ordinariness of the initiation of these dialogues is an indication of mutual recognition by the participants.[11] In other words, we know that the one speaking recognizes the individual whom they are addressing by the words that they choose to use.

In Gen 4 the initial questions the Deity asks assume an understanding of the actions that have come before.[12] The Deity may not have "regarded" Cain's offering but the Deity is aware of the man and the fact that he is not pleased with something that has come to pass. In Gen 16 contact is made between Divine and human and for the first time Hagar is spoken to directly using her proper name. As Westermann explains it, "Contact is made and an existing sense of solidarity is preserved; rejection of the salutation means rejection of this solidarity."[13] Considering all that has happened to Hagar in the household wherein she resides, responding to a stranger in the wilderness does not seem to be the most opportune moment to speak. Yet without hesitation Hagar replies.

In the following three Abraham dialogues each verbal initiation contains a personal proper name. In Gen 17 the Deity announces that Sarai's name is, in fact, Sarah. The introductory question of Gen 18 indicates the Divine knows the name of a woman whom they have yet to physically meet.[14] And in Gen 15 the first divine utterance is the command to "fear

---

[9] In Gen 15 "Fear not" is jussive ms. Genesis 32 "Send me away" is imperative ms.

[10] Matthews, *More Than Meets the Ear: Discovering the Hidden Contexts of Old Testament Conversations*, 23.

[11] Sidnell, *Conversation Analysis: An Introduction*, 199.

[12] Westermann, *Genesis 1-11: A Commentary*, 299.

[13] Westermann considers the greeting "where have you come from/where are you going?" to be found only in narratives involving small circles of characters making the interaction that much more personal. Westermann, *Genesis: A Practical Commentary*, 125.

[14] Wenham argues for a rhetorical classification to the question. He states, "Like [Genesis *added by ET*] 3:9 'Where are you?' and [Genesis, *added by ET*] 4:9, 'Where is Abel your

not" followed by Abram's proper name and then a form of divine self-identification to assure the human of the existing relationship.

Finally, Gen 32 is our "stand-alone" dialogue. The narrative description of combat gives way to a verbal wrestling. The command "Send me away!" is one of the simplest and most direct examples of a relational statement. Without individual identification the statement established that one will not release the other from their physical relationship. Opening statements such as these, have, as Sidnell explains, "a kind of special capacity to get the conversational ball rolling by virtue of the conditional relevance they establish."[15] Through turn-taking analysis it becomes possible to discern the identities of the wrestling partners and their relationship to each other.

Sidnell observed that the initiation of dialogue is often hidden from view with "complete ordinariness; they are so much a part of us that we hardly notice them."[16] There are unique elements in each one of our conversations as well as components that will set them apart from other passages, speeches and dialogues, yet how the conversation actually starts is relatively simple in the language used. What is common for all six is that, regardless of the previous narrative, it is the Deity who speaks first and each statement expresses a recognition of the human condition and acknowledges some kind of an existing relationship with that human. Notwithstanding the dialogue's rather innocuous beginnings, the human participants, regardless of moral, social or ancillary status, are shown to be worthy of a relationship with the Divine. That relationship is expanded in the conversation that follows.

B. PROPER NAMES

As the Deity creates and names in Gen 1-3 a world is formed and the general community of humankind is fashioned. Genesis 4 produces the first use of a human proper name and the first use of a proper name within Divine spoken dialogue.[17] Much scholarship has focused on origination

---

brother?' [Gen 18:9, *added by ET*] is not a real question, for the questioner knows the answer. In this case, it rather shows something about the questioner and indicates the real recipient of the message about to be given." Wenham, *Genesis 16-50*, 47.

[15] Sidnell, *Conversation Analysis: An Introduction*, 198.

[16] Ibid., 197.

[17] Genesis 4:9 "Where is Abel thy brother?" The exclusion of *ha-ADAM* has been explained in chapter 1 "Proper Names."

of a name, its etymology and meaning.[18] However, the use of a proper name can be more than the sum of its parts. How a proper name is used can, in many cases, define an individual's true identity, their social status and/or explain their relationship with others. We will now examine the proper names and their usage in the dialogues under consideration.

1. Genesis 4: Cain and Abel

The birth of Cain in Gen 4:1 is a complete birth report conforming to the standard elements of a conception notice, a birth notice, and an etymological speech introduced by his mother Eve.[19] Eve's statement "I have gotten a man from YHWH" (קניתי איש את-יהוה) however, has sent scholars to the mat searching for explanations to this unique statement.[20] For Van Wolde, Eve's declaration highlights the relationship between the Deity and humankind. She states, "YHWH gives life to Cain, together with the mother Eve. This first implicitly narrated action of YHWH signifies that the relation between YHWH and Cain is installed by YHWH at the birth of Cain."[21] Van Wolde sees Eve's statement as a reassurance that even though humankind is no longer in the presence of the Deity, as they were in the Garden, they are still important enough to warrant a personal connection and relationship. The birth of Abel, on the other hand, almost immediately overturns this suggested relationship. "The birth of Abel contains no conception element or etymological element but is a simple birth notice that combines the birth and naming elements."[22]

Following the birth and identification of Abel the names of the brothers are alternated exactly four times within vv. 2-5. The chiastic structure of the verses is extremely interesting.[23] "When the verbs are the same, the subject changes; when the verb changes, the subject remains the same[... added by ET] What is achieved throughout is an emphasis on

---

[18] For insight into naming and etymology contained within individual birth narratives, see Finlay, *The Birth Report Genre in the Hebrew Bible*. With regards to Gen 17 specifically see Joseph Fleishman, "On the Significance of a Name Change and Circumcision in Genesis 17," *JANES* 28 (2001): 21.

[19] Finlay, *The Birth Report Genre in the Hebrew Bible*, 77.

[20] For a detailed examination of the discussion see Westermann, *Genesis 1-11: A Commentary*, 290-92.

[21] Ellen Van Wolde, *Words Become Worlds: Semantic Studies of Genesis 1-11* (Leiden: Brill, 1994), 50.

[22] Finlay, *The Birth Report Genre in the Hebrew Bible*, 77.

[23] Craig, "Questions Outside Eden (Genesis 4.1-16): Yahweh, Cain and Their Rhetorical Interchange," 112.

the similarity and contemporaneity of the pairs of actions. Neither Cain nor Abel occupies the centre of the stage."[24] If the stress is on similarity, what then is the difference that causes the conversational discord?

Finley explains, "The birth report of Abel differs significantly from the others in the superstructure, for reasons of developing the narrative."[25] Another point to acknowledge is that, after the structure and the Deity's first speech to Cain, Abel is no longer a stand-alone named individual. In other words, "The entire emphasis is on Abel's being a brother: he does not *have* a brother, he *is* a brother only."[26] Cain is never labeled as such. Abel's name is, therefore, "not really the name of a person but an appellative, constructed out of the story."[27]

Within the Gen 4 narrative two names are used and are, for the most part, equal in weight and tone. According to the dialogue, however, Abel,

---

[24] Francis I. Andersen, *The Sentence in Biblical Hebrew* (The Hague: Mouton, 1974), 122-23.

[25] Finlay, *The Birth Report Genre in the Hebrew Bible*, 79. The meaning behind the names Cain and Abel are not germane to this argument. However, I do acknowledge that most scholars agree that the name Abel and the meaning behind it are a foreshadowing of his limited existence. Sarna's JPS commentary states "Hebrew *havel* means 'breath, nothingness.' The name may augur his destiny; or, if it was given after his death, it may be a reflection of his fate. *Havel* is often used to express the fleeting nature of life. The name may alternatively, or perhaps simultaneously, contain a reference to his vocation in that Syriac *hablâ* means 'herdsman.'" Sarna, *Genesis*, 32. The fact that the name Abel belongs only to narrative (he is not mentioned in the genealogies) and does not appear outside of Gen 4:1-16 strengthens the argument.
As for the name Cain, the name is not so easily defined or it's etymological reasonably explained. Scholars have found multiple theories to explain the name: von Rad states "the name of the first-born, means 'spear' and is also attested in early Arabic as a personal name. The etymology with which the mother justifies the name, however, is quite obscure." Von Rad, *Genesis: A Commentary*, 103. Cassuto argues "The Aramaic word cited is recognizable, even by its form, as a denominative noun, and in any case connotes also a *refiner*, who works in *silver* and *gold*. In Biblical Hebrew, קַיִן *qayin* signifies a 'weapon', which has been given *form* by the craftsman (ii Sam. xxi 16). The conclusion to be drawn from all this is that the name of Adam's first son means: a creature [literally, 'a formed being,' *added by ET*]." Cassuto, *A Commentary on the Book of Genesis*, 197-98. Speiser comments "If the name is cognate with Ar. *qayin* 'metalworker,' the indicated derivation would be more in order in v. 22. But this is plainly yet another case of sound symbolism." Speiser, *Genesis*, 30. Cotter explains that Eve "proclaims that she has created a man in the same way as YHWH (*qānîtî 'îš 'et-YHWH*, 4:1) and names him Cain (*qayin*, 'Smith') in a way that both foresees his alienation from the land and creates a similarity in sound with the verb *qānîtî*." Cotter, *Genesis*, 41. Westermann argues that the name Cain is a clear example of a personal name within the context of Gen 4 but is not a particular motivator for the story. See Westermann, *Genesis 1-11: A Commentary*, 285.

[26] Six times Abel is mentioned in vv. 8-11 and each time he is referred to as a brother of Cain. Van Wolde, *Words Become Worlds: Semantic Studies of Genesis 1-11*, 59.

[27] Westermann, *Genesis 1-11: A Commentary*, 289.

as a proper name, is only verbally declared in reference to Cain his
brother. This does not specifically diminish Abel's individual relationship
with the Deity; it does however, relegate the name to a submissive position within the equation that highlights Cain's relationship with the
Divine. Cain, as a proper name, is used in connection with a declaration
made known to the world regarding the curse and subsequent protection
of the Deity. As a whole the proper name Cain identifies this particular
individual as the only one to receive these promises.

2. Genesis 16: Hagar, Sarai, Ishmael, El-Roi

Within the isolated dialogue of Gen 16 the use of a proper name takes
on special significance. Between vv. 7 and 14 there are four names spoken: Hagar, Sarai, Ishmael and *El-roi*. Brichto notes that "the status of
the characters and their importance — in varying degrees — to YHWH,
and to Abram, and to one another, is[... *added by ET*] underlined by the
narrator's[... *added by ET*] use of the personae's proper names and their
epithets."[28] By examining the names listed above and how they are
employed we can see the intention behind their use.

From the start of the Abraham cycle Hagar has not been spoken to or
identified as a named individual by either Sarai or Abram. Her identity
is therefore incomplete due to the absence of her spoken name.[29] Schneider goes so far as to recognize that "humans treat her only as an object,
never addressing her by name."[30] With the Deity being the first to address
Hagar by name Gossai comments that "the stark and telling difference
between human and divine recognition of one's personhood is seen in
16:8, where Hagar is addressed by name by the angel of Yahweh. Even
as a slave, an outsider, and oppressed person, Hagar has an identity which
is divinely given."[31]

With this divine identification there are, however, some detractors.[32]
While the Deity has uttered the name which Sarai and Abram have avoided,

---

[28] Brichto, *The Names of God: Poetic Readings in Biblical Beginnings*, 214.

[29] Hemchand Gossai, *Power and Marginality in the Abraham Narrative* (Lanham, Md.:
University of America Press, 1995), 6.

[30] Schneider, *Mothers of Promise: Women in the Book of Genesis*, 117.

[31] Gossai, *Power and Marginality in the Abraham Narrative*, 6.

[32] Again, the meaning of the name is not part of the argument here. However, many
scholars see it as important to the overall narrative explanation. Sarna suggests that
through Hebrew word play, Hagar's name suggests a meaning of "stranger" and "harsh
treatment." Sarna, *Genesis*, 119. Other commentaries suggest an uncertain meaning
"perhaps 'wanderer,' from Arabic *hajara*, 'to migrate'; or 'town,' from Sabean and
Ethiopic *hagar*, originally meaning 'splendid.'" *Women in Scripture: A Dictionary of*

Hagar's identity is immediately tied with that of Sarai and her position within the household, that of Sarai's handmaid. (ויאמר הגר שפחת שרי) "The deity acknowledges what Sarai and Abram have not: the person-hood of this woman. Yet the appositive, 'maid of Sarai,' tempers the recognition, for Hagar remains a servant in the vocabulary of the divine."[33] Therefore, even though Hagar is identified by a messenger of YHWH by her proper name, her status is contingent on the use of the second proper name, Sarai, used here as an adjectival marker.

The third proper name used in this dialogue is Ishmael. In vv. 10-12 the dialogue does not focus specifically on Hagar but on the son she is carrying. However, when his name is called and explained[34] the name reapplies the focus to Hagar's situation, i.e., "YHWH has heard of your afflictions." (כי-שמע יהוה אל-עניך) The proper name Ishmael, while refer-ring to an unborn child, in fact further identifies Hagar as a unique indi-vidual.[35] The child's name "is not based on the caprice of the parents,

---

Named and Unnamed Women in the Hebrew Bible, the Apocryphal/Deuterocanonical Books, and the New Testament, ed. Carol L. Meyers (Grand Rapids, Mich.: Eerdmans, 2001), 86. See also Drey, "The Role of Hagar in Genesis 16," 181-83.

[33] Phyllis Trible, "The Other Woman: A Literary and Theological Study of the Hagar Narratives," in Understanding the Word: Essays in Honor of Bernhard W. Anderson, ed. James T. Butler, Edgar W. Conrad, and Ben C. Ollenburger, JSOTSup 37 (Sheffield: JSOT Press, 1985), 226. Schneider expands, "Many treat the reference to Hagar as a *shiphchah* as evidence that the narrator is trying to demean her, but its use by the nar-rator, Sarah, and Abraham functions to explain her status and relationship to the other figures in the text. Later Sarah will refer to Hagar with a term that may be more demean-ing, but in the beginning of Hagar's story the narrator uses *shiphchah* to describe what the situation is. Sarah uses it to identify who she means to give to Abraham. The mes-senger of the Deity uses the term so Hagar knows who is being addressed." Schneider, *Mothers of Promise: Women in the Book of Genesis*, 105.

[34] In his dissection of the Birth Genre, Finlay discusses the naming aspect of Ishmael's birth narrative stating that "there is no etiological element in the birth report itself, but there is at least an implied etiology in the announcement in Gen 16:11." Finlay, *The Birth Report Genre in the Hebrew Bible*, 99. For Finlay's full discussion see pages 96-104. Speiser notes that the further discussion of Ishmael in vv. 11 and 12 is "to account for the place of the Ishmaelites in the scheme of things, the role of the Bedouin who are always in evidence on the border between the desert and the sown, a group as defiant and uncontrollable as the young woman from whom the narrative drives them." Speiser, *Genesis*, 121. Interestingly scripture does not bear out the bleak abandonment of the Ishmaelites. For example, when Isaac and Ishmael bury their father there is no sign of conflict (Gen 25:9). One of David's sisters married an Ishmaelite (1 Chr 2:17), and an Ishmaelite and a Hagrite were administrators for David (1 Chr 27:30-31).

[35] Contrary to Dozeman's interpretation of the passage. Thomas B. Dozeman, "The Wil-derness and Salvatin History in the Hagar Story," *JBL* 117 (1998): 34. Nikaido states, "When the motif of oppression appears in the Bible, one can be assured that God will take up the cause of the oppressed." Nikaido, "Hagar and Ishmael as Literary Figures: An Intertextual Study," 229.

but determined by God himself. The boy shall be called *Yisma'el* 'because Yahweh has heard (שמע) of your mistreatment' and, therefore, will care for you."[36] The *you* in both cases is not the unborn boy but Hagar. Her salvation "will be her son, a son whose name will be a constant reminder to her of the heed God once paid to her misery."[37]

Within this dialogue is a singular example of a human leaving a mark upon the Deity in the form of a name. Hagar becomes the only human to name the Divine thus giving us our fourth proper name contained within the passage. (ותקרא שם-יהוה הדבר אליה אתה אל ראי) Attempts to actually understand, let alone translate, the name have been "almost inexhaustible."[38] Von Rad states:

> The names by which Hagar attempts to fix her recollection of this encounter with God are obscure. The God who was revealed to her she calls "God of seeing," which refers to the miracle of God's seeing Hagar and prophesying a great future for her child. But one thinks immediately she saw the one who saw her. The "for" in the statement is not quite 'logical' only because God permitted himself to be seen by her can she make any utterance about God.[39]

Sarna continues the explanation:

> The vocalization of the second element occasions a marvelous ambiguity that permits the following translations of the name: "God of seeing," that is, the all-seeing God; "God of my seeing," that is, whom I have seen; "God who sees me." Most likely, the several meanings are intended to be apprehended simultaneously. When God "sees," it is, of course, that He shows His concern and extends His protection; when Hagar "sees," she experiences God's self-manifestation.[40]

Putting translation issues aside, what is most interesting about the incident described through Hagar's speech is the fact that "it connotes naming rather than invocation. In other words, Hagar does not call *upon* the name of the deity [as is done in Gen 12:8; 13:4, *added by ET*]. Instead she calls the name, a power attributed to no one else in all the Bible."[41]

---

[36] Gunkel, *Genesis*, 187.
[37] Dennis, *Sarah Laughed*, 70.
[38] Brichto, *The Names of God: Poetic Readings in Biblical Beginnings*, 216. Most scholars agree that the translations of *El-roi* are "not clear." Suggestions for meanings include "God of seeing" or "God who sees," or "God of a vision." For example see, Speiser, *Genesis*, 118-19. Westermann, *Genesis 12-36: A Commentary*, 246-49. Humphreys, *The Character of God in the Book of Genesis: A Narrative Appraisal*, 103.
[39] Von Rad, *Genesis: A Commentary*, 194.
[40] Sarna, *Genesis*, 121.
[41] Trible, *Texts of Terror: Literary-Feminist Readings of Biblical Narratives*, 18. Emphasis original. Teubal suggests "the Desert Matriarch," an entity separate from Hagar, is the

In the dialogue of Gen 16 Hagar is properly named for the first time yet her identity is compromised by the use of Sarai's name. Ishmael's name is declared but only in relation to his mother's tribulations. Finally, the Deity is called a proper name though it is impossible to understand or translate. In the process, the names used reveal the perception of the individuals involved, i.e., Hagar is seen as a proper and complete individual by the Deity; Sarai's name is used to identify Hagar's social status; the name Ishmael "reveals Yahweh's self-perception; he is a God who hears"[42] and by naming the Deity *El Roi*, "God who sees," Hagar reveals her perception of the Deity. Proper names in this dialogue therefore take on special significance through their distinctive use in identifying an individual's relationship with other humans and with the Divine. With this divine identification and the dialogue that follows "even though Hagar takes a risk in returning to the status of slave, her new identity is now predicated on the belief that God sees, God hears, and God shapes the future."[43]

3. Genesis 17: Sarai/Sarah, Ishmael, Isaac

In Gen 17 all named individuals are inactive participants in the dialogue between the Deity and Abraham. "Sarah does not appear or carry out any actions in Gen 17, and yet her life is changed by the conversation between the Deity and Abraham."[44] Her life is altered not through the change of a name but through the use of proper names.

Schneider contends that the announcement of Sarai's new name Sarah in v. 15 (שרי אשתך לא-תקרא את-שמה שרי כי שרה שמה) is not in actuality a change.[45] Instead, she argues, it is a correction proclamation of a divinely designated identity.

---

one who identifies the Deity as El-Roi. Savina J. Teubal, "Sarah and Hagar: Matriarchs and Visionaries," in *Feminist Companion to Genesis*, ed. Athalya Brenner (Sheffield: Sheffield Academic Press, 1993), 247. Drey argues against 'the Desert Matriarch' designation. See Drey, "The Role of Hagar in Genesis 16," 191.

[42] Turner, *Genesis*, 79.

[43] Gossai, *Power and Marginality in the Abraham Narrative*, 19.

[44] Schneider, *Sarah: Mother of Nations*, 60.

[45] The change of name from Sarai to Sarah is, for most scholars, directly linked with that of Abram's name change at the beginning of the same chapter. For example: "The name changes of the ancestors to Abraham and Sarah (17:5, 15) imply both the authority of the giver of the new name (cf. 3:20) and the new destiny or mission indicated by the new name (cf. 32:29)." *The Harper Collins Bible Commentary*, ed. James Luther Mays, Rev. ed. (San Francisco, Calif.: Harper San Francisco, 2000), 93. While I am not arguing against this link, I am only interested in the names that are contained within our

The way the Hebrew presents it is not a change, since the text does not use that terminology, as it does with Abraham (17:5). Instead the Deity states, "Sarai, your wife, you will no longer call her name Sarai because Sarah is her name" (17:15). This is worded as though the Deity is not changing her name but correcting Abraham, as if he has been calling her the wrong name all along.[46]

Most scholarship does not see this textual difference.[47] Schneider's argument, however, proves correct when viewed through the lens of the use of proper names.

To understand Schneider's subtle textual variance is to understand that Sarai/Sarah is not being given a new identity, instead Abraham and the

---

dialogue parameters and therefore am required to analyze the change of Sarai/Sarah as distinct from that of Abram/Abraham. Comparisons will be made when necessary.

[46] Schneider, *Mothers of Promise: Women in the Book of Genesis*, 36. Schneider is spotlighting the use of the verb היה "to be" in v. 5 and its absence in v. 15. In Abram's case the proper name Abraham "will come to be." For Sarai, the name Sarah, the text indicates, does in fact already exist.

[47] Von Rad insists that "linguistically, 'Sarai' is only an archaic form of the later formation 'Sarah' and probably means princess.'" Von Rad, *Genesis: A Commentary*, 202. Westermann agrees and states that the new name, with its interpretation of 'princess' is "explanation enough." Westermann, *Genesis: A Practical Commentary*, 132. Humphreys examines the names by comparing the root as a noun and as a verb. "'Sarah,' which is not far from 'Sarai, resonates with a tension between two words that sound alike. At least a reader at home in classical Hebrew hears in it echoes of two words; the one a noun *śarah* meaning 'princess or lady'; and the other a verb *śarah* meaning 'to contend, to struggle, to strive.' The suggestions of royalty are appropriate for the woman from whom 'kings of peoples will come into being.' The contention and striving suggested echo the evolution of her relationship with her handmaid Hagar and also with her husband." Humphreys, *The Character of God in the Book of Genesis: A Narrative Appraisal*, 109. Also see Speiser, *Genesis*, 127.
Speiser states that "linguistically, *śārā* embodies the common feminine ending whereas *śāray* preserves an old and specialized feminine form." Ibid., 125. Discussions regarding the meaning of the new name also focus on echoes in classical Hebrew with similar sounding words; the noun *sarah* meaning "princess or lady" (Judg 5:29; 1Kgs 11:3; Isa 49:23; Lam 1:1 and Esther 1:18) and the verb *s-r-h* meaning "to contend, to struggle, to strive" (Gen 32:29; Hos 12:4-5). "No interpretation of the matriarch's name is given, but the succeeding blessing about 'kings/rulers' who will issue from her suggests an implicit midrash based on word play, for Hebrew *sar*, 'prince, ruler,' is often paired with *melekh*, 'king.' Further, there may well be an oblique reference to Sarah as the progenitrix of the future Israel, for in Genesis 32:29 that name is said to derive from Jacob's having 'striven with being divine and human.' The Hebrew verb stem used there is *s-r-h*." Sarna, *Genesis*, 126. Humphreys adds, "The contention and striving suggested echo the evolution of her relationship with her handmaid Hagar and also with her husband. And both connotations may look ahead as well to what is yet to come in her story as it unfolds in relations to Hagar, to Abraham, and to God. God again meaningfully plays with words as he renames the husband and wife." Humphreys, *The Character of God in the Book of Genesis: A Narrative Appraisal*, 109.

reader are being forced to comprehend her true identity.[48] "What is new is that God tells Abraham explicitly that Sarah is to be the mother of the covenant-continuing son and so blesses her with a blessing that will allow her to become mother of nations and of kings of different peoples."[49] With the identity of the covenant mother categorically assured in v. 16, Abraham's reaction in v. 17 illustrates his ignorance regarding the Deity's divine intentions for Sarah. This misunderstanding leads to the Deity's use of additional proper names Isaac[50] and Ishmael in vv. 19-21. Arranged in a chiastic structure, the names directly address Abraham's ignorance and matches his misgivings, doubts and concerns point for point.[51]

Verse 19a solidifies the identity of the mother of promise. Verse 19b identifies Isaac as the promised son and emphasizes the term covenant twice in the latter part of the same verse. The apex of the chiasm is v. 20. The fate of Ishmael, the now identified non-covenant and non-biological

---

[48] Humphreys agrees somewhat in that the name Sarah is "marking a profound change in her situation and identity." Humphreys, *The Character of God in the Book of Genesis: A Narrative Appraisal*, 109. Cotter states that a different name "whether through marriage or religious profession, is, then or now, a powerful means of adopting a new identity." Cotter, *Genesis*, 109.

[49] Cotter, *Genesis*, 110. The Deity blesses Sarah twice in v. 16 by stating "I shall bless her" and "I shall give you a son from her." Wenham explains, "This may sound quite prosaic, but every word is significant. Back in 15:3 Abraham had complained 'You have not given me descendants.' Since then the Lord has given him the land (15:18) and a covenant (17:2) but no son except Hagar's. Now there is to be a son for him from Sarah. Indeed, the nations and kings promised to Abraham in v. 6 are to be descended from Sarah." Wenham, *Genesis 16-50*, 25.

[50] Wenham suggests the following regarding the history of the name. "The name Isaac is typical of early second-millennium Amorite names, consisting of a verb in the imperfect and a divine name (cf. Ishmael or Israel). Thus it is usually surmised that the full name of Isaac was Isaac-el, just as the full name of Jacob was probably Jacob-el. If יצחק אל is the correct full name of Isaac, then it may be translated 'The god El laughs/smiles/looks with favor.' Like the name Ishmael, it records divine mercy in granting the child's birth. Another possibility is that Isaac is not a shortening of Isaac-el but a name in its own right and refers to the laughter and pleasure of the parents over the child. Hence it could be interpreted '(The father) laughs/smiles.' However, as usual with names, the Bible is not interested in a historic etymology so much as in the associations evoked by the name. Wherever the name Isaac is discussed, it is associated with the verb צחק 'to laugh' or in the piel 'make sport of' and reflects the skeptical laughter of his parents when told of his birth (v. 17; 18:12-15) or Ishmael's mistreatment of him (21:9)." Wenham, *Genesis 16-50*, 26.

[51] The paraphrased structure is as follows:
A   Sarah shall bear a son 17:19a
   B   With Isaac I will establish my covenant 17:19b
      X   Ishmael I have blessed 17:20
   b   I will establish my covenant with Isaac 17:21a
a   Sarah will bear at the appointed season 17:21b

son of Sarah, is expounded.[52] Verse 21a then mirrors 19b as the Deity reiterates the name Isaac and his covenant status all of which is due to the one divinely proclaimed Sarah who "will bear to thee in that appointed season in the following year" in v. 21b.

Sarah's divine identity, corrected by the Deity in v. 15, is justified in vv. 19-21 through the chiastic structure and the use of names contained therein. It is not simply the fact that Sarai/Sarah is the only woman in the Hebrew Bible to have her name changed or that the action is taken by the Deity. Schneider observes that Sarah's "name change occurs before her shift in status, [that of, *added by ET*] making her the mother of the heir to the promise. This name change again indicates that there is something about Sarai herself that is important, not just the act that Abraham is her spouse."[53] Through dialogue and the use of multiple proper names Sarah's maternity has been revealed to be as important as Abraham's paternity.[54]

4. Genesis 18: Sarah

The dialogue of chapter 18 contains one proper name and a lot of laughter. "Where is Sarah, thy wife?" (איה שרה אשתך) is similar in tone to the question asked of Hagar in Gen 16:9.[55] The use of the proper name in the opening question of chapter 16 gives Hagar recognition of her personhood. In chapter 18 the question has a similar effect of focusing the coming dialogue on Sarah.[56] Prior to the initiation of our dialogue Sarah is on the periphery of the narrative actions.[57] This changes dramatically as the Divine voices the question. Within the conversation that follows the name Sarah is used by the Deity four times.[58] Laughter is also repeated four times within the conversation.[59] Each time, the verb צחק

---

[52] The Deity informs Abraham that "I will cause him to be fruitful and to become a great many. Twelve princes shall he beget and I will give to him a great nation." (Gen 17:20) Schneider states, "The Deity, as all along, has nothing against Ishmael, and even from the announcement of his birth has intended a role for him (16:11-12)." Schneider, *Sarah: Mother of Nations*, 59.

[53] Ibid., 57.

[54] Turner, *Announcements of Plot in Genesis*, 77.

[55] Comparisons can also be made to Gen 4:9 when the Deity asks, "Where is Abel your brother?" Hamilton, *The Book of Genesis: Chapters 18-50*, 12.

[56] Brichto, *The Names of God: Poetic Readings in Biblical Beginnings*, 232.

[57] Humphreys, *The Character of God in the Book of Genesis: A Narrative Appraisal*, 116.

[58] The narrator uses the name an additional four times. The ninth reference to Sarah is with a pronominal in v. 15, "but thou didst laugh."

[59] According to Gunkel, "in the whole context, the word 'laughter' is supposed to impress us. Therefore, it is repeated four times." Gunkel, *Genesis*, 197.

"to laugh" is uttered it is feminine and directly associated with Sarah, the only parent mentioned in the dialogue.[60]

In v. 10 the Deity declares that Sarah will have a son. (והנה-בן לשרה אשתך) Her reaction and comments in vv. 10-12 "lay the foundation for a wordplay on the name of the son"[61] (ותצחק שרה בקרבה) as contained in the reference to the still unnamed Isaac and Sarah's definitive connection to him.[62] The impression left with most scholars is the rebuke Sarah receives for her denial but little else develops from the wordplay.[63] Yet the wordplay never varies. Sarah and laughter are and will be directly related.[64]

While both Gen 17 and 18 are recorded dialogues between Abraham and the Deity, this time the promise as voiced by the Deity is actually heard by Sarah. Fretheim observed that the "divine appearance at the familial tent — where Sarah is most likely to be present — seems especially designed to reinforce the promise of a son by conveying the word directly to Sarah herself [... added by ET] That the visitors begin the conversation with reference to Sarah reinforces this point."[65] From the first mention of Sarah's proper name to the last reference of laughter in this dialogue, the use of a proper name in Gen 18 expands on Gen 17's recognition of Sarah's true identity and maternal destiny.

5. Genesis 15: Abram, Adoni YHWH, Eliezer, YHWH

Within the visionary dialogue of Gen 15 there are names that are not easily defined or explained and yet they describe the Divine/human relationship as that of master to servant. In v. 1 of the conversation the patriarch is addressed as Abram by the Deity, the first time the Deity has called the

---

[60] Fretheim, *Abraham: Trials of Family and Faith*, 111.

[61] Coats, *Genesis*, 137-38. Speiser agrees. He states there is nothing equivocal "where Sarah is concerned. She is depicted as down-to-earth to a fault, with her curiosity, her impulsiveness, and her feeble attempt at deception. It must not be forgotten, however, that this vivid sketch has been colored, at least in part, by the supposed origin of the name Isaac." Speiser, *Genesis*, 131.

[62] Coats states, "The extensive play on the verb *shq* ('laugh') sets the basis for giving a name, but the name is not announced, and no reference to the destiny of the child can be found. This unit does not develop the pattern in full." Coats, *Genesis*, 138.

[63] Ibid., 138.

[64] Wenham argues that the repetition of laughter in the narrative "assumes the etymology of Isaac [from, *added by ET*] the previous chapter and sees no need to repeat it [with Sarah, *added by ET*]." Wenham, *Genesis 16-50*, 47.

[65] Fretheim, *Abraham: Trials of Family and Faith*, 111.

patriarch by his proper name.[66] The descriptive qualifiers do not represent this as unusual or unexpected, but are indicative of an established relationship. For the Divine, the object of calling Abram's name is to declare that the man should "fear not" and to introduce a more expansive and specific covenantal promise.

Abram's response in v. 2 specifically identifies the Divine as "(My) lord YHWH" (אדמי יהוה). While this is a familiar form of address in the prophetic books it is rare in the Pentateuch.[67] There is also the difficulty in definitively declaring אדמי יהוה or יהוה as a title or a proper name.

Surveying the term's use throughout the scriptures, Ha designates "(My) lord Yahweh" a title for the Deity.[68] Revell follows Ha up to a point. The scholars diverge when Revell examines each portion of the "title." He states that the use of the identification of "(my) lord" "alone, or in combination with the name 'Yahweh,' shows that the two were used distinctly as terms of address. It seems clear that, a part of the motivation for the use of '(my) lord' in this way was the desire to use the first person pronoun incorporated in the form to recall the speaker's close relationship to God."[69] He goes on to state that when used in written form the combination "(My) lord Yahweh" "has a value distinct from the name Yahweh."[70]

Scholars of Exod 6:3 (ושמי יהוה לא נודעתי להם) are quick to identify YHWH as a proper name.[71] Commentaries on Genesis, however, are a

---

[66] The narrator has identified Abram by name on numerous occasions since Gen 11:26. The first person to address Abram by name is Melchizedek, king of Salem, in Gen 14:19 as he blesses him upon his return from Lot's rescue. The final time Abram is referred to directly as Abram is Gen 17:5 when the Deity changes his name to Abraham. The covenantal promise, as given in chapters 12 and 13, is given to Abram but done using only pronouns.

[67] Ha notes that of the four Pentateuchal uses of the term "Gen. 15 claims two, vis. vv. 2 and 8, while the other two are Dt. 3:24 and 9:26. It is significant that of the other 280 occurrences of the title in the OT, 257 are found in the prophetic literature — 216 in Ezekiel, 22 in Isaiah, 20 in Amos, 12 in Jeremiah, and one each in four minor prophets — while the Deuteronomistic historical book have only 12 and the Psalter 7." Ha, *Genesis 15: A Theological Compendium of Pentateuchal History*, 68-69.

[68] Ibid., 68.

[69] E.J. Revell, *The Designation of the Individual: Expressive Usage in Biblical Narrative* (Kampen: Kok Pharos, 1996), 216.

[70] Revell does admit, however, that when the collective term is used in spoken references its value is uncertain. Ibid., 198.

[71] James Plastaras, *The God of Exodus: The Theology of the Exodus Narratives* (Milwaukee, Wisc.: Bruce, 1966), 86. Also see Donald E. Gowan, *Theology in Exodus: Biblical Theology in the Form of a Commentary*, 1st ed. (Louisville, Ky.: Westminster John Knox, 1994), 90. Revell, *The Designation of the Individual: Expressive Usage in Biblical Narrative*, 197.

bit more reticent to attach the same personal significance to the term YHWH.[72] Sarna's remarks that the Deity's Gen 15:7 statement "I am YHWH" (אני יהוה), walks right up to the "proper name" designation and then shys away. He states, "This is the first use of this solemn, introductory, self-identifying formula. It is not the disclosure of a hitherto unknown name, but an emphasis on the unimpeachable authority behind the accompanying declaration."[73]

While the exact determination of Adoni YHWH and YHWH as proper names cannot be decided here, it must be noted that there is evidence to suggest it could, at least, be considered a proper name. Due to this consideration we can explore the relationship that exists between Abram and the Divine. To that end Plastaras argues that "one must not underestimate the importance of a divine name. The science of comparative religion indicates that an unknown or unnamed god never becomes the object of genuine worship. Without a name, the god remains a distant impersonal force."[74] Revell explains, "The designation of God most often used in address is the name 'Yahweh'[... added by ET] The phrase '(My) lord Yahweh' (אדמי יהוה), which depicts the speaker's relationship with God as a master-servant relationship, is used as a vocative where the speech is of particular concern to the speaker."[75] In Gen 15, Abram's visionary and very intimate dialogue with the Deity, it stands to reason that if the Deity is to call Abram by name, Abram may return the acknowledgement by calling the Deity by name.[76]

---

[72] For example, Speiser deems YHWH "a name" but only to designate the occurrences of its use to "permit us to attribute certain portions to *J* with relative confidence." Speiser, *Genesis*, 114.

[73] Sarna, *Genesis*, 114. It is also interesting to note Gowan's more philosophical explanation. He states, "[The, *added by ET*] use of 'Yahweh' as the personal name of God thus falls between two extremes to be found in religion and philosophy. The one assumes the reality and power of the god are contained in the name itself, so that one can conjure with it. The opposite extreme claims God so far transcends all language that he cannot have a name. For Israel the former extreme made God subject to human manipulation, and they understood that to be impossible, so the holiness of his name had to be protected. But they also seem to have recognized that to claim God could not be named would make him impersonal or pantheistic[... *added by ET*] Once monotheism had triumphed within Judaism, it would seem that a proper name would no longer be necessary[... *added by ET*] as they no longer spoke the name 'Yahweh.'" Gowan, *Theology in Exodus: Biblical Theology in the Form of a Commentary*, 90.

[74] Plastaras, *The God of Exodus: The Theology of the Exodus Narratives*, 87.

[75] Revell, *The Designation of the Individual: Expressive Usage in Biblical Narrative*, 214.

[76] In reference to the Deity's pronouncement in Exod 6:3 Gowan wrote, "God becomes a person to us, whom we can address and whom we feel we know to some extent, when he gives us a name by which we can call him." Gowan, *Theology in Exodus: Biblical Theology in the Form of a Commentary*, 90.

Another possible proper name used in Gen 15 is that of Eliezer in v. 2. (ובן־משק ביתי הוא דמשק אליעזר). Translation difficulties prove nearly insurmountable in this case however.[77] Turner stated that "while 15.2b is not understandable, perhaps the best construction we can put on it is that there possibly was a character in Abram's entourage called Eliezer who was a *ben mešeq bêtî*, whatever that was."[78] Gunkel argued that "the consonants אליעזר are customarily understood as the name of Abraham's chief servant. Since, however, this name occurs only here, not even in chap. 24, this interpretation is questionable to an extreme degree."[79]

Taking into account the difficulties in demarcating Adoni YHWH, YHWH and Eliezer as proper names yet allowing for the consideration of said names, the following dynamic may be set up within the visionary dialogue. Abram is named by the Deity, Abram then responds by using a master/servant name to identify his conversation partner. Abram's response includes the name of another individual involved in a lower master/servant relationship. Once this second relationship is clarified by the higher authority the Deity self-identifies as YHWH and Abram once again responds to the master from a subservient position using the name Adoni YHWH.

Even if a case cannot be made for the use of proper names, other than Abram, in this dialogue, there are two elements that cannot be argued. First is the fact that the vision is framed in the prophetic formula style authenticating a Divine conversational partner[80] and secondly Abram, through the use of his address recognizes this fact.[81]

6. Genesis 32: Jacob/Israel

For most commentators the name change of Jacob to Israel as contained in Gen 32:29 (ויאמר לא יעקב יאמר עוד שמך כי אם־ישראל) engenders a discussion regarding the meaning of the names and recognition of Jacob's character. According to Turner, like Abram/Abraham and Sarai/

[77] Wenham laments translation attempts of the passage. "This phrase is very difficult and widely regarded as corrupt and impossible to correct. The major problem concerns the interpretation of 'my heir.' The minor problem is the qualifying phrase ('he is Damascus, Eliezer'). משק is a *hapax legomenon* of uncertain meaning, and nowhere else is Abraham's heir called Damascus or Eliezer." Wenham, *Genesis 1-15*, 328.
[78] Turner, *Genesis*, 73.
[79] Gunkel, *Genesis*, 179.
[80] Ha, *Genesis 15: A Theological Compendium of Pentateuchal History*, 69.
[81] Ibid., 70.

Sarah before him, "Jacob's new name does not announce any change in his life, but simply registers that he continues much as before."[82] In this case the etymology of the names is of some help in discerning the importance of the names but not as housed in the conventional scholarly discussions.

The traditional consensus is that the name Jacob designates its bearer as a cheat and trickster.[83] The new name Israel is then variously interpreted to mean a "victorious fighter against God and people,"[84] "may El persevere,"[85] or as a name of honor recalling the triumphant struggle.[86] The arguments strive to change Jacob's deceitful character to that of a worthy patriarch and progenitor of Israel as a nation.[87] This argument,

---

[82] To strengthen this argument is the fact that, while the name change occurs in Gen 32:28 the narrator continues to refer to the patriarch as Jacob throughout the remaining story. Turner, *Genesis*, 143.

[83] For example see: von Rad, *Genesis: A Commentary*, 321. Wenham, *Genesis 16-50*, 297. Humphreys, *The Character of God in the Book of Genesis: A Narrative Appraisal*, 194.

[84] Gunkel, *Genesis*, 350.

[85] Speiser clarifies, "But both Jacob and Israel are treated here symbolically, to indicate the transformation of a man once devious (Jacob) into a forthright and resolute fighter." Speiser, *Genesis*, 255.

[86] Von Rad, *Genesis: A Commentary*, 321. The variant interpretations stem from an imprecise understanding of the grammar. Sarna explains that the "grammatical structure [of the name Israel, *added by ET*] has no exact analogue among biblical personal names[... *added by ET*] In biblical times there already seem to have been traditions connecting the name *yisra'el* with either sovereignty or rectitude. Hosea 12:5, in reference to our narrative, says of Jacob *va-yasar*, which can only derive from *s-w-r*, by-form of *s-r-r*, 'to have dominion,' as proven by Judges 9:22 and Hosea 8:4. This suggests that the prophet took the name to mean 'He had dominion over a divine being.'" Sarna, *Genesis*, 404-05.
Wenham argues, "The etymology of Israel offered by the text relates ישראל 'Israel' to the verb שרה 'to struggle, fight.' So the word literally means 'El (God) fights.' This is not exactly the same as 'you have struggled with God,' but it should be remembered that popular etymologies in the Bible generally take the form of a play on the name rather than a precise historical etymology. It has also been thought that the notion of 'God fighting' is incompatible with Israelite theology, so that the real meaning of Israel must be different." Wenham, *Genesis 16-50*, 296. Curtis agrees with Wenham. He explains that a definition of "he struggles with God" or "he prevails with God" "runs against the analogy of other names involving an imperfect verb and a theophoric element since in virtually all those instances the theophoric element is the subject of the verb rather than the object." Edward M. Curtis, "Structure, Style and Context as a Key to Interpreting Jacob's Encounter at Peniel," *JETS* 30 (1987): 134. Arnold also follows. "The name 'Israel' itself likely employs a word meaning 'rule, judge' rather than 'strive,' and is thus 'God rules' or 'God judges.'" Bill T. Arnold, *Genesis*, New Cambridge Bible Commentary (Cambridge: Cambridge University Press, 2009), 285.

[87] Westermann, *Genesis: A Practical Commentary*, 229. Sarna expounds that, "since names in the Bible are inextricably intertwined with personality and destiny, the change

however, is limited by the descriptive verbs שרה "to persist/strive" and
יכל "to prevail." "The explanation [of the new name, *added by ET*] sets
God and men as the object of the key verb, a point that cannot be justified
in an analysis of the name. The name suggests that the story should be
interpreted as a struggle between Jacob and God, but that point alone
does not do justice to the explanation. Israel is by nature, by name, the
one who struggles with both God and man."[88] Therefore the new name
Israel does not describe his future but his past and present situation. He
has, in fact, been striving with others his entire life.[89] As we saw with
Sarah, the new name is not an indicator of character, per se, but of the
status of the individual before the Deity.

While the meaning behind the names has selected weight it is not the
most significant aspect to the use of the name. During the struggle Jacob
demands a blessing from his attacker. Before that blessing is given he
must state his name. In an earlier episode, Gen 27, Jacob was asked the
same question. His response was a categorical lie in which he answered
"I am Esau your first born."[90] This time, however, he answers with
abrupt honesty. Arnold sees this response as a "near confession since
'Jacob' echoes the verb to deceive."[91] Von Rad judges the facts, "The
ancients did not consider a name as simply sound and smoke. On the
contrary, for them the name was closely linked with its bearer in such a
way that the name contained something of the character of the one who
bore it. Thus, in giving his name, Jacob at the same time had to reveal
his whole nature."[92] Wenham explains that "To bestow a blessing, the
blesser must know who he is blessing."[93] Jacob's revelation before his
assailant admits his guilt in cheating his brother. The assailant now knows,
from Jacob's own lips, with whom he is dealing.

For Jacob's assailant the only power he has within the dialogue is
the authority to change the patriarch's name to Israel and to bless him.

here signifies a final purging of the unsavory character traits with which *ya'akov* has
come to be associated." Sarna, *Genesis*, 227.
[88] Coats, *Genesis*, 230.
[89] Turner, *Genesis*, 142-43. Humphreys states, "This new name is less a mark of a
new and dramatic change in Jacob than a recognition of who and what he has been."
Humphreys, *The Character of God in the Book of Genesis: A Narrative Appraisal*,
194.
[90] Genesis 27:18-19.
[91] Arnold, *Genesis*, 285.
[92] Von Rad, *Genesis: A Commentary*, 321.
[93] Wenham, *Genesis 16-50*, 296.

According to Barthes, a revealed name in this case, is "clearly related to blessing."[94] Once the confession "Jacob" has been stated a new name can be revealed. It is the name by which the Deity can now bless the patriarch. This bestowal of the blessing, as contained in the new name, regardless of its interpretative translation, becomes the climax of the episode.[95] The juxtaposition of the assailant's refusal to provide Jacob/Israel with a proper name in v. 30 keeps the conversational focus on the Divine blessing, not on the messenger who gives it.[96] For this dialogue the use of a name parallels the giving of a divine blessing to an individual who is willing to divulge his true human nature.

The purpose of this examination has been to determine if a proper name has more meaning within dialogue than traditional narrative analysis allows. By removing the overarching narrative and lessening the influence of the customary scholarship, we have observed within the Cain dialogue that the use of a proper name specifically identifies one human. This divine identification is not just for the one being protected. It also acknowledges that identity to the world. In the wilderness dialogue Hagar's proper name recognizes her as a complete individual who has a privileged relationship with the Deity separate from that of the covenant couple. For Sarah, her proper name proves her import to the overall story. She is more than just Abraham's wife or a mother to be. The use of her name, repeated and emphasized, reveals her true identity and destiny. She is an individual who is not on the Deity's periphery. Genesis 15 employs the name Abram to reveal a covenant and to stress the master/servant relationship that exists between the Divine and the patriarch. While a proper name in Gen 32 engenders a great deal of discussion regarding a human's ability to know their Deity, declaration and knowledge of a name is instrumental within the act of a blessing. A name may have an etymological reason propelling it into the narrative. It may be a symbol or type of things to come for a biblical character. How a name

---

[94] Barthes, *Image, Music, Text*, 136.

[95] Sarna, *Genesis*, 227.

[96] Multiple scholars argue that to know the name of the Deity will give the human power over the bearer. For example see Gunkel, *Genesis*, 350. Coats, *Genesis*, 230. George W. Ramsey, "Is Name-Giving an Act of Domination in Genesis 2:23," *CBQ* 50 (1988): 25. Ramsey, however, concludes that "Instead of thinking of name-giving as a *determiner* of an entity's essence, the Hebrews regarded naming as commonly *determined by* circumstances. The naming *results from* events which have occurred." Ibid., 34. Emphasis in the original.

is used within dialogue, however, shows the Divine/human relationship to be personal, sometimes private, other times very public, but always individualized.

C. DIALOGUE ANALYSIS[97]

The next section of this thesis will, in some cases, require a dramatically new perspective with regards to the examined passage. It must be remembered that we have dislodged the following passages from the overall narrative through line. For the most part, narrative elements are not part of the analysis nor do they influence the interpretation of dialogue. I do not examine the deeper significance of narrative elements such as cultic performance or hospitality protocol. Instead, I treat the performance or protocol as a response to direct speech when there is a direct correlation.[98]

I concede that complete eradication of narrative is impossible to achieve. I also understand that examining dialogue out of context can, in some cases, be detrimental. It is not my goal, however, to fragment the text to such a degree as to render my findings useless to further scholarship. On the contrary, by examining the dialogue in this isolated manner I hope to give future scholars new building blocks from which they can extend their own findings.

---

[97] To review, these are the analytical definitions as they will be used in this thesis:
Dialogue or Conversation, as defined using cultural anthropology guidelines, is a verbal communication between two or more individuals with interaction carried out for social purposes rather than as an exchange of goods and services. For ease of expression, the terms *dialogue* and *conversation* will be used interchangeably. Other forms of communication, those termed *non-verbal*, or narrative description elements will be considered where they play a definitive role within the verbal exchange.
Narrative or Narrative Elements are "plot, story, point of view, and character [descriptions... *added by ET*] These compositional techniques are integrated into the overall organizational structure of the narrative that the narrator supplies."
Direct Discourse, also known as *speech* is when the narrator or author inserts a character's utterances into a narrative. This "usually occurs as part of a dialogue between two characters but occasionally appears as a monologue." While technically, the biblical narrator is relating these non-live dialogues, instances of direct discourse will be treated as defined as dialogue and conversation above.

[98] In future research I hope to take this form of conversation analysis and apply it to multiple dialogues which also have elements such as cultic performance, hospitality protocol and positioning theory. In that monograph I will examine these components in more depth and also compare their significance to each other to see if a form or formula for, say, Divine/Human Cultic Performance Dialogue can be found.

1. Genesis 4:3-15: Cain's dialogue

a. *Adjacency Pairs and Turn Taking*[99]

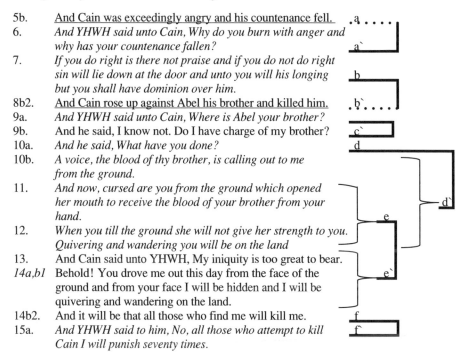

5b.   And Cain was exceedingly angry and his countenance fell.

6.   *And YHWH said unto Cain, Why do you burn with anger and why has your countenance fallen?*

7.   *If you do right is there not praise and if you do not do right sin will lie down at the door and unto you will his longing but you shall have dominion over him.*

8b2.   And Cain rose up against Abel his brother and killed him.

9a.   *And YHWH said unto Cain, Where is Abel your brother?*

9b.   And he said, I know not. Do I have charge of my brother?

10a.   *And he said, What have you done?*

10b.   *A voice, the blood of thy brother, is calling out to me from the ground.*

11.   *And now, cursed are you from the ground which opened her mouth to receive the blood of your brother from your hand.*

12.   *When you till the ground she will not give her strength to you. Quivering and wandering you will be on the land*

13.   And Cain said unto YHWH, My iniquity is too great to bear.

14a,b1   Behold! You drove me out this day from the face of the ground and from your face I will be hidden and I will be quivering and wandering on the land.

14b2.   And it will be that all those who find me will kill me.

15a.   *And YHWH said to him, No, all those who attempt to kill Cain I will punish seventy times.*

b. *Analysis*

With the first line of dialogue, Gen 4 avoids the obvious. Without reference to Abel or his regarded offering, the Deity confronts Cain echoing the narrator's words. Verse 6 (למה חרה לך ולמה נפלו פניך) repeats in verbal form the narrative elements of 5b (ויחר לקין מאד ויפלו פניו) (a-aˋ) but turns the same words into a question using the repeated interrogative למה. Humphreys suggests that since the Deity does not wait for a reply this first verse of dialogue is intended to be interpreted as a rhetorical question[100] indicating that "Yahweh wants Cain to know he is aware of

---

[99] Underlined elements are considered narrative. Italicized elements are considered Divine utterances. Regular typeface elements are considered human responses. Dotted adjacency lines are narrative connecting to dialogue elements.

[100] In the case of a rhetorical question I use Bar-Efrat's definition: a rhetorical question as, "a question which is not asked for the sake of achieving an answer, since the answer is well known to the speaker. The purpose of the question is to persuade the

what he feels."[101] It can be said that the dialogue echo acts as a bridge from the previous action.[102] The questions in v. 6 "presumes an understanding of what has preceded which passes a moral condemnation on Cain; the question implies a reproach and does not see that Cain's resentment is justified."[103] This may be the first time the Deity has spoken to Cain but the questions asked and how they are asked support the argument that the Deity is well aware of the individual human.[104]

The awareness evidenced in the questions of v. 6 supports the second divine expression in v. 7. The statement of v. 7a (הלוא אם-תיטיב שאת ואם לא תיטיב לפתח חטאת רבץ), however, is murky.[105] Most scholars agree that Gen 4:7 is one of the most difficult and obscure passages in the Bible.[106] Westermann goes so far as to state that "all explanations or attempts at emendation of the text have failed."[107] One of the difficulties is the identification of the object of the Deity's address in v. 7 (הלוא אם-תיטיב שאת). According to Humphreys it is unclear as to whether the Deity is "addressing Cain's initial gift, stating that it was not good but it is in his power to do good in giving gifts to him? Or is it addressed to Cain's anger — presumably not in Yahweh's eyes an appropriate response to his response to their gifts?"[108] BDB indicates that the noun שאת can be translated as "exaltation, dignity, swelling and/or uprising." The most common translation of Gen 4:7 "is there not acceptance" is considered dubious.[109] There is an essence of forgiveness, or uplifting of countenance, and/or cheerfulness in the original that is hard to express in the translation, all of which makes determining its emphasis difficult.[110]

---

audience by implying that the answer is self-evident or known to everybody and therefore not to be doubted or discussed." Bar-Efrat, *Narrative Art in the Bible*, 211.

[101] Humphreys, *The Character of God in the Book of Genesis: A Narrative Appraisal*, 56.

[102] Van Wolde, "The Story of Cain and Abel: A Narrative Study," 30.

[103] Westermann, *Genesis 1-11: A Commentary*, 299.

[104] Craig calls this a "new mode of exchange" between the Deity and a human. He notes that "in the garden, YHWH initiated speech through a prohibition. Outside Eden YHWH's speech is not represented until *after* the narrator reports Cain's disposition." Craig, "Questions Outside Eden (Genesis 4.1-16): Yahweh, Cain and Their Rhetorical Interchange," 114.

[105] Perry calls v. 7 "one of the most cryptic passages in Scripture." Perry, "Cain's Sin in Gen. 4:1-7: Oracular Ambiguity and How to Avoid It," 264.

[106] For detailed analysis of the passage see Cassuto, *A Commentary on the Book of Genesis*, 208-13. Also see Westermann, *Genesis 1-11: A Commentary*, 298-301.

[107] Westermann, *Genesis 1-11: A Commentary*, 299.

[108] Humphreys, *The Character of God in the Book of Genesis: A Narrative Appraisal*, 57.

[109] BDB, 673.

[110] Westermann notes that the expression translated as "make a lair at the door" or "crouching at the door" is unique in that "it lies completely outside the admonitory or warning

Verse 7b (ואליך תשוקתו ואתה תמשל-בו) is relatively simple when compared with 7a. There is a minor translation difficulty in the imperfect verb
תמשל. "The force of *timšol* is debated and can range across 'will/may/
must rule.' Varied translations reflect the difficulties in pinning down a
term that may owe a significant dimension of its impact to its very scale
of possibilities."[111] Westermann opts to translate the verb as "must master" but also contends that it is not definitive. "One can also interpret the
sentence as a question (the absence of the particle introducing a question
would be grammatically possible): 'But you, will you be its master?' The
sentence would then have echoes of a warning"[112] Westermann does
admit that there is not a great deal of difference between the statement
and the question. However, according to turn-taking pairing, a question
would beg for an adjacent verbal response from Cain. If interpreted as a
statement, and therefore a promise, the narrative action of v. 8b2 (ויקם
קין אל-הבל אחיו ויהרגהו) is the pairing with the narration acting as the
adjacent pair. (b-b`) The statement of v. 7b then, becomes a promise of
outcome from the Deity to the human if the individual takes the correct
action. The choice "clearly lies with [Cain. *added by ET*]"[113] Cain's
response, as the rest of the dialogue explains, is incorrect action.

style of the two verses… there is no similar expression anywhere in the Old Testament." He goes on to argue against sin being the object of the participle with the weak
claim that it is unlikely because "it is difficult to imagine such personification (demon-
izing) of sin in so early a text." Westermann, *Genesis 1-11: A Commentary*, 299-300.
Another obstacle to a clear translation is the word חטאת which is translated as sin or
sin-offering. It is a feminine noun widely attested in scripture but enters the text for
the first time in this verse. In this clause the active participle רבץ means to lie down
or stretch out as with domestic animals. Word order emphasizes חטאת, "sin," as the
object of the action to lie down. BDB therefore indicates that when רבץ is combined
with the noun חטאת it should have the added weight of "no exceptions" because the
animal is equivalent to a "crouching beast." BDB, 308, 918.
If we take חטאת to be the object of the action in 7b then we must agree that due to
the conjunctive ו it is also the object of the following action/noun תשוקה. The noun
תשוקה is translated as a strong "longing" such as a man for a woman or vice versa and
reflects the admonition to Eve in Gen 3:16. Here *sin* is again the object but expresses
the figurative translation in stronger terms, such as the longing "of a beast to devour."
There is nothing passive about the essence of this translation. The warning from the
Deity to Cain is then twofold: sin will be waiting and it will be waiting for the individual who does not choose to do right.

[111] Humphreys, *The Character of God in the Book of Genesis: A Narrative Appraisal*, 57.
[112] Westermann, *Genesis 1-11: A Commentary*, 300.
[113] Craig argues that "Cain's responsibility is stressed through second-person pronouns:
unto you its desire is and you must master it." Craig, "Questions Outside Eden
(Genesis 4.1-16): Yahweh, Cain and Their Rhetorical Interchange," 115.

Coats states that the second dialogue section (vv. 9-15) "can be defined in terms of a gradual reduction in tension."[114] He is interested in following the Deity's reaction to the guilt of the human. Westermann sees a description of punishment to fit the crime of murder and observes that the Deity conducts the interaction directly with Cain, in other words face to face. Westermann also notes that "it is only in Gen 1-11 in the whole of the Old Testament that God acts directly as judge in this way."[115] The choice of language reflects this construct.

Some see the Deity as an "interrogator,"[116] others see the question asked in v. 9a as rhetorical, implying rebuke.[117] Following the single word sentence (ויהרגהו) "And he killed him" v. 9 introduces, in quick succession, a tightly intertwined Divine/human dialogue where the Deity seems to be immediately present. (c-c`) The text indicates little or no delay between Cain's action of killing and the Deity's question. The question (אי הבל אחיך) "Where is Abel your brother?" then becomes a "means for discovery by Yahweh and for him to come to terms with what has happened. On the other [hand, *added by ET*], their effect is also to urge the one questioned, and the reader, to view what has happened from the perspective of Yahweh's interest or stake in it."[118] The question "Where is your brother?" contains two important points. First, Cain does not exist on his own, he has a brother. And second, there is one who has an interest in interrogating him.[119] In this one question Cain is offered the opportunity to confess these two relationships, one with his brother and one with the Divine.

Cain's "brazen" response in v. 9b (לא ידעתי השמר אחי אנכי) lies in the face of his divine relationship and rejects any fraternal responsibility.[120] (c-c`) Cassuto sees the meaning of the lie as an intensification of sin begun in Gen 2. He states that, "When there is a murder there is usually a lie which serves to cover it up. Actually one of the most important settings of the lie as a cover up for a fact is the context of murder and its

---

[114] Coats, *Genesis*, 64.

[115] Westermann, *Genesis 1-11: A Commentary*, 303.

[116] La Sor, Hubbard, and Bush, *Old Testament Survey: The Message, Form, and Background of the Old Testament*, 81.

[117] Cassuto, *A Commentary on the Book of Genesis*, 217. Also see Craig, "Questions Outside Eden (Genesis 4.1-16): Yahweh, Cain and Their Rhetorical Interchange," 121.

[118] Humphreys, *The Character of God in the Book of Genesis: A Narrative Appraisal*, 58.

[119] Westermann, *Genesis 1-11: A Commentary*, 304.

[120] Cassuto, *A Commentary on the Book of Genesis*, 217. Craig states that "Cain reveals in his lie and arrogant rhetorical question [9b1, *added by ET*] a preoccupation with self" and that his response 'I am not my brother's keeper' (9b2) "attempts to gain the upper hand in the conversation with an offhand counter-question." Craig, "Questions Outside Eden (Genesis 4.1-16): Yahweh, Cain and Their Rhetorical Interchange," 122.

consequences."[121] La Sor calls Cain's response "an impertinent witticism"[122] but Westermann gives him a bit more credit. He says Cain "is correct in his retort inasmuch as it is not really his job to be looking after his brother constantly. He is incorrect when he obscures the situation where he should have been his brother's keeper."[123] Humphreys also has some admiration for Cain and calls him "not unskilled in rhetorical combat." He goes on to explain that Cain's "statement followed by a question suggests [that, *added by ET*] if Yahweh's questions attempt to shift his perspective, Cain's urges that his initial perspective be entertained as well."[124] Taking v. 9 as a whole we see the relationship between Deity and human to be tense not only in a tight structural form but also in the dialogue pairing, with each participant challenging the other to varying degrees.

Verse 10a gives no indication that the Deity has answered Cain's question. Cassuto suggests that "What have you done?" (מה עשית) is a "rhetorical question resembling an interjection"[125] mostly due to the understanding that the answer is already known to the Deity. Westermann on the other hand sees the Deity's question as "confronting Cain and his cantankerous lie and saying to him face to face: 'What have you done!' This does not evoke a retort from Cain which could pin him down on his lie; instead it expresses the perplexity which the deed must arouse in everyone."[126]

Westermann then declares the statement of v. 10b to be "one of the monumental sentences in the Bible"[127] (קול דמי אחיך צעקים אלי מן-האדמה). The blood that has been shed is calling out, accusing in a most descriptive way compared to the terse report of murder. For Westermann "the most important word in the sentence is אלי, 'to me.' It is no empty sentence that the blood of the victim cries out; there is someone there to whom it cries out. Cain cannot hide his deed... The murderer has no escape when faced with [the question of v. 10a, *added by ET*] because there is someone who hears the victim's blood crying out."[128]

[121] Westermann, *Genesis 1-11: A Commentary*, 304.
[122] La Sor, Hubbard, and Bush, *Old Testament Survey: The Message, Form, and Background of the Old Testament*, 81.
[123] Westermann, *Genesis 1-11: A Commentary*, 304.
[124] Humphreys, *The Character of God in the Book of Genesis: A Narrative Appraisal*, 58.
[125] Cassuto, *A Commentary on the Book of Genesis*, 218.
[126] Westermann, *Genesis 1-11: A Commentary*, 305. Note, there is no evidence in the *banyan* of a confrontational tone.
[127] Ibid., 305.
[128] Ibid., 305. Cassuto agrees with this position but for different reasons. For him the instance of hemistich parallelism in reverse order binds vv. 10 and 11 together; "the

Instead of allowing Cain time to respond, the Deity voices "a pointed two-word question followed by an extended statement"[129] that runs through the end of v. 12. Coats identifies this multi-verse statement as a formal accusation due to the virtue of its legal wording.[130] The Deity does not allow for any kind of human reply. Instead the statement continues immediately from question (v. 10a), to accusation (v. 10b) to judgment (vv. 11-12). (d-d`) The Deity, in effect, answers the question of 10a by reporting to have heard the blood of the slain brother in 10b (קול דמי אחיך צעקים אלי מן-האדמה).

The next adjacency pairing begins in v. 11 (e-e`) with the first hint of an emphatic emphasis (ועתה ארור אתה מן-האדמה). Cassuto explains, "the ועתה belongs to the framework and is not part of the curse."[131] He therefore reasons that this exclusion, combined with the past participle ארור, serve to make the subject אתה emphatic.[132] The causative connotation of the preposition מן attached to האדמה is the element accusing Cain of the sin he has committed. It is the cry of the blood that overcomes Cain and his hubris.[133]

The כי that begins v. 12 is, according to Cassuto, a "phrase that usually serves to introduce the conclusion."[134] For Cassuto, the emphasis of the passage is the curse of "quivering and wandering" (נע ונד) that will follow Cain for the rest of his life. Westermann and others make the point that the phrase definitely does not describe the life of a wandering shepherd or the nomadic tribes of the area. The meaning describes "an existence that is hunted and hounded."[135]

Westermann declares these dialogue verses (11-12) to be not so much about the lifestyle resulting from the curse, as they are "saying something about the consequence of the deed"[136] originally perpetrated by Cain. He states:

blood of thy brother" calls "from the ground" and then "from the ground" "the blood of thy brother." For Cassuto the climax comes at the end of v. 11. He states, "At the end there comes a word that stands alone, and it's very isolation at the conclusion of the verse lends it emphasis: *from your hand.*" Cassuto, *A Commentary on the Book of Genesis*, 218

[129] Humphreys, *The Character of God in the Book of Genesis: A Narrative Appraisal*, 58.
[130] Coats, *Genesis*, 64.
[131] Cassuto, *A Commentary on the Book of Genesis*, 306.
[132] Ibid., 218.
[133] Westermann, *Genesis 1-11: A Commentary*, 305.
[134] Cassuto, *A Commentary on the Book of Genesis*, 218.
[135] Westermann, *Genesis 1-11: A Commentary*, 307-08. The verb נוד is defined as "to move hither and thither." It can have the meaning "to flee," Jer 4:1, in the qal, and "to drive out" in the hiphil, Ps 36:12. Also see Cassuto, *A Commentary on the Book of Genesis*, 221.
[136] Westermann, *Genesis 1-11: A Commentary*, 306.

The curse affects the individual. Its effect is to separate or cut off [as an, *added by ET*] individual is set apart from the community[... *added by ET*] There is no case attested where a collective is cursed; this is always a secondary usage. It can only be an individual who is cursed in 4:2-16[... *added by ET*] This makes the sign of Cain comprehensible; so too the punishment that Cain receives and his complaint about its severity. He is expelled from the community of other people[... *added by ET*] Among those people who live alienated from God and limited by mortality and fallibility there is the exceptional possibility of life under the curse. This is embodied in Cain.[137]

In a similar vein, Sailhamer sees this portion of dialogue as focusing on the theme of repentance. He states that "the meaning of this passage turns on how we understand Cain's reply in v. 13. Did Cain complain that his 'punishment' was too great to bear? Or should we understand his reply to be that his 'iniquity' was too great to forgive?"[138]

According to Westermann, Cain's brief but clever defensive response (גדול עוני מנשׂא) to the curse is in the form of a lament[139] whose theme, in vv. 13-14b1, (e-e`) is the mitigation of threatened punishment.[140] Cain acknowledges his sin/punishment/iniquity is too great to tolerate but, as Humphreys points out, "it is not clear just how much Cain acknowledges in saying 'my *'awon* is too great for bearing.' [He, *added by ET*] directs Yahweh's attention to his punishment and even elaborates on it, as he transposes banishment from the ground's face to being hidden from Yahweh's face, and as he expands being a fugitive and wanderer in to being free game to any who find him."[141] Juxtaposed to this concept,

---

[137] Ibid., 307.

[138] Sailhamer, *The Pentateuch as Narrative: A Biblical-Theological Commentary*, 113-14.

[139] Westermann, *Genesis 1-11: A Commentary*, 309. According to Westermann the lament "can be recognized as a real lament in that it contains, even if only by way of hint, all three elements of the lament (God-lament, I-lament, enemy-lament)." Coats describes vv. 11-12 as a curse formula. Coats, *Genesis*, 65.

[140] Westermann, *Genesis 1-11: A Commentary*, 308. To determine the situation of mitigation we must analyze the understanding of the Hebrew word עוֹן. For Westermann עוֹן is "a concept of sin[... *added by ET*] which sees 'sin' as an isolated phenomenon. It is characteristic of the Hebrew עוֹן that it describes an event which can include 'sin' and 'punishment.' The word עוֹן describes this complexity in which the stress, is according to the context, now on the one aspect, now on the other." According to Westermann, when therefore Gen 4:13 is translated: "My punishment is too great...," the meaning "sin" is included, not excluded. Ibid., 309.

[141] Humphreys, *The Character of God in the Book of Genesis: A Narrative Appraisal*, 59. Garcia-Treto follows and explains, "Cain's protest appeals to bonds which even Yahweh is forced to recognize. In effect, the ground for Cain's complaint is precisely that the bonds of common humanity, and of humankind with God, are not broken; in fact, they cannot be broken, not even for the guilty." Francisco O. Garcia-Treto, "Crossing the Line: Three Scenes of Divine-Human Engagement in the Hebrew

Cassuto claims that v. 13 could not be a plea for mitigation because "Cain's heart is now filled with remorse; he realizes the enormity of his crime, and accepts the judgment."[142] For Westermann there has been no admission of guilt or remorse, only the declaration that the separation from community will be too great to bear. Whether Cain is filled with remorse or concerned for his separation from the community, the question becomes should mitigation be considered?

The force of the curse of banishment is recognized in v. 14a when 'the ground's face' (מעל פני האדמה) is understood to be the geographical area "where Cain and Abel lived their lives and which at the same time provided the means for life to be lived, for nourishment, prosperity, security, protection. Banishment meant the confiscation of the whole basis of life and with it exposure to such danger of death as to be equivalent to surrender to death or worse."[143] When read in this light Cain's lament in vv. 13-14b1 describes the enormity of his alienation and why it will be so hard to bear. 'To be driven away from the ground and from before the Deity' (גרשת אתי היום מעל פני האדמה ומפניך אסתר) "is to have all relationships, particularly with the family broken. Moreover, it is to have one's relationship with the Lord broken."[144] Cassuto wants to find some redeeming value in Cain stating that he "acquiesces in all this as a just punishment for his crime, and to indicate his submission to the judgment he repeats the words of the Lord's decree."[145] Westermann, however, explains the need for the repetition of the curse of 'quivering and wandering' as looking for the function of the whole dialogue. He states:

> The narrative of Cain contains the cry of the blood of the victim and the lament of the murderer condemned for life. The cry and the lament are part of human existence; they are a defensive reaction to life threatened. Just as in v. 10 the blood of the one murdered does not cry in the void, so too the defensive lament of the murderer is heard. The person as a creature, and no matter what one's situation, remains within earshot of the creator; that is the meaning of the cry and the lament.[146]

Bible," in *Teaching the Bible*, ed. Fernando F. Segovia and Mary Ann Tolbert (Maryknoll, NY: Orbis, 1998), 108.

[142] Cassuto, *A Commentary on the Book of Genesis*, 222. He claims that "because עון *'āwōn* ['iniquity,' *added by ET*] is, as a rule, used with נשא *nāśā'* [literally, 'lift', 'carry, *added by ET*] in another sense, namely, 'to forgive iniquity'" therefore, even though נשא is not identifiable in this passage he claims this use of עון must include the essence of forgiveness making remorse on Cain's part necessary.
[143] Westermann, *Genesis 1-11: A Commentary*, 310.
[144] Coats, *Genesis*, 65.
[145] Cassuto, *A Commentary on the Book of Genesis*, 224.
[146] Westermann, *Genesis 1-11: A Commentary*, 309.

To determine the meaning within this dialogue and the relationship between the human and the Divine we need to examine the final adjacent pairing.

By v. 14b1 we have a broken Divine/human relationship (e-e`) with words from Cain that express fear due to a lack of divine protection. Cain's statement in v. 14b2 (והיה כל-מצאי יהרגני) is, for the human, a statement of fact. Now that the verdict of judgment has been delivered and the protection of the Divine and the community removed, there is nothing standing between Cain and those who seek retribution. In an adjacency pair context the human statement cries out for a Divine response. (f-f`) In v. 15a the Hebrew states YHWH spoke to him (ויאמר לו יהוה). This speech, however, is different from the previous ones due to the manner in which the proper name is used. The Deity identifies Cain but the Divine is not addressing him directly (לכן כל-הרג קין שבעתים יקם). Cassuto notes that the wording is "*if anyone slays Cain*, not *if anyone slays YOU*, because this is a proclamation addressed to all mankind."[147] The use of the proper name here is to inform all of humankind that the Deity is aware of one single individual and that individual, no matter what the crime, is still protected to a certain extent by the Deity.[148]

The verb נקם "avenge, take vengeance" is used, according to most commentaries, in a juridical form. The justification for this usage is "to prevent a person, even a murderer, from becoming a prey for other people. The sentence is meant to forestall blood vengeance; the 'sevenfold' is to act as a deterrent."[149] The choice of "seventy times" or "sevenfold" is also significant. The Deity is indicating that vengeance will be taken "in perfect measure, with the full stringency of the law."[150] The significance to the juridical use of the verb combined with the use of the proper name identifies Cain and his protection under a legal ordinance as he is cast out into the world. Westermann, who does not see repentance in Cain's actions, does, however, admit to a limited mitigation on the Deity's part in v. 15a. He says, "The mitigation, or limitation, of the punishment

---

[147] Cassuto, *A Commentary on the Book of Genesis*, 225. Emphasis original. Note: Westermann translates לכן and the beginning of the Deity's answer in v. 15 as "'No!' (= 'not so': read לא כן)[... but states that it, *added by ET*] refers only to the consequence that Cain draws from the fate that is his lot, not to the expulsion as such that was imposed by the curse." Westermann, *Genesis 1-11: A Commentary*, 311.

[148] Van Wolde, "The Story of Cain and Abel: A Narrative Study," 28.

[149] Westermann, *Genesis 1-11: A Commentary*, 311.

[150] Cassuto, *A Commentary on the Book of Genesis*, 226.

in v. 15 is not really modifying what was pronounced in vv. 11-12, but parries the consequences of the life of an outcast which Cain feared."[151]

In this first Divine/human relational dialogue we have an interesting dynamic. The Deity of Gen 1-3 who created and commanded all things is challenged in direct discourse with a human. The first two adjacent pairs combine verbal speech from the Deity with human reaction narrative. In both cases, however, the Divine's verbal statements express patterns of awareness of the actions taken by Cain. The third pairing catches the human in a lie and denial as to his relationship with the Deity who is questioning him. Cain's brazen interrogation of the Divine rejects his fraternal responsibility and imposes his perspective on the Deity. The pairing of section d-d` is all contained within one divine speech. In this case the movement is progressive with the Deity first questioning Cain's actions (10a), then answering the question with knowledge that Cain will not or does not have the opportunity to give (10b). To further elucidate the situation the Deity then continues from accusation to judgment. The progression of vv. 11 and 13 provide the initiation of the fifth pairing. Whether there is repentance in Cain's nature will be debated for millennia to come. That is not at question here. What is observed, however, is that Cain, now under condemnation, once again forces the Deity to view the situation through the human lens with his response in vv. 13-14b1. The final pairing of this Divine/human relational dialogue is a declaration of perceived human fact, that all who find Cain will attempt to kill him. The Deity responds with a mitigation of the above mentioned judgment. While the human is still cursed to quiver and wander, those who kill him will be avenged.

For this Divine/human relational dialogue the thrust and parry of conversation is confrontational. The human requires the Deity to view the situation from his point of view. The Divine still holds the upper hand but is willing to concede, if in a very limited fashion, to Cain's distress. The human must still pay for his crimes but he has voiced his opinion and been heard by the Deity. Regardless of the moral decline of the human Cain, he is still under the auspices of the Divine.

---

[151] Westermann, *Genesis 1-11: A Commentary*, 310. Gordon argues, "A sevenfold talion is threatened against anyone who harms Cain, and the scale of the mercy is not explained simply by saying that it is not until after the flood that capital offences are punished with capital sentences (see 9:5-6). The logic sevenfold talion would say that Cain, who killed his brother Abel, should be far more susceptible to the law of talion than any assassin of Cain the murderer." Robert P. Gordon, "The Ethics of Eden: Truth Telling in Gen 2-3," in *Ethical and Unethical in the Old Testament*, ed. Katherine Dell (New York: T&T Clark, 2010), 19.

2. Genesis 16:7-14: Hagar in the wilderness

a. *Adjacency Pairs and Turn Taking*

8a1. *And he said, Hagar Sarai's handmaid, Where have you come from*

8a2. *and where will ye go?*

8b. And *she said, I am fleeing from Sarai my mistress.*

9. *And the messenger of YHWH said to her, Return to your mistress and bow down under her hands.*

10. *And the Messenger of YHWH said to her, I will cause your seed to multiply. And I will not count its abundance.*

11. *And the messenger of YHWH said to her, Behold, you are pregnant and you will bring forth a son and will call his name Ishmael because YHWH has heard your affliction.*

12. *And he will be a wild ass of a man. His hand will be against all men and they will be against him. Amid all his brothers will he dwell.*

13. And she called the name of YHWH who was speaking to her God who sees me, because she said, Also, have I not continued to see after he has seen me?

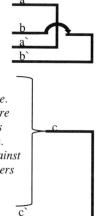

b. *Analysis*

Sarna labels the Deity's encounter with Hagar as "not fortuitous but deliberate and purposeful."[152] With the opening statement in v. 8 (הגר שפחת שרי), we are told that the Divine knows the exact identity of the woman with whom the Deity is speaking; not just by the use of her proper name but with the naming of her mistress and social status. Unlike Abram and Sarai who will never identify Hagar by name, the Divine speaks to her in a most personal way and asks her two very pointed questions. (a, b) The interrogations (אי-מזה באת ואנה תלכי) however, are not just about her situation at that single moment in time. Von Rad sees the questions as a reflection of her past and her future.[153]

With the initiation of dialogue by the Deity, Hagar is not reduced, as might be expected, to quivering silence. Instead, the appearance of the Divine and the questions asked have drawn Hagar to speak for the first time. Her first response is to answer truthfully — but not completely (מפני שרי גברתי אנכי ברחת). She does acknowledge her past social status which still has a claim upon her.[154] She does not, however, recount the

---

[152] Sarna, *Genesis*, 120.

[153] Von Rad, *Genesis: A Commentary*, 193.

[154] Regarding the term "my mistress" Schneider states, "This verse indicates that Hagar, like the messenger, considers herself still in some sort of slave status to Sarai." Schneider, *Sarah: Mother of Nations*, 55.

abuse she has suffered.[155] Hagar simply states where she has come from. (a-a`) Where she is going is left unanswered. The response focuses only on her past, to the effect of confessing that she envisions no future.[156] Verse 9, however, displays the Deity's inclination "to both the past and the future, though focusing on the future."[157]

Verse 9 (שובי אל-גברתך והתעני תחת ידיה) is an interesting adjacent pair in that the Divine's commands answer the Divine's question of v.8a2 by reversing Hagar's action of fleeing with a mandate to return. (b-b`) Humphrey's sees this specific response in the context of the larger Sarai-Hagar narrative. He understands the command to be an underscoring of "the motif of authority/power/control in this unit."[158] Wenham also considers the Divine command in the context of the whole narrative. For him "this apparently harsh intervention is viewed by the narrator as an act of divine grace that salvages at least temporarily something from the wreck of human relationships described in the first scene."[159] Trible, however, states that within the Divine response of v. 9 and the dialogue of 'return and submit' Hagar has been found by the Deity "in order to tell her where she is going. And the Divine command merges origin and destiny."[160]

Often commentators see this command as insensitive or oppressive[161] and justifiably so. However, it cannot be stressed enough that the command is then qualified with a blessing.

> Given [Hagar's, *added by ET*] contempt of Sarai (16:4-5) her future stands in danger (in view of 12:3), so she must get this matter resolved before true freedom for her becomes possible. At the same time, she will not return defenseless and she will not return with the same

---

[155] The "harsh treatment" dealt to Hagar by Sarai in v. 6 is the verb ענה. This same verb is used in Exod 1:11-12 to describe the treatment the Hebrews received at the hand of the Egyptians and in Exod 22:21-22 in the laws prohibiting abuse of widows and the fatherless. BDB, 776.

[156] Turner states, "escaping from Sarai is her only aim; she does not know where she is going." Turner, *Genesis*, 78. Von Rad states, "Hagar answered the first question openly and defiantly; to the second she has nothing to say." Von Rad, *Genesis: A Commentary*, 194.

[157] Fretheim, *Abraham: Trials of Family and Faith*, 96.

[158] Humphreys, *The Character of God in the Book of Genesis: A Narrative Appraisal*, 101.

[159] Wenham, *Genesis 16-50*, 9.

[160] Trible, *Texts of Terror: Literary-Feminist Readings of Biblical Narratives*, 16.

[161] Reis argues the Deity's speech in vv. 9-11 is not oppression as much as a revelation of Hagar's character. She states, "The repeated use of the formula 'And the angel of the Lord said' indicates that Hagar obdurately makes no response to the angel's speeches[... *added by ET*] To return to certain abuse is not an attractive proposition, even if the order comes from an angel; Hagar does not budge." Pamela Tamarkin Reis, "Hagar Requited," *JSOT* 87 (2000): 90.

dependent status as before. She will go back to Abraham and Sarai with strong promises received directly and personally from God. With these promises in hand, Hagar will no longer be dependent upon God's promises to Abraham and Sarai as she stands on her own in her relationship with God.[162]

The address in v. 9 seems intolerably harsh; however, the intervening of a promise in v. 10 precedes language of salvation in v. 11 and the added descriptive clarification of v. 12.[163] All of which leads to the third adjacent pairing of this dialogue.

The blessing promised in v. 10 (הרבה ארבה את-זרעך ולא יספר מרב) comes to Hagar; not a man, a husband or a patriarch. Of all the women in the book of Genesis, she is the only one to receive this divine promise directly and one of just four people "to hear the language of the promise from God's own lips."[164] Darr comments that "surely these words are intended to comfort Hagar. After all, a divine promise of numerous offspring is no small thing, even if it does not carry with it a concomitant pledge that those children will inherit land on which to live."[165] Gunkel even declares the blessing "a superabundantly rich reward for the hardship."[166] Unlike the more general promise to Abram in chapters 12 and 15, the promise to Hagar in v. 10 is specified with annunciation details supplied in v. 11.

With the announcement "Behold you are pregnant" (הנך הרה) in v. 11, the Deity acknowledges Hagar's intimate secret.[167] Unlike Sarai, Rachel and Hannah who rail on the Divine as well as their husbands regarding

---

[162] Fretheim, *Abraham: Trials of Family and Faith*, 96-97.

[163] Ngan states, "YHWH's word may be read not as an indictment against Hagar but as a directive for her to choose life over death." Ngan, "Neither Here nor There: Boundary and Identity in the Hagar Story," 81. Dennis, *Sarah Laughed*, 67. Where dialogue analysis sees the vv. 9-12 as part of an adjacent pairing, many scholars consider the tie that binds vv. 9-11 together to be the fact that each verse begins with the same introduction "And the messenger of YHWH said to her." For example, Westermann explains the delineation as a "mechanical repetition." Westermann, *Genesis: A Practical Commentary*, 125. Brichto considers the repetition to be emphasizing the distancing of God from Hagar even though the command, incentive to return and the promise of a son is extremely personal. Brichto, *The Names of God: Poetic Readings in Biblical Beginnings*, 215.

[164] Dennis, *Sarah Laughed*, 67. Abram has heard the promise in Gen 12:2 and 15:5. The Deity will repeat the promise to Isaac (26:2-6, 24) and Jacob (28:13-15; 35:9-12; 46:3-4). Joseph receives it second hand from his father (48:3-4).

[165] Darr, *Far More Precious Than Jewels: Perspectives on Biblical Women*, 140.

[166] Gunkel, *Genesis*, 188.

[167] This is unusual in that, as Wenham observed, "in other biblical oracles, the statement about pregnancy usually refers to the near future; here the angel comments on Hagar's present condition." Wenham, *Genesis 16-50*, 10.

their affliction of barrenness, there is no record of Hagar ever crying out to the Deity or anyone else for a child. While birth announcements frequently include a prophecy regarding the child's destiny,[168] the unsolicited pronouncement by the Divine[169] pays heed to Hagar's past affliction and assures her a future through her unborn son.[170]

As the Deity continues in vv. 11b and 12, attention is given to Hagar's suffering in the annunciation of the name of her son. Ishmael, the messenger claims, will be named (כי-שמע יהוה אל-עניך) "because YHWH has heard your afflictions." These are not Ishmael's afflictions although they do foreshadow his life to a certain extent. The referenced suffering is Hagar's.[171] Sarna notes that "here the name is given a special twist and is interpreted as 'God has paid heed to your suffering.' This constitutes a unique phrase in the Hebrew, it being an amalgam of two distinct idioms. Generally, God 'sees (r-'-h) suffering,' as in Gen 29:32 and Exod 4:31, and 'heeded (sh-m-') their outcry,' as in Exod 3:7 and Deut 26:7."[172]

Westermann designates the future of Ishmael and his descendants to be "a clan oracle like 9:25-27." [173] Brichto labels the verse an "aside" that is for the reader's edification and not for Hagar.[174] There is, however, significance to v. 12 and the description of Ishmael as a "wild ass of a man" (פרא אדם). The connotation being that he will be an individual and live a life unfettered by social convention.[175] While the words focus on Ishmael's future, the Deity is also reflecting on Hagar's life, both past and future.[176]

---

[168] Finlay, *The Birth Report Genre in the Hebrew Bible*, 92-93.
[169] Wenham asserts that it is only with this declaration that Hagar realizes the Divine identity of the messenger before her. "The mysterious identity of the one who can make such harsh demands and make such amazing promises is at last apparent when the angel of the Lord gives a birth oracle, an annunciation that was to become a hallmark of angelic prediction in the Bible." Wenham, *Genesis 16-50*, 10.
[170] Trible, *Texts of Terror: Literary-Feminist Readings of Biblical Narratives*, 17.
[171] While outside the scope of this thesis, it would be interesting to track the names of children as a reflection on the mother and the entity who makes the annunciation of the name.
[172] Sarna, *Genesis*, 121. Westermann noted that the naming of Hagar's son in v. 11, combining the verbs to see and heed, directly contradicts the command for Hagar to return and submit to Sarai in v. 9 and confirms that Hagar has lived through misery and confirms her action of flight. Westermann, *Genesis: A Practical Commentary*, 126.
[173] Westermann, *Genesis: A Practical Commentary*, 126.
[174] Brichto, *The Names of God: Poetic Readings in Biblical Beginnings*, 447n19.
[175] Wenham noted the use of "wild ass" "is used in the OT as a figure of an individualistic lifestyle untrammeled by social convention (Jer 2:24; Hos 8:9)." Wenham, *Genesis 16-50*, 11.
[176] Sarna indicates that ëwild ass" is used to reflect on the mother. "Hagar, the abused slave woman subjected to the harsh discipline of her mistress, will produce a people free and undisciplined." Sarna, *Genesis*, 121.

Gunkel acknowledges the continued dichotomy of "being against every man" (ידו בכל) by stating that the foretelling "means that this independent Ishmael is a son worthy of his defiant mother who did not want to take the yoke either and who cast off the secure life because it was a life in subjection."[177] The Divine dialogue that contains a command to return and submit is followed by a blessing for the victim, an annunciation of a son whose name acknowledges the cruelty she has endured, and a prophecy of a future for Hagar and her son that will be anything but meek and dutiful.

Hagar's response to these divine statements of vv. 10-12 (c-c`) illustrates that she has, according to Sarna, become "spiritually stirred by her revelatory experience. She has become conscious of God's concern for the downtrodden."[178] Regardless of the actual point of Hagar's spiritual awakening, v. 13 (ותקרא שם-יהוה הדבר אליה אתה אל ראי) is an extraordinary moment in Hebrew scripture. With all that has passed in the dialogue so far it is interesting to note that Hagar does not take time to analyze the Deity's words.[179] "Instead, she names the Lord who sees. The narrator introduces her words with a striking expression that accords her a power attributed to no one else in the Bible. Hagar 'calls the name of the Lord who spoke to her.' She does not invoke the Lord; she names the Lord. She calls the name; she does not call *upon* the name."[180] By literally calling the name of the Divine "He sees me" Hagar has testified of her personal experience with the Divine.[181] The difference here is that

---

[177] Gunkel, *Genesis*, 188. Trible agrees "the word *face* builds upon his mother's action when she said, 'From the *face* of Sarai my mistress I am fleeing' (16:8). In Ishmael, Hagar's story continues." Trible, *Texts of Terror: Literary-Feminist Readings of Biblical Narratives*, 17. Emphasis original. Sarna makes an interesting comment with regard to Ishmael and Ishmaelite reception. "It is noteworthy that the image of Ishmael in the Bible, as distinct from later Jewish literature, is by and large not a negative one. He is not an inveterate enemy of Israel. In fact, there seems to have been some intermingling between the tribe of Simeon and the Ishmaelites, for the clans of Mibsam and Mishma are associated with both, as proved by Genesis 25:13 and 1 Chronicles 4:25. The Ishmaelites do not appear among the victims of David's raids into the south lands, even though these incursions encroach upon their habitat, as is clear from 1 Samuel 27:8 and Genesis 25:18. David's sister married 'Jether the Ishmaelite,' according to 1 Chronicles 2:17, and among the administrators of crown property under David were 'Obil the Ishmaelite' and 'Jaziz the Hagrite,' according to 1 Chronicles 27:30f." Sarna, *Genesis*, 122.

[178] Sarna, *Genesis*, 121.

[179] Dozeman states, "The reader expects an etiology of the name Ishmael after that annunciation." Instead, Hagar names the Deity and the location of the encounter. Dozeman, "The Wilderness and Salvatin History in the Hagar Story," 26.

[180] Trible and Russell, *Hagar, Sarah, and Their Children: Jewish, Christian, and Muslim Perspectives*, 41. Emphasis in the original.

[181] Sarna states, "The name is inextricably bound up with existence and with the nature and character of the Being who bears it. Hagar gives expression to her personal discovery

where the Deity "heard" (שמע) Hagar's afflictions she now responds that
the Deity has "seen" (ראה) her distress.[182]

Humphreys analyzes the impact of Hagar's choice of naming the Deity
"The God who sees me" in this manner:

> In her apparent use of a form of the verb *ra'ab*, "to see," Hagar reverses
> and intensifies the way Yahweh's messenger spoke of Yahweh's atten-
> tion to her. He had said "Yahweh has heard your affliction," playing
> on the name of Ishmael as "God (*'el*) hears." Language of hearing is
> not unexpected in narratives dealing with God's engagement with
> humans. If anything it is striking how readily and easily God and
> humans talked and listened to each other to this point. Whatever we
> make of her name for Yahweh and the explanation she gives of it, we
> are struck by the presence of the verb "to see (*ra'ab*)." It appears
> once in the name and twice in its explanation (three times in her seven
> words here)[... *added by ET*] She speaks, it appears, not of hearing or
> being heard, but of seeing and possibly of being seen. Might we see
> Hagar here as claiming for all her apparent submission, a certain privi-
> lege? Lowest in the hierarchy of authority/power/control, she makes
> what is a unique claim in speaking of her engagement with Yahweh.
> Yahweh has yet to speak to Sarai. He has spoken to Abram but neither
> Abram nor the narrator has claimed in so many words that Abram saw
> Yahweh/God. In fact, Hagar's claim here [in v. 13, *added by ET*]
> stands out not only in this text but as one of the few such claims in all
> of the Hebrew Bible. For all her social marginality, Hagar constructs
> God and their encounter in ways that privilege her.[183]

The effect of claiming to have been seen by the Deity is Hagar's way of
asserting a relationship with the Divine that Sarai does not have.[184] The
response also harkens back to the use of her proper name by the Deity
who acknowledges her personhood when Sarai has not. Hagar's final
response also serves to combine the understanding that both Hagar and
the Divine have "plainly" observed and are aware of each other.[185] Hagar

by designating God after the particular aspect of His providence that she has experienced." Sarna, *Genesis*, 121. Reis explains, Hagar is "astonished by the long-sight-
edness of the being who appears to her; he is indeed a 'god of seeing,' for he can see
beyond her to her descendants." Reis, "Hagar Requited," 92.

182 When used in this manner "to see" most often equates to the act of "caring." Wenham,
Genesis 16-50, 11.

183 Humphreys, *The Character of God in the Book of Genesis: A Narrative Appraisal*,
103-04.

184 Rulon-Miller argues, "Hagar's speech to Yahweh is natural, direct, and spirited. She
answers his questions in a matter-of-fact manner, and seems enthusiastic, even triumphant, when she tells him the name she has created for him. Nina Rulon-Miller, "Hagar:
A Woman with an Attitude" in The World of Genisis: Persons, Places, Perspectives,
ed. Philip R. Davies and David J. A. Clines, JSOTSup 257 (Sheffield: Sheffield Academic Press, 1998), 77.

185 Dennis, *Sarah Laughed*, 72.

names the Deity whom she encountered "Deity of my seeing," that is, "the Divine who saw me (in my distress)." "This would be a satisfactory conclusion, but v. 13b adds another explanation, whose text is obscure"[186] There is no standard translation for 13b. For example, כי אמרה הגם הלם ראיתי אחרי ראי has been interpreted as "Have I seen God and lived after seeing him?"[187] "Did I not go on seeing here after he had seen me?"[188] and "The God who sees me lives."[189] While the text is formidable to translators, it must be stressed that the statement at least speaks of a mutual seeing on the part of both Hagar and the Divine and includes the idea of still living after having been seen by the Deity. For a woman who is denied a personal identity by those with whom she lives, the divine care she has been shown throughout this dialogue exceeds the human abandonment she has suffered.[190]

Once Hagar is removed from those who control virtually every aspect of her life a personal relationship can materialize and that relationship, it turns out, is with the Divine. When examined, the dialogue pairs do not identify Hagar as only a handmaid to Sarai, in terms of her son or as the mother of Abraham's first born.[191] "The Deity's treatment of Hagar and the promises to, and demands of, her signify the Deity's understanding of the role and importance of her character."[192] Gossai observed,

> The return of Hagar to Sarai is not a return to the status quo. While the messenger's words might appear to be a reconstruction of an identical slave-mistress relationship as existed before, in fact Hagar is now aligned with a different source of power. Hagar now has the confidence of Yahweh, and while Sarai and Abram are covenanted with Yahweh, Yahweh's "preferential option" for the poor is evident here.[193]

Mutual recognition is illuminated in each of our three adjacent pairs.

---

[186] Westermann, *Genesis: A Practical Commentary*, 126. Sarna uses "formidable," Fretheim "difficult," Wenham states the text "merely expresses astonishment" and "much perplexity," Westermann says the "text is difficult," while Gunkel simply states the text is "nonsensical." Additional comments can be found in the following: Sarna, *Genesis*, 121. Fretheim, *Abraham: Trials of Family and Faith*, 97. Wenham, *Genesis 16-50*, 11. Westermann, *Genesis: A Practical Commentary*, 126. Gunkel, *Genesis*, 188.

[187] Wenham, *Genesis 16-50*, 11.

[188] Speiser, *Genesis*, 117.

[189] Brueggemann, *Genesis*, 153.

[190] Gossai, *Power and Marginality in the Abraham Narrative*, 14.

[191] Humphreys, *The Character of God in the Book of Genesis: A Narrative Appraisal*, 119.

[192] Schneider, *Sarah: Mother of Nations*, 54.

[193] Gossai, *Power and Marginality in the Abraham Narrative*, 16.

With the initial utterance of speech the Divine acknowledges Hagar to be a complete individual worthy of proper identification. Her social status is also acknowledged. The first adjacent pairing then reiterates the experience of the human being and the limited future she sees. The second pairing, answering the Divine question of future plans, is provided not by the human but by the Deity. Hagar will return and submit to the past she has run from. Harsh as this sounds, the third paring exhibits a Divine/human relationship not seen anywhere else in Genesis. For the humiliation she has endured and will have to endure, Hagar will not be a slave, handmaid or Egyptian only. She will be a mother of abundance. Her son will be free and strong against those who try to enslave him. Her unspoken thoughts, feelings, and pains have been heard and addressed in a way that allows her to state that the Deity has "seen" her as no one else in the scriptures has. The Divine/human relational dialogue, in this case, states unequivocally that the individual human is seen, heard and known by the Deity in a way that others cannot begin to acknowledge.

3. Genesis 17:15-22: Sarai renamed

a. *Adjacency Pairs and Turn Taking*

15.   *And Elohim said unto Abraham, Your wife Sarai, you will not call her Sarai because her name is Sarah.*

16a.   *And I will bless her and also you will have a son from her* a   b

16b.   *and I will bless her and she will be to nations; kings of peoples will come from her.*   d

17a.   <u>And Abraham fell upon his face and he laughed</u>   .a`. . .

17b.   and he said in his heart, Will a son be born to one who is one hundred years old and will Sarah who is ninety bear? b`

18.   And Abraham said unto Elohim, O that Ishmael might live before you.   c

19a.   *And Elohim said, Indeed, Sarah your wife will bear you*   b`` *a son and you will call his name Isaac*

19b.   *and I will set my covenant with him, a covenant forever and with his seed after him.*   d`

20.   As for Ishmael, I have heard you. Behold I will bless him and cause him to be fruitful and he will become many. Twelve princes will he father and I will give to him a great nation.   c`

21.   I will set my covenant with Isaac whom Sarah will bear   d`` to you at the appointed season in the following year.

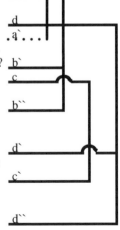

b. *Analysis*

The opening verbal statement of dialogue in Gen 17 is unique within the conversations we are examining. This initial statement by the Deity, changing Sarai's name to Sarah (שרי אשתך לא-תקרא את-שמה שרי כי שרה שמה), has no adjacent pair in Abraham's verbal response, actions or any divine counterpoint.[194] Per our discussion of proper names most scholars see the name change as identifying Sarah as a "princess" now worthy of covenantal motherhood. Abraham, however, has no comment, verbal or otherwise, to make regarding the change in his wife's name. It is v. 16 that "throws him for a loop" and begins the turn-taking in earnest.

The dialogue of v. 16 contains multiple blessings for Sarah as the Deity introduces the promise of a son by and kingly increase to the matriarch.[195] While most commentaries continue to focus on the patriarchal emphasis of the dialogue,[196] Speiser makes a surprising "Sarah-centered" observation:

> The passage is concerned with Sarah, whereas her son is as yet incidental. Indeed, if it were not for redundancy in the Heb. verse as it stands (the repetition of "I will bless her"), no reference to the blessing of Isaac would have been suspected at this point. There is also the inherent possibility that the second instance is to be construed as part of a subordinate clause: "And when I have blessed her, she shall give rise to nations."[197]

What makes the two blessings made to Sarah by the Deity in v. 16 so interesting is not just their utterance but the fact that the emphasis is, in fact, on Sarah. Five times in the verse and within each subordinate clause, Sarah is identified as the individual who will receive or be active in the blessings[198] (וברכתי אתה וגם נתתי ממנה לך בן וברכתיה והיתה)

---

[194] Coats argues that the change to Sarai's name is included here to match, through wordplay, Abraham's name change in verse 5. Coats, *Genesis*, 135.

[195] Westermann suggests that the parallel blessing as given to Abraham in Gen 15:1-6 "illustrates the harmonization of the two promises." Westermann, *Genesis: A Practical Commentary*, 132.

[196] Humphreys states, "The fruit of the second blessing is more centered on her in terms of her fruitfulness: From her will be nations, kings of peoples. In each case the transformed meaning of her life is stated in terms of seed, male seed, a son, and kings of peoples. The one who seemed beside the point now receives meaning in terms of a son she will bear." Humphreys, *The Character of God in the Book of Genesis: A Narrative Appraisal*, 109.

[197] Speiser, *Genesis*, 125.

[198] Once as a personal pronoun (object), once as subject of the verb, once as the suffix of the verb and twice as the feminized preposition "from her."

לגוים מלכי עמים ממנה יהיו). The emphasis is no longer on "God's oath
for possession of land; here the promise seems more directly attached
to multiplication of descendants. Moreover, the content of the everlast-
ing covenant becomes explicitly the promise for a son by Sarah."[199]
While the promises are spoken to Abraham, the text does not assimilate
Sarah under Abraham.[200] Through the declaration of promised blessings
in v. 16 Sarah has been expressly assured participation in the divine
covenant the Deity made with Abraham. As Schneider says, "There is
nothing subtle about the Deity's intentions or stance on the matter,"[201]
all of which makes the pairing of vv. 16a and 17a more interesting
(a-a`).

The adjacent pairing of vv. 16a and 17a (a-a`) is not a strong one
initially. Laughter, however, can be considered a verbal utterance, especially in light of what we will witness in the next chapter, and when the
surrounding dialogue is analyzed, the pairing of vv. 16a and 17a
becomes more apparent. In Gen 17:3 the Deity appeared to Abram to
discuss details of the covenant, Abram's only reaction was to fall on
his face (ויפל אברם על-פניו). Most scholars interpret this as an expression
of awe, submission and faith.[202] Abram's name is changed and the following verses reaffirm the covenantal promise and deliver the Law of
Circumcision. Throughout the divine speeches Abraham has no verbal
reaction. Here in v. 17a, reacting to the knowledge of Sarah's upcoming pregnancy, he falls on his face and this time laughs (ויפל אברהם
על-פניו ויצחק) (a-a`).[203]

Scholars debate the interpretation of v. 17a in various ways that often
indicate their level of respect for the man and the office of patriarch.
Westermann argues that "the gesture of falling down in reverence is
Abraham's first and most important reaction. His 'laughing' plays on
the name of the son."[204] Turner suggests that Abraham laughs "with a
laugh of exasperation and words of incredulity. The first action (17:3)
shows his comfort with Ishmael as the focus, reinforced by thirteen years

[199] Coats, *Genesis*, 135.
[200] The blessings given to Sarah are not exactly parallel to the promise given to Abraham.
[201] Schneider, *Sarah: Mother of Nations*, 58.
[202] Sarna asks if the laughter is that of "joy, surprise, doubt — or perhaps a little of each?" Sarna, *Genesis*, 123.
[203] Brichto claims, "the point of locating this act of grateful obeisance at this juncture [in v. 17, *added by ET*] is to signal a skepticism on Abraham's part, a skepticism explic-itly thought... It is to this almost-expressed skepticism that God replies." Brichto, *The Names of God: Poetic Readings in Biblical Beginnings*, 228.
[204] Westermann, *Genesis: A Practical Commentary*, 132.

of non-communication from Yahweh. The second registers just how resistant to change he is."[205] Cotter goes so far as to state that:

> when God told Abram to face him [in the opening verses of chapter 17, *added by ET*] he — Abram — did not listen, did not walk in God's way. His posture should bespeak of worshipful obedience. Instead it bespeaks the opposite. In 17:17-18, Abraham is still in that posture of not listening to the God who is addressing him. He is distracted, laughing to himself about the silly things this divinity says to him.[206]

This initial pairing is the catalyst for the second pairing.

The declaration that Sarah will have a son engenders the twofold question Abraham utters in v. 17b. Spoken within his heart,[207] (הלבן מאה-שנה יולד ואם-שרה הבת-תשעים שנה תלד) Abraham may utter questions of awe, surprise or doubt. Regardless of how the academic chooses to describe the response, "the double question essentially describes two conditions that in combination produce a state of affairs that is manifestly inimical to the notion of Abraham and Sarah producing a child."[208] (b-b`) What is interesting from an adjacency pair perspective is the Deity's rebuttal to Abraham's internal monologue. Whether Abraham's actions and thoughts are internal or verbal, classified as awe, surprise or doubt, they are not rebuked by the Deity. Instead, the dual question is answered with assurance[209] in v. 19a (אבל שרה אשתך ילדת לך בן וקראת את-שמו יצחק) (b-b`-b``). The promise is emphatically reiterated with details heretofore unknown — the name of the promised son.

---

[205] Turner, *Genesis*, 83. Dennis suggests Abraham's laugh is in response to the "absurdity" of the suggestion that the aged patriarch and his wife could become pregnant. Dennis, *Sarah Laughed*, 47.

[206] Cotter, *Genesis*, 111. Furthermore, Wenham contends that the actions taken by Abraham in v. 17 express the astonishment and confusion of a 100 year old man. He states, "The narrative makes Abraham's astonishment very clear in three ways. First, 'Abraham fell on his face,' a gesture of awe, amazement, and gratitude. In itself, prostration is ambiguous: clearly it indicates that Abraham found the remarks about Sarah more amazing than his own name change and the command to circumcise his household. But is he showing faith? 'And laughed,' his second astonished response, indicates the opposite; he is not simply laughing with joy, as Jacob maintains. Sarah's laughter in Gen 18:12-15 clearly expresses unbelief. Yet the very word ויצחק 'and laughed' spells 'and Isaac.' So in laughing at God's promise, Abraham unwittingly confirms it. Third, he is so overcome by the announcement that he can hardly think straight. The way he frames his doubt, 'Can a man... give birth?' combines two different constructions for a double-barreled question. To smooth his grammar, various emendations have been proposed. However, they are unnecessary. Probably the confused syntax reflects Abraham's inward confusion." Wenham, *Genesis 16-50*, 25-26.

[207] See dialogue analysis for a discussion regarding unvocalized speech.

[208] Sarna, *Genesis*, 126.

[209] Ibid., 126.

In the third adjacent pairing Abraham's verbal reaction (in v. 18) is to "direct God's interest (typically!) to what is already a certainty, i.e., to Ishmael."[210] Abraham raises the possibility of Ishmael as his heir[211] (לו ישמעאל יחיה לפניך). Some scholars interpret this request as an indication that Abraham has, to this point, understood Ishmael to be the promised covenant son.[212] Wenham states that, "Superficially, this is just a prayer that God's care and protection will be granted to Ishmael, but in not taking up the promise of a son through Sarah, Abraham shows his reservations."[213] In response to Abraham's plea[214] for Ishmael, Trible notes that the Deity begins the reply (c-c`) "with an asseverative particle (*'abal*) that holds both positive and negative meaning. It affirms and it refutes. Translations capture the nuance with phrases such as 'No, but' and 'Yes, but.'" Trible continues, "From God's perspective Ishmael has the wrong mother. To be sure, he will be blessed, becoming the father of twelve princes and a great nation, but he will not be the child of the covenant."[215] The promise given to Ishmael is similar to the covenant that will be made with Isaac. Even though Ishmael is promised princes and nationhood the word covenant, however, does not appear in v. 20.[216]

---

[210] Von Rad, *Genesis: A Commentary*, 103.

[211] Schneider, *Sarah: Mother of Nations*, 59. It is interesting to note here that while "the text refers to Ishmael as Abraham's son (16:15; 17:23, 25-26), Abraham never labels Ishmael his son. Yet, Abraham pleads for Ishmael to the Deity (17:18), circumcises him as soon as he learns of that command (17:25), never asks for a son by Sarah, and does not encourage the probability of such an event (Gen 20)." Schneider, *Mothers of Promise: Women in the Book of Genesis*, 34.

[212] Fretheim states, "Abraham seems to be satisfied that [Ishmael, *added by ET*] is the fulfillment of God's promise of a son (17:17-18); Isaac is almost an unwelcome afterthought." Fretheim, *Abraham: Trials of Family and Faith*, 110. Trible sees the verse as a plea "for the legitimacy of Ishmael." Trible and Russell, *Hagar, Sarah, and Their Children: Jewish, Christian, and Muslim Perspectives*, 42. Coats suggests that Abraham's first questions in v. 17 are "simply a complaint, capturing the incredulous character of the promise. The second [question in v. 18, *added by ET*] is an appeal for Ishmael as the son of the promise." Coats, *Genesis*, 135. Brueggemann explains, "We are now able to see the function of Ishmael as a threat to the promise. Abraham is no longer pressed to believe in an heir to be given, for he already has one, albeit in a devious way. Abraham is willing to stake his future on Ishmael. He does not fully understand the promise and its strange character. The laugh and the reference to Ishmael (vv. 17-18) are attempts to avoid the deep and unsettling claim God now makes on him." Brueggemann, *Genesis*, 156.

[213] Wenham, *Genesis 16-50*, 26.

[214] Schneider states that Abraham "Makes a case for Ishmael." Schneider, *Sarah: Mother of Nations*, 59. Turner argues that "Abraham's passionate doubting of whether a couple of their age could possibly procreate (17:17), constitutes a plea for Ishmael." Turner, *Genesis*, 82.

[215] Trible and Russell, *Hagar, Sarah, and Their Children: Jewish, Christian, and Muslim Perspectives*, 42.

[216] Westermann compares the blessings to clarify that divine blessing can extend beyond Israel even without the defining term 'covenant.' Ishmael "receives the promise of

In the final adjacent pair of dialogue the Deity dramatically reaffirms the original statement (וברכתיה והיתה לגוים מלכי עמים ממנה יהיו) made in v. 16b (d-d`-d``). Trible states, "God is adamant. Only Sarah can bear the legitimate heir; only Sarah can keep genealogy alive; only Sarah can give birth to the child of the covenant."[217] Furthermore, the Divine states that the everlasting covenant will be made with Isaac and only with Isaac (v. 19b v. 21 והקמתי את-בריתי אתו לברית עולם לזרעו אחריו ואת-בריתי אקים את-יצחק). Finally, as if to erase all doubt from Abraham's mind, the Deity declares an exact time for the event to take place in the following year in v. 21b[218] (תלד לך שרה למועד הזה בשנה האחרת). Nearly the entire dialogue, with its internal adjacent pairs (b and c), is circumscribed by this final pairing which pulls the primary focus back to Sarah (d-d'-d``).

This dialogue and the adjacent pairs contained therein give remarkable attention to a woman who is traditionally seen as a secondary character in the patriarchal narrative.[219] The Deity's opening statement receives no response in the dialogue. It is the incredible news that a ninety year old woman will, in fact, have a child that provokes the patriarch to respond. Attempted justifications for the reaction of laughter aside, there has to be some element of disbelief as the second pairing delineates a son and his name. The third pair brings the human perspective to the forefront once again. Abraham indicates that he has a son who may or may not prove to be an heir. The pairing of c-c` declares this son to have a promised blessing of twelve princes and a great nation but the all-encompassing adjacent pair proves, once and for all that nations, kings and people will come from the son whom Sara will bear. A son who will be named Isaac. Though the dialogue is between the Deity and Abraham, with Sarah not physically present, this conversation is, in actuality, about her; the role she will play, the son she will have. Abraham's participation is, in a sense, reduced to that of only dialogue partner.

---

increase as requested by Abraham in v. 18; it is Isaac, however, in whom the 'covenant' of God with Abraham is to be continued. The promise for Ishmael contains the same combination of blessing and increase as in v. 16, as well as a clear reference to Ishmael's history." Westermann, *Genesis: A Practical Commentary*, 132.

[217] Trible and Russell, *Hagar, Sarah, and Their Children: Jewish, Christian, and Muslim Perspectives*, 42.

[218] Wenham states that this last phrase "raises the tension of the narrative and injects a feeling of suspense and drama into it." Wenham, *Genesis 16-50*, 27.

[219] Humphreys, *The Character of God in the Book of Genesis: A Narrative Appraisal*, 109.

4. Genesis 18:9-15: Abraham, visitors and Sarah

a. *Adjacency Pairs and Turn Taking*

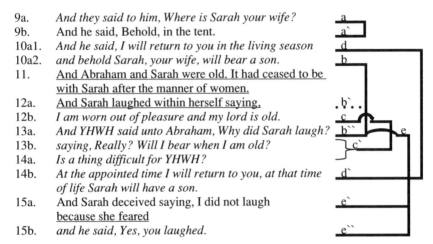

9a.	*And they said to him, Where is Sarah your wife?*
9b.	And he said, Behold, in the tent.
10a1.	*And he said, I will return to you in the living season*
10a2.	*and behold Sarah, your wife, will bear a son.*
11.	And Abraham and Sarah were old. It had ceased to be with Sarah after the manner of women.
12a.	And Sarah laughed within herself saying,
12b.	*I am worn out of pleasure and my lord is old.*
13a.	*And YHWH said unto Abraham, Why did Sarah laugh?*
13b.	*saying, Really? Will I bear when I am old?*
14a.	*Is a thing difficult for YHWH?*
14b.	*At the appointed time I will return to you, at that time of life Sarah will have a son.*
15a.	And Sarah deceived saying, I did not laugh because she feared
15b.	*and he said, Yes, you laughed.*

b. *Analysis*

The dialogue of Gen 18 is the first time we have two human participants speaking with and reacting to the Deity.[220] The Divine responses are also varied in their reception and direction, i.e., Sarah speaks, albeit internally, and the Deity responds to her comments by addressing Abraham. Scholars often approach this dialogue as a doublet of the Gen 17 account[221] and, while there is merit to the argument, it must be noted that in this conversation Sarah is no longer an absent, passive participant. Therefore this dialogue is not in existence to simply mirror the disbelief of Sarah and Abraham.[222]

---

[220] The visitors who arrive at Abraham's tent will be identified as the Divine visitors when speaking in the plural and where the speaker becomes singular in v. 10a will be entitled the Deity.

[221] Sharon Pace Jeansonne, *The Women of Genesis: From Sarah to Potiphar's Wife* (Minneapolis, Minn.: Fortress, 1990), 22.

[222] Brueggemann calls Abraham and Sarah "models of disbelief." Brueggemann, *Genesis*, 158. Turner states, "The repetition here of the prediction concerning Sarah's impending pregnancy is not redundant. Not only does it provide an insight into Sarah's attitude to the promise, but also underlines Abraham's reaction. Sarah's spontaneous laugh, like Abraham's previous outburst, has all the characteristics of a response to unbelievable news. She has not heard of such a thing before. Yet Abraham has known of it for some time. His wife's reaction reveals that he has never told her." Turner, *Genesis*, 84.

The narrative preceding this dialogue emphasizes the domestic setting
and integrates Sarah's attendance while still keeping her separate from
the action.²²³ The Divine visitor's initial question in v. 9a (שרה איה
אשתך) can be viewed two ways, as a genuine question or a rhetorical
one.²²⁴ Whether the scholar views the question from the Divine visitors
as guests who have enjoyed Sarah's labors but not yet met her or as a
question put forth by Divine visitors who know the name of a woman
they have never met is not the point. The response from Abraham in
v. 9b is (הנה באהל) (a-a`). It does not occur to him to ask how the Divine
visitors know Sarah's name. Sarah's presence has not been requested by
the Deity before and yet Abraham does not question why they might
want to know where she is now.²²⁵ He simply and directly answers the
query. The initial adjacent pair establishes Sarah's potential participation

The scriptures carry no record of Abraham recounting his divine dialogue as recorded
in chapter 17 with Sarah. Schneider states that Sarah's "reaction indicates that Abraham has neglected to inform her of this promise." Schneider, *Mothers of Promise:
Women in the Book of Genesis*, 31. There is no way to know if this was deliberate or
not. It is however important to note that the scriptures seem to indicate that Sarah is
at a disadvantage in knowing the divine identity of the visitor who is speaking about
her and to recognize that, at this juncture, the Deity has not self-identified in Sarah's
presence. Any response from Sarah must be considered with this uncertainty in mind.
Gunkel, *Genesis*, 197.

223 Trible describes Sarah as standing "surreptitiously outside the tent." Trible and Russell,
Hagar, Sarah, and Their Children: Jewish, Christian, and Muslim Perspectives, 43.
Wenham has Sarah simply listening at the tent door with the Divine visitor's back to
the tent. The object of this description, he argues, regardless of the literal positions of
the participants, is that Sarah's reaction cannot be physically seen by the Divine visitor.
"The fact that he can discern Sarah's reactions without seeing her proves his status
and guarantees his message." Wenham, *Genesis 16-50*, 48. Brichto sees a connection
with the birth announcement of Gen 17. "The aside that Sarah was standing at the
opening of the tent, which was situated behind the numen's back, is functionally parallel to Abraham's lying face to the ground in Chapter 17." Brichto, *The Names of God:
Poetic Readings in Biblical Beginnings*, 232. Matthews suggest that Sarah's location is
identified due to observance of the hospitality code. "The doorway, like the city gate,
was a conduit for trade and hospitality and could only be crossed with the permission
of the owner." This argument will put her outside the tent, listening to the men within.
Victor H. Matthews, "Hospitality and Hostility in Genesis 19 and Judges 19," *BTB* 22
(1992): 5. For a complete explanation of Matthews' hospitality protocols see Victor
H. Matthews, "Hospitality and Hostility in Judges 4," *BTB* 21 (1991).

224 Wenham states, "Like [Gen, *added by ET*] 3:9 'Where are you?' and [Genesis, *added
by ET*] 4:9, 'Where is Abel your brother?' it is not a real question, for the questioner
knows the answer." Wenham, *Genesis 16-50*, 47. Janzen argues that it would be
improper for strangers to address a woman or wife directly in the biblical culture.
Therefore, he states, the initial question is posed to Abraham. J. Gerald Janzen, *Abraham and All the Families of the Earth: A Commentary on the Book of Genesis 12-50*
(Grand Rapids, Mich: Eerdmans, 1993), 54-55.

225 Dennis, *Sarah Laughed*, 49. See also Schneider, *Sarah: Mother of Nations*, 68.

in the following exchange and focuses the reader and the dialogue participants on the real recipient of the message about to be given — Sarah.[226]

According to Speiser, v. 10a exposes the true nature of the visitors to
be Divine. He states that as "one of the visitors now acts as spokesman.
[His, *added by ET*] statement is the first direct intimation that the visitors
might not be what they seemed at first."[227] The divine nature of the conversation, in truth, begins here. The revelation that Sarah will have a son
in v. 10a2, according to Darr, is "intended for *her* ears, since Abraham
already had received the good news."[228] The statement then begins a
"tumble-down" conversation between Sarah and the Divine with Abraham
acting as a type of translator or somewhat of a go-between.

The narrative of verse 11 turns to Sarah "in the doorway of the tent"
and gives an extraordinarily precise description of both Abraham and his
wife. In two clauses the couple is described as 'old in days' and Sarah as
past menopause (ואברהם ושרה זקנים באים בימים חדל להיות לשרה ארח
כנשים). Previously in the narrative Sarah's reason for childlessness had
been described in terms of infertility, not age related.[229] For narrative and
dialogue purposes v. 11 is important as it provides background to the
adjacent pairing and the reactive dialogue that follows. It is not, however,
considered part of the dialogue.

The second adjacent pair is demonstrated in Sarah's reaction to v. 10a2
(b-b`-b``). Verse 12a states, "And Sarah laughed" in response to hearing
she will have a son (ותצחק שרה). It is a simple statement that has provoked

[226] Don Seeman, "'Where Is Sarah Your Wife?' Cultural Poetics of Gender and Nationhood in the Hebrew Bible," *HTR* 91 (1998): 108.

[227] Speiser, *Genesis*, 130. Sarna follows Speiser stating, "The supernatural character of
the visitors now asserts itself. The statement is not meant to be literal. It simply means,
as Ramban noted, that by this time next year the prediction will have been fulfilled."
Sarna, *Genesis*, 130.

[228] Darr, *Far More Precious Than Jewels: Perspectives on Biblical Women*, 102. Emphasis original. Wenham agrees and adds, "The promise is for Sarah alone here, and
the phrasing (והנה) makes it fulfillment sound even closer." Wenham, *Genesis 16-50*,
48.

[229] See Gen 11:30 and Westermann, *Genesis: A Practical Commentary*, 135. Brueggemann suggests that the reference to the couple's great age is to reinforce the fact that
"Abraham and Sarah have by this time become accustomed to their barrenness. They
are resigned to their closed future. They have accepted that hopelessness as 'normal.'"
Brueggemann, *Genesis*, 159. Schneider argues, "The placement of this verse is particularly important. Someone definitely considered it relevant for the reader to know
and remember the age and status of Abraham and the status of Sarah's fertility before
letting the reader know her response. If the onset of menopause for Sarah were not
relevant for understanding the following comments, then this information would not
have been included. But it is here to help readers understand Sarah's reaction." Schneider,
Sarah: Mother of Nations, 69.

much scholarship and friction. Is it unfaithfulness, derision, disbelief in
the Deity or a natural reaction to extraordinary news?[230] It is true that
some scholarship excuses Abraham's laughter in chapter 17 and others
judge Sarah's response with a much more critical eye.[231] A decisive
meaning behind the words of v. 12a will never be settled upon. In light
of adjacent pairs, however, we will see that this simple statement does
engender some very specific responses and reassurances from the Deity.[232]

There is another segment of v. 12a that is heavily commented upon. It
is the description that Sarah laughed "within herself" (ותצחק שרה בקרבה).
Humphreys explains:

> Whether she so contained the words that follow is not as clear... There
> is no "she said in her heart" to parallel the notice in Genesis 17:17.
> Yet there is no "and she said" either, only le'more, the Hebrew equivalent

---

[230] Von Rad stated, "Sarah did not basically renounce Yahweh with conscious unbelief;
her laugh is rather a psychologically understandable incident, just as unbelief so often
expresses itself." Von Rad, *Genesis: A Commentary*, 207. Gunkel states, "Sarah considers the men's statement a joke like those old women are accustomed to hear[...
added by ET] syntactically, she conceives of the matter as a fact and is amused by it."
Gunkel, *Genesis*, 197. Speiser goes so far as to label Sarah's reaction an "impetuous
reaction, one of derision." Speiser, *Genesis*, 131. Westermann was adamant, "Genesis
18:12 states explicitly Sarah's reason for laughing; it is a natural reaction." Westermann, *Genesis: A Practical Commentary*, 136. Claassens argues, "Sarah's laughter
becomes the means by which she momentarily transcends her circumstances. For a
moment at least, Sarah is able to enter a different reality where she becomes a subject
whose inner thoughts and desires are revealed." L. Juliana M. Claassens, "Laughter
and Tears: Carnivalistic Overtones in the Stories of Sarah and Hagar," *PRSt* 32
(2005): 300.

[231] Residuals of this way of thinking persist today. "Sarah's incredulous laughter at this
announcement parallels Abrahams' laughter in 17:17; however, Sarah's laughter,
unlike that of Abraham, is judged negatively by Yahweh as revealing a lack of trust
in the divine word." *The Harper Collins Bible Commentary*, 94.
The scholarly arguments regarding Sarah's response, however, are expanding. As
Brichto explains, "The smile in each case (17:17 and here) is a wry smile, to be sure;
a skeptical smile, expressing disbelief in a promise the mortal so desperately would
want to believe, and the negative force of 'jeer' or even 'scoff' is perhaps too strong
to convey the skepticism of a smile on the part of one receiving tidings too good to be
true." Brichto, *The Names of God: Poetic Readings in Biblical Beginnings*, 232. Humphreys states, "There is no thought given to the possibility that her words express a
delighted surprise, and her laughter is joy at news she could no longer hope to hear.
We do not find out whether her surprised laughter and her words express delight or
disbelief." Humphreys, *The Character of God in the Book of Genesis: A Narrative
Appraisal*, 118. Schneider admits that the text does not define the nature of Sarah's
laughter. She does, however, then argue that Sarah's laughter can be described as an
expression of belief and joy at the announcement and the fulfillment of a lifelong
desire. Schneider, *Sarah: Mother of Nations*, 69, 72, 92.

[232] Claassens suggests it is "Sarah's laughter that invites dialogue from God." Claassens,
"Laughter and Tears: Carnivalistic Overtones in the Stories of Sarah and Hagar," 300.

of quotation marks, which can be used for both what one says to
another and one's reflections to oneself. Do her words represent her
thoughts, or were they uttered aloud in surprise — even in disbelief or
doubt or suppresses anger — at the absurdity of what she had just
heard announced to Abraham concerning her? In the extended narrative this is the first time she gets any direct indication that Yahweh has
special designs for this family of which she is a part, and that her part
will be critical to Yahweh's design.[233]

The significance of Sarah's laughter (12a) and comments (12b) is that
they are voiced in some fashion. The Deity, without possibly hearing a
verbal reply or seeing her reaction, will acknowledge her response[234] with
multiple replies that affect three out of the five adjacency pairs in this
dialogue. (b-b`-b``, c-c`, e-e`-e``)

   The first Divine response (i.e. second adjacent pair) to Sarah's laughter in v. 13a has the Deity asking Abraham for an explanation as to why
his wife has laughed. (למה זה צחקה שרה) (b`-b``) Some scholars consider
this Divine response a rebuke or 'formal accusation'[235] against Sarah.
Humphreys takes a rather antiquated view when he declares that the
Deity:

> takes [Sarah's laughter and comments, *added by ET*] as a challenge to
> him, basically a doubt regarding what he might be able to bring about.
> Sarah's possibly spontaneous and quite natural surprise is transposed
> by him into doubt and a challenge, and Yahweh again addresses her
> husband rather than her. *In this interchange about birth and the biology
> of reproduction, Yahweh seems more comfortable talking to another
> male.*[236]

The Divine response, while not directed to Sarah, is direct in its adjacent
pairing. The Deity's request for an explanation is unequivocally invoked
due to Sarah's reaction to the incredible news that she may yet give birth
(b-b`-b``).

---

[233] Humphreys, *The Character of God in the Book of Genesis: A Narrative Appraisal*, 117.
Also see Hatav's article which argues that "the infinitival *lemor* may be used to interpret any communication act." Hatav, "(Free) Direct Discourse in Biblical Hebrew,"
21.

[234] Rulon-Miller, *Hagar: A Woman with an Attitude*, 71.

[235] Coats, *Genesis*, 138. Also see Brichto, *The Names of God: Poetic Readings in Biblical
Beginnings*, 233.

[236] Humphreys, *The Character of God in the Book of Genesis: A Narrative Appraisal*,
117. Emphasis original. Rulon-Miller suggests Sarah's "laugh may express her thought
that it would be 'too awesome' even for Yahweh to cure Abraham's impotence or his
life-ling desire for her." Rulon-Miller, *Hagar: A Woman with an Attitude*, 71.

The third adjacent pairing (c-c`) finds the Deity's response to Sarah's second concern is just as specific as the first. Sarah's comments in v. 12b (אחרי בלתי היתה לי עדנה ואדנח זקן) deal exclusively with what she physically knows; for her, at least, pleasure[237] is rare, if not non-existent and that both she and her husband are old. Fretheim argues that comments by the narrator in v. 11 soften Sarah's reactions of v. 12, "making it more understandable, as does her observation about the end of sexual pleasure. The issue for Sarah is no longer barrenness, but age."[238] Again, a comparison can be made with Abraham's response in Gen 17:17. His first reaction is to mention the unlikelihood of a hundred year old man siring a child (הלבן מאה-שנה יולד). He then addresses the fact that Sarah, the designated covenant mother, is ninety years old and it is highly improbable that she will ever conceive (ואם-שרה הבת-תשעים שנה תלד). Brichto observes an interesting inverted comparison between Abraham and Sarah. He states, "Sarah, too, begins with her own inadequacy, and only then thinks of her husband's."[239] As is human nature, both the patriarch and his wife address the Divine with corporeal real-life impediments. As the dialogue is paired (v. 12b with vv. 13b-14a) (c-c`), we see that, rebuke or not, the Deity addresses Sarah's concerns in a manner that reveals the marvelous and miraculous purpose for the dialogue as a whole. Sailhamer observed:

> The subtle changes in the wording of Sarah's thoughts reveal that the Lord was not simply restating her thoughts but was interpreting them as well. In this way the writer is able to give the reader a deep insight into the meaning of the passage. First, the Lord restated Sarah's somewhat ambiguous statement ("After I am worn out, will I now have pleasure?") as simply, "Will I really have a child?" Then he took Sarah's statement about her husband ("My husband is old," 18:12) and reshaped it into a statement about herself ("I am old," v. 13). Finally, he went beyond her actual words to the intent of those words: "Is anything impossible with the Lord?" (v. 14). By means of these questions to Abraham, the underlying issue in the narrative is put before the reader, that is, the physical impossibility of the fulfillment of the promise through Sarah.[240]

[237] Scholars debate the specific meaning of *pleasure* from the joy of children to sexual pleasure. See Schneider, *Sarah: Mother of Nations*, 71. Also see Jeansonne, *The Women of Genesis: From Sarah to Potiphar's Wife*, 23.

[238] Fretheim, *Abraham: Trials of Family and Faith*, 113. Fretheim sites Gen 11:30 and 16:2 as further examples of Sarah's barrenness.

[239] Brichto, *The Names of God: Poetic Readings in Biblical Beginnings*, 232-33.

[240] Sailhamer, *The Pentateuch as Narrative: A Biblical-Theological Commentary*, 166.

Sarah's question in v. 12b reflects her understanding of her body and her world, especially her view of Abraham and the couple's procreative abilities.

The strength of these adjacent pairs (both b and c) is shored up by the adjacent promises in v. 10a and 14b which surround Sarah's fears and disbelief (d-d`). Before divulging the promise of a son for Sarah the Deity informs Abraham, in v. 10a1, that he will "surely return in the living season" (שוב אשוב אליך כעת חיה). This statement, while somewhat uncertain in meaning,[241] is reiterated in the wording of v. 14b (למועד אשוב אליך כעת היה). Most studies of this narrative unit overlook commenting on this verse. If mentioned at all it is simply declared a repeat of v. 10[242] or a partial birth announcement.[243]

Brueggemann called the final pairing of this Divine/human relational dialogue (e-e`) "a curious dialogue… filled with pathos"[244] Here in v. 15 Sarah speaks directly with the Deity.[245] It is the one and only dialogue exchange between them.[246] This final adjacent pair mirrors the initial 'laughter' pairing (b`-b``) but turns both statements into a negative (e`-e``) (לא כי צחקת 15b לא צחקתי כי יראה 15a).

Interestingly, in the case of the first laughter pairing (b`-b``), the dialogue concerned Sarah but the Divine response was addressed to Abraham.

[241] Sarna explains that the phrase only occurs here and in 1 Kings 4:16f. The context is similar but the "at the/this time" element could be referring to a full year or a nine month pregnancy. Sarna, *Genesis*, 130.

[242] Gunkel, *Genesis*, 197.

[243] Coats, *Genesis*, 137.

[244] Brueggemann, *Genesis*, 160. Gunkel suggests that with the repeated promise Sarah realizes who is speaking. She then "becomes intimidated and lies." Gunkel, *Genesis*, 197. Von Rad calls Sarah's utterance an "audacious lie" born of confusion." Von Rad, *Genesis: A Commentary*, 207.

[245] Schneider notes that "the text confirms that Sarah laughs earlier but not who she fears or who uses her laughter as proof. Most translations assume that the Deity is the speaker, though the text does not state this explicitly." Schneider, *Mothers of Promise: Women in the Book of Genesis*, 32. Contrary to popular scholarship, Schneider suggests that it is Abraham with whom Sarah is speaking and of whom she is afraid. "[Abraham, *added by ET*] sells her to Pharaoh's harem. Abraham is prepared to let Hagar treat Sarah with disrespect when Hagar becomes pregnant (16:5). Though Sarah probably does not know it, Abraham is also the one who has not informed her that the Deity promised her a son, and that he has originally rejected the offer (17:18). Another thing she does not know is that her husband is the one who laughs (17:17) and does not say a word when she is blamed for what he does (18:13, 15). Therefore, it is just as plausible, in fact more likely, that Abraham is the one who says, 'No, you did laugh.', and that Abraham is the one whom Sarah fears." Schneider, *Sarah: Mother of Nations*, 73.

[246] Dennis, *Sarah Laughed*, 50.

In that instance her husband did not respond. Here in v. 15a we see Sarah takes the initiative and responds to the Deity's question[247] (לא צחקתי כי ויראה). Brichto argues that "she responds guiltily — speaking as much for Abraham as herself — with denial. A denial that is not a lie, for neither she nor Abraham actually expressed the doubt in word or smile."[248] Fretheim agrees with Brichto stating that Sarah's laughter is more likely an attempt to withdraw the laughter because she now realizes who is speaking.[249] Phillips, however, deems Sarah's response a lie but argues it is justified. She argues, "As with Abraham, the Lord addressed what [Sarah, *added by ET*] had expressed only inwardly. That accounts for her fear and the subsequent audible lie."[250]

The Deity responds that her laughter is a fact[251] (לא כי צחקת) (e-e`-e``). For Sarna and many scholars Sarah's laughter and denial question the Deity's sovereignty and power.[252] Fretheim, contrary to most negative views of this dialogue, presents a refreshing take on the theory. He argues, "In effect, God is saying: do not deny the laughter, but continue to laugh and in time it will be transformed. In effect, the denial means that [Sarah's, *added by ET*] laughter does not stand in the way of her becoming a mother and she need not fear that it will."[253] Whether the scholar chooses to label the verbal exchange in v. 15 as a withdrawal, guilty denial or Divine rebuke the adjacency of the direct pairing shows

---

[247] Humphreys states Sarah responds because she is "not willing to be erased this time." Humphreys, *The Character of God in the Book of Genesis: A Narrative Appraisal*, 117.

[248] Brichto, *The Names of God: Poetic Readings in Biblical Beginnings*, 233-34.

[249] Dennis argues that "Sarah's fear is the only clue we are given in the story that she at least has penetrated God's disguise." Dennis, *Sarah Laughed*, 52. Westermann believes that the Deity is revealed in the response. "Now Sarah is frightened; her fear takes the form of trying to deny that she laughed. Now that she realizes what she has done, she would like to undo it. The [Deity, *added by ET*] responds: you cannot undo what is done." Westermann, *Genesis: A Practical Commentary*, 136. Sarna explains Sarah's in this manner, "No wonder, for she had laughed not out loud but to herself, and her innermost thoughts had been read!" Sarna, *Genesis*, 131. Fretheim simply states, "Fear can be a natural response in the midst of the experience of such divine words." Fretheim, *Abraham: Trials of Family and Faith*, 114. Coats sees a different aspect to the exchange. He states, "The exchange offers a threat to the safety of the prospective mother by virtue of the challenge Yahweh presents to her." Coats, *Genesis*, 138.

[250] Phillips, *Incredulity, Faith, and Textual Purposes: Post-Biblical Responses to the Laughter of Abraham and Sarah*, 26.

[251] Fretheim explains that "This exchange keeps both Sarah and Abraham on the same level regarding the reception of the promise and will link up with her response to the naming of Isaac." Fretheim, *Abraham: Trials of Family and Faith*, 114.

[252] Sarna, *Genesis*, 127.

[253] Fretheim, *Abraham: Trials of Family and Faith*, 115.

once again that the Deity responds with a wider view than the human individual had imagined. The Deity heard the laughter even if it was uttered within Sarah.

The Divine/human relational dialogue of chapter 18 is interesting due to the direct and indirect turn taking that creates the conversation. Abraham, active in the first adjacent pairing, establishes Sarah's proximity to the dialogue and then becomes a passive partner. Sarah, who is finally present, moves from the periphery to the center as she responds to the Divine declaration of a son. Her internal monologue is then recounted and questioned by the Deity. All of which is enclosed by a double promise of Divine return to signal the conception of her soon to be son. While the initial adjacent pair regarding her laughter is not addressed to her. Sarah takes it upon herself to comment on this pairing. Her verbal reaction ultimately results in the only dialogue exchange between the covenant matriarch and the Deity. It may not be the conversation she had hoped for but it is a direct retort to her statement.

Once again Divine/human relational dialogue is focused on an individual who expresses doubts, fears and possibly incredulity. Each of these verbal expressions is responded to and/or resolved by the Divine's paired utterances. Sarah may not have known about her covenant roll before this chapter but she has been assured of her place and her importance within the covenant through this dialogue exchange.

5. Genesis 15:1-17: Abram's visionary dialogue

a. *Adjacency Pairs and Turn Taking*

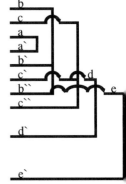

1b1.	*Fear not Abram,*
1b2.	*I am your shield*
1b3.	*and your very great reward.*
2a1.	And Abram said, Adoni YHWH, what will you give to me
2a2.	Since I am childless
2b.	and the heir of my house is Eliezer of Damascus.
3a.	And Abram said, Behold you have given me no seed
3b.	and behold a son of my house will inherit.
4.	*And Behold the word of YHWH came to him saying, This one will not inherit because he who comes from your bowels will inherit.*
5.	*And he brought him outside and said, Look to the heavens and count the stars if ye are able to count them and he said to him, Thus your seed will be.*

7.   *And he said to him, I am YHWH who brought you out*
      from Ur of Chaldees and gave you this land as an
      inheritance.
8.   And he said, Adoni YHWH, how will I know that I will
      inherit it?
9.   *And he said to him, Take to me a heifer three years old*
      and a she-goat three years old and a ram three years old
      and a turtle dove and a young pigeon.
10.   And he took all of these and he cut them in two in the
      middle and he laid each part side by side but the bird he
      did not divide.
13.   *And he said to Abram, Surely you will know that your seed*
      will be a stranger in a land which is not theirs and they
      will serve them and they will oppress them four hundred
      years.
14.   *And the nation which they will serve I will judge and*
      afterwards they will leave with great possessions.
15.   *And you will die in peace and be buried at a good old age*
16.   *And the fourth generation will return here because the*
      iniquity of the Amorites is not complete as of now.

b. *Analysis*

Genesis 15 is the first chronologically recorded dialogue between the
Deity and Abram. Though there is an ethereal quality to the conversation
our examination will show there is little difference in the adjacency elements of the dialogue from those of the 'everyday' conversations we have
surveyed.

For many scholars, a study of Gen 15 focuses on balancing the sections
of narrative and dialogue.[254] Much of it, however, tends to be strictly
comparative in nature with little examination of the actual dialogue content.[255] If the conversation is treated as one continuous dialogue, Abram

---

[254] Wehnam stated that the "scenic construction is typical of Hebrew narrative, but here
the scenes simply serve as setting for the dialogue." Wenham, *Genesis 1-15*, 326.
Gunkel argues, "The passage is hardly to be called a 'narrative.' There is no development of plot." Gunkel, *Genesis*, 182. Coats goes so far as to declare the chapter to be
"composed entirely of speeches." Coats, *Genesis*, 123.

[255] For example, Williamson observes, "In the first section Yahweh makes three statements
(vv. 1b, 4 and 5b), the latter two resulting from Abraham's negative response (vv. 2-3)
to Yahweh's opening pledge (v.1). In the second section Yahweh again makes three
statements (vv. 7, 13-16 and 18b-21) and once more the latter two are responses to
Abraham's negative rejoinder (v. 8) to Yahweh's opening pledge (v. 7)." Williamson,

is not a passive recipient of the promise[256] and development in the relationship between the two participants can be seen. Abram's striking response to the Divine promise of reward is to question[257] followed by the Deity's assurance and action taken by both parties. To examine the dialogue as a whole is to examine an intimate relationship between the human and Divine.

"Fear not Abram, I am a shield to thee and thy very great reward" (אל-תירא אברם אנכי מגן לך שכרך הרבה מאד). So begins the first dialogue between Abram and the Deity. To emphasize the personal nature of this conversation the Deity begins by addressing Abram by his proper name.[258] The Deity's statement 'fear not' is seen by scholars as alternately, a commandment,[259] a reassurance[260] and an oracle.[261] The addition of the terms *shield* and "great reward" usher in discussions of military metaphors.[262] At this moment in the scriptures, however, there is in fact no threat to Abram or his family.[263] If there is no threat there is no need for fear or a protective shield in a military sense. As for a great reward, the promise is so vague it begs for clarification which is exactly how Abram responds.[264] (a-aˋ, b-bˋ, c-cˋ) Humphreys argues that this is "not the sort

---

Abraham, Israel and the Nations: The Patriarchal Promise and Its Covenantal Development in Genesis, 122-23.

[256] Brueggemann, *Genesis*, 141.

[257] Fretheim, *Abraham: Trials of Family and Faith*, 35.

[258] It is interesting to note that this is the first time the Deity has done so. All other references using the proper name have been by the narrator or by Melchizedek (Gen. 14:19). The only other time the Deity calls Abram by this name is to change his proper name to Abraham.

[259] The form of the verb is Qal jussive 2ms.

[260] Lipton, *Revisions of the Night: Politics and Promises in the Patriarchal Dreams of Genesis*, 187.

[261] Wenham explains, "This is a very common phrase in the OT, frequently introducing an oracle of salvation." Wenham, *Genesis 1-15*, 327.

[262] Van Seters states, "This same genre oracle with the same components may be found among the oracles of Esarhaddon and Ashurbanipal. There can be no question, from an examination of these, that they are all a form of oracle given to the king before a military campaign as an assurance of victory. They appear to be in response to the king's prayer of lament about the threats of the enemy, and they demand trust in the deity's power to bring victory." Van Seters, *Abraham in History and Tradition*, 254.

[263] The conflict of chapter 14 has concluded with a blessing from Melchizedek and a refusal to allow the King of Sodom even a modicum of power over Abram.

[264] Coats calls the verse 'vague.' Coats, *Genesis*, 124. However, von Rad sees no ambiguity in the statements. He interprets the reward or gift as a statement regarding future posterity. Von Rad, *Genesis: A Commentary*, 183. Turner follows von Rad "seeing it as referring to posterity — this is certainly the main focus of Abraham's riposte." Turner, *Announcements of Plot in Genesis*, 72. Ha concludes, "Not only is

of response his sovereign patron would expect"[265] and yet the Divine response to human query is direct and specific.

As Abram begins his address he uses the identifier Adoni YHWH (אדני יהוה). This rare form of address[266] has significance on two levels. First, the compound designation in the title is employed to draw attention to and to give prominence to the following clauses.[267] Second, The address Adoni YHWH highlights Abram's status with the Divine. Sarna argues that the title suggests a master-servant relationship.[268] Westermann sees Abram's first vocal response to the Divine as a prayer.[269] Von Rad is opinionatedly descriptive of Abram's responses. He states, "Abraham demurs resignedly. His despondent skepticism in the face of the assurance of divine protection and the exceptionally great divine gift borders almost on blasphemy; and yet it contains a timorous reference to the real subject of his anxiety, his childlessness."[270] Scholars focusing on genre classify vv. 2 and 3 as a lament built upon individual complaint statements.[271] In response, Abram chooses to speak of the challenges inherent

---

its form unclear but there is also no clear indication of what it is for. This was why Abraham had still to ask, 'What will you give me?'" Ha, *Genesis 15: A Theological Compendium of Pentateuchal History*, 43.

[265] Humphreys, *The Character of God in the Book of Genesis: A Narrative Appraisal*, 93.

[266] "This formula occurs only here and in v. 8 in Genesis. אדני 'sovereign' is a characteristic mode of address to God in intercessory prayer. It is not found in Genesis outside of the Abraham cycle." Wenham, *Genesis 1-15*, 327. Ha expands on this understanding by stating, "Almost all the non-prophetic texts employ the title to address YHWH either in a prayer or dialogue with Him. While this usage differs from the normal prophetic uses of the title dealt with above, it is not unknown among the prophets." Note: Ha lists exceptions as 1 K. 2:26 and Pss. 68:9 with potentially 71:16 and 73:28. Ha, *Genesis 15: A Theological Compendium of Pentateuchal History*, 69.

[267] Revell, *The Designation of the Individual: Expressive Usage in Biblical Narrative*, 216.

[268] He says, "This Hebrew divine title, rarely used in the Torah, appears here for the first time. It is used in a context of complaint, prayer, and request. Here the word of 'Lord' is *'adoni*, 'my Lord,' not the divine name YHWH, and its use suggests a master-servant relationship. Abram does not permit his vexation to compromise his attitude of respect and reverence before God." Sarna, *Genesis*, 113.

[269] Westermann, *Genesis: A Practical Commentary*, 118.

[270] Von Rad, *Genesis: A Commentary*, 183. Wenham follows von Rad to a degree calling Abram's question 'pitiful.' Wenham, *Genesis 1-15*, 334.

[271] Van Seters states "There is no difficulty with the genre of vv. 2-3, which are easily recognized as a lament." Van Seters, *Abraham in History and Tradition*, 255. Also see Westermann, *Genesis: A Practical Commentary*, 118-19. Coats argues that v. 2 "is strictly speaking not yet a complaint. It is a request, apparently, for a surety or sign related to the promise. The motivation for the request, however, anticipates a complaint." He goes on to flesh out the definition using v. 3 as an example. "With a new speech formula, v. 3 makes the complaint specific." Coats, *Genesis*, 124.

in the Deity's assertions of v. 1. "Abram brings Yahweh's rather lofty language to earth and to a question that focuses on the concrete particulars of his family situation."[272]

In the first adjacent pairing the divinely promised reward is directly countered with Abram's first verbal question (v. 2a1) to the Deity, "What will you give me?" (מה-תתן-לי) (a-a`). From Abram's point of view great reward is a matter of physical possessions.[273] Where the Divine has stated, 'Fear not," Abram responds with his greatest fear, is childlessness (v. 2a2) (ואנכי הולך ערירי) (b-b`) and the equivalent, no seed (v. 3a) (הן לי לא נתתה זרע) (b-b`-b``). In response to the Deity's promise of a shield, Abram explains that he has a shield already in place against his childlessness in the form of Eliezer (v. 2b) (ובן-משק ביתי הוא דמשק אליעזר) (c-c`) who has been designated the son of his house (v. 3b) (והנה בן-ביתי יורש אתי) (c-c`-c``). Abram's questions beg a definition of *reward* from the Deity.[274] Ha explains that "in terms of literary function, Abraham's question in v. 2 appears to be his way of requesting a sign from YHWH to confirm the promise in v. 1 by assuring its long-term value for him."[275] With this in mind, Abram's introduction of Eliezer as an heir is the patriarch's definition of a solution. He is, in effect, challenging the Deity to either deny the solution or provide a concrete description of promised reward.[276] Abram's declaration, that a member of his household will inherit,[277] squarely assigns his personal lack of seed to the Deity.

Wenham follows Coats with a slight expansion. The *behold* and "so that" in v. 3 add "a note of exasperation to the complaint." Wenham, *Genesis 1-15*, 328.

[272] Humphreys, *The Character of God in the Book of Genesis: A Narrative Appraisal*, 93.

[273] See Gen 13.

[274] Brichto states, "Reward is a matter of material possessions enjoyed in good health over a long lifetime. What good [Abram, *added by ET*] asks are such 'goods' to a man like himself who is barren." Brichto, *The Names of God: Poetic Readings in Biblical Beginnings*, 205-06. Turner argues that Abram's "complaint is not that God has given him no reward whatsoever, but concerns the *degree* or *amount* of the reward." Turner, *Announcements of Plot in Genesis*, 72. Emphasis original.

[275] Ha, *Genesis 15: A Theological Compendium of Pentateuchal History*, 45.

[276] Humphreys states, "[Abram, *added by ET*] can ask 'hard questions.' Having acted upon Yahweh's call, he now calls on Yahweh to act." Humphreys, *The Character of God in the Book of Genesis: A Narrative Appraisal*, 94.

[277] Commenting on the definition of inheritance within these verses Sarna stated that the term *heir* here "reflects a society in which a servant can become heir to a childless couple. Numerous ancient Near Eastern documents provide for the adoption of a stranger who inherits the estate in return for the performance of filial duties. These include paying the adoptive parents the proper respect, maintaining the household, taking care of their physical needs and comforts in their old age, and performing the funerary rites at their death. In such cases, the adopted son cannot be deprived of a share of the inheritance even if there are subsequently natural-born sons. Thus, God's

By examining the specific elements within the dialogue we see that "v. 3 is not a mere repetition of v. 2 but marks a real progression of thought."[278] Humphreys makes the argument:

> There is a complex interplay in tone and substance between Yahweh's and Abram's words in this brief episode. A certain indirectness is followed by a directness in each case. It is as if each speaker expects the other to get the point without having it stated, only then to feel the need to drive it home with a directness that may reflect a studied inattention to the implied point.[279]

In v. 1 the Deity stated a promise, which engendered a request from Abram for clarity producing the adjacent pairs a, b and c. Abram's "double protest" of "no seed" and "Eliezer could inherit" in vv. 2 and 3, triggers a double assurance response from the Deity.[280] In vv. 4 and 5 the Deity clarifies the promise and gives what amounts to "a concrete proposal."[281] Fretheim shows that the Deity "speaks directly to Abraham's concerns, with 'heir' repeated and word order designed to emphasize the point"[282] (v. 4) (לא יירשך זה כי-אם אשר יצא ממעיך הוא יירשך) (d-dˋ). Verse 5 (הבט-נא השמימה וספר הכוכבים אם-תוכל לספר אתם כה יהיה זרעך) then drives the point home with an "object lesson"[283] in response to Abraham's comments of vv. 2 and 3 (e-eˋ). Ha states that the opening narrative clause of v. 5 "is somewhat strange since there is no indication of YHWH and Abraham being 'inside' any place."[284] The point, most

emphatic and unambiguous reply in verse 4 can only mean that the patriarch despairing of having children, had decided to resort to the adoption of his servant but has not yet acted. God assures him that this will not be necessary." Sarna, *Genesis*, 113.

[278] Ha, *Genesis 15: A Theological Compendium of Pentateuchal History.*

[279] Humphreys, *The Character of God in the Book of Genesis: A Narrative Appraisal*, 95.

[280] Brueggemann, *Genesis*, 140.

[281] Ha, *Genesis 15: A Theological Compendium of Pentateuchal History*, 45. Sometimes called a "sign." See Brueggemann who argues, "While alike in substance there is one difference between the approach of God in verse 1 and verses 4-5. The second approach includes a *sign*, a clue to the movement of God[... *added by ET*] The multitude of stars is received by Abraham as a sign of the power of God in his life. The sign is not proof or demonstration, but it is a sacrament to those who can discern the connection between the concrete visible and the promised." Brueggemann, *Genesis*, 144-45.

[282] Fretheim, *Abraham: Trials of Family and Faith*, 36. Wenham labels the response "an emphatic affirmation that a real son will inherit from him." Wenham, *Genesis 1-15*, 329.

[283] Humphreys, *The Character of God in the Book of Genesis: A Narrative Appraisal*, 94.

[284] Ha continues, "The strangeness may be ironed out by pointing out that there is no place intended in the clause under consideration." Ha, *Genesis 15: A Theological Compendium of Pentateuchal History*, 45.

scholars suggest, in not exactly where Abram was but that the visual experience reinforces the verbal promise given by the Deity.[285] As Fretheim explains, "The reference to the stars is a rhetorical move to make a point about the promise in the face of his questions: God keeps promises. The image of the stars does not center on issues of power, but on stability and, repeatedly, on sheer numbers."[286] The one who comes directly from Abram's bowels will become as innumerable as the stars he is unable to count.[287] With all of Abram's concerns "one aspect is unambiguously clear. Abram will father a son (15:4), and the numerous progeny promised in 15:5 will come through him."[288] Abram's direct questions have been addressed, answered and supported with verbal responses and visual aids.

Immediately following the announcement of his innumerable descendants we are told 'Abram believed the Lord' (והאמן ביהוה) in v. 6a. Belief is the very point which leads Abram to question the Divine in vv. 2 and 3.[289] For many scholars v. 6 is a conclusion to the dialogue[290] and the verses that follow become a discussion of ritual.[291] This dialogue, however, has been built upon divine statements countered by human request

---

[285] Sarna, *Genesis*, 113. Van Seters suggests, "if the words 'he brought me outside' introduce a visionary experience the time of day suggested by the appearance of the stars is not a true dramatic element or any indication of a narrative tradition. But it does link up with the prophetic reports forms of vv. 1 and 4." Van Seters, *Abraham in History and Tradition*, 256. Noegel makes an interesting observation regarding this "taunt." He argues that since the sun has yet to set (v. 12) Abram will not be able to count stars (v. 5) because they are not out yet. This, he contends, makes the statement "if you are able" a test. "The question is made even more poignant by the fact that we are not told that Abram ever attempted to count them." Scott B. Noegel "A Crux and a Taunt: Night-Time Then Sunset in Genesis 15" (Sheffield: Sheffield Academic Press, 1998), 132.

[286] Fretheim adds "The rhetorical shift from dust (13:16) to stars also suggests stability and perhaps security." Fretheim, *Abraham: Trials of Family and Faith*, 36.

[287] Westermann argues "The countless stars, is an extension of the promise of a son to include the promise of many descendants; it presupposes the combination of the two." Westermann, *Genesis: A Practical Commentary*, 119. Also see Gunkel Gunkel, *Genesis*, 179.

[288] Turner, *Genesis*, 74. With regard to the larger scheme of the extended narrative, however, Brueggemann argues "The response of God to Abraham is not a fool-proof argument like the brief of a lawyer. It comes in two parts: (a) in verse 4, the word again; and (b) in verse 5, a sign, a glance at the heavens. But the sign proves nothing." Abram may be promised a son but he still does not hold one in his arms. Brueggemann, *Genesis*, 143.

[289] Turner, *Announcements of Plot in Genesis*, 72.

[290] For example see von Rad, *Genesis: A Commentary*, 185. Coats, *Genesis*, 124. Brueggemann, *Genesis*, 144. In slight contrast Cotter calls v. 6 a "clear turning point of the story." Cotter, *Genesis*, 100.

[291] A thorough discussion of the significance of ritual (or not) is beyond the scope of this thesis.

for clarity.[292] Even after the narrative comments of v. 6 interrupt the conversation this pattern continues. Von Rad observed:

> On the one hand, it is clear that a new narrative context begins with v. 7, for the self-introduction of the divinity, according to all comparable passages (cf. Gen. 28:13; Ex 3:6; 6:2), makes sense only at the beginning of the self-revelation. On the other hand, it is obvious that the redactor is attempting to unite the event about to be described closely to the one that has preceded [sic, *added by ET*]; for a narrative cannot have begun with v. 7 only.[293]

Following this argument we can see that Abram moves from a state of questioning belief to the issue of knowing. Once past v. 6 he believes, now his adjacent pairs demand a sign, so that he might know.[294]

The Deity opens his second promise to Abram in v. 7 by stating "I am YHWH." Fretheim explains, "In swearing by the divine self, God does justice to the relationship"[295] with Abram. Here the Divine expands the relationship with a promise of land[296] and knowledge. Similar to v. 1, v. 7 describes the Deity offering another great promise. This time it is the inheritance of land. Abram's paired response in v. 8 is another question (במה אדע כי אירשנה) (f-f'). This question differs from the question in v. 2 in that it is not classified as a lament.[297] Abram is confirming that he does not possess the land,[298] similar to being childless, and is asking for another confirming sign.[299]

---

[292] Fretheim states, "Abraham's faith has been enabled by what God has just said; indeed, God's word has created Abraham's faith. Abraham's faith has not been generated from within himself of through his own resources. More specifically, this faith-event occurs because God particularizes the promise for Abraham by addressing the specific situation opened up by Abraham's question." Fretheim, *Abraham: Trials of Family and Faith*, 36.

[293] Von Rad, *Genesis: A Commentary*, 186.

[294] Brodie, *Genesis as Dialogue: A Literary, Historical, and Theological Commentary*, 228.

[295] Fretheim, *Abraham: Trials of Family and Faith*, 39.

[296] Turner argues that "The narrative's attention moves away from progeny to land. This provides Yahweh with the opportunity to reveal that his leading goes back to Terah's initial move from Ur and not simply Abram's from Haran (15:7)." Turner, *Genesis*, 74.

[297] Wenham argues that "to ask for a sign does not imply unbelief or any conflict with v. 6. On the contrary, to refuse a proffered sign can indeed demonstrate lack of faith." Wenham, *Genesis 1-15*, 331.

[298] Van Seters, *Abraham in History and Tradition*, 258. Also, Turner states, "Now that Yahweh has removed Lot as his heir, Abram has no tangible foothold on nationhood other than Yahweh's promise. This has always been the case with the land promise. Abram's response to Yahweh's repletion of the promise, 'O Lord God, how am I to know that I shall possess it?' (15:8), confirms that he still does not possess it." Turner, *Genesis*, 75.

[299] "The promise itself takes on a rather stereotyped structure. Abram's response is now much less a complaint than a simple request for surety." Coats, *Genesis*, 124.

The Deity's direct answer to v. 8 is provided in vv. 13-16[300] (g-g`). The Deity responds with an infinitive absolute form of knowledge (v 13 ידע תדע). Brodie argues that, "unlike the question of believing, where it is [narrated, *added by ET*] that Abram believed (15:6), it is never said, as directly, that Abram knew. But he asked how he should know (15:8), and he was told with emphatic directness, 'Know! Know that your descendants…' (15:13)."[301] The Deity then expands the response through the final verses of the dialogue.[302] Verse 13 states his seed will be strangers in a land, oppressed and humbled for a period of time (כי-גר יהיה זרעך בארץ לא להם ועבדום וענו אתם ארבע מאות שנה). In v. 14 this land will be judged and Abram's seed will be freed with great possessions[303] (וגם את-הגוי אשר יעבדו דן אנכי ואחרי-כן יצאו ברכש גדול). Verse 15 holds a personal promise for Abram. He will die in peace at an advanced age (ואתה תבוא אל-אבתיך בשלום תקבר בשיבה טובה). Abram's question of knowing is answered by the Deity through very specifically promised acts that will come to pass.

The final adjacent pair in this dialogue is reminiscent of Gen 4. There we observed that narrative actions taken by Cain resulted in the opening of divine dialogue. Here in Gen 15 we have a verbal Divine directive followed by narrative actions taken by Abram (h-h`). Wenham calls the Deity's statement in v. 9 an "enigmatic command"[304] (קחה לי עגלה משלשת). The imperative form of the verb carries a commission to gather animals of various species. Abram's actions of v. 10 then go beyond the original instructions.[305] While Abram's narrative actions are outside direct dialogue, the command of v. 9 and Abram's execution of the command through v. 10 make it a strong adjacent pair. When scholars focus on the

---

[300] Fretheim, *Abraham: Trials of Family and Faith*, 37.

[301] Brodie, *Genesis as Dialogue: A Literary, Historical, and Theological Commentary*, 230.

[302] Note that von Rad calls these verses a "rupture [of, *added by ET*] the exciting predatory events" of the ritual described in vv. 9-12 and 17. Von Rad, *Genesis: A Commentary*, 186. Van Seters simply states vv. 13-16 are "'usually considered additional." Van Seters, *Abraham in History and Tradition*, 259. Westermann considers the verses an oracle formulated as revelation to explain the coming history of Israel. Westermann, *Genesis 12-36: A Commentary*, 226. On this point also see von Rad, *Genesis: A commentary*, 187.

[303] Cotter classifies the historical points contained in vv. 13-16 as "three stages of suffering followed by three stages of redemption." Cotter, *Genesis*, 101.

[304] Wenham, *Genesis 1-15*, 331.

[305] Westermann, *Genesis 12-36: A Commentary*, 225. This is not to say that Abram's actions are not warranted in light of other sacrifice narratives. I am simply observing actions taken that are not in response to a direct point of dialogue.

ritualistic aspects of this chapter they see the rite in vv. 9-11 as the answer to Abram's v. 8 request.[306] If, however, we follow the adjacent pairing a different picture emerges. The Deity's sweeping statements in v. 7 have been countered with Abram's questions and concerns of v. 8 (f-f`). The knowledge he requests (g) comes after (g`) the fulfillment of the required ritual (h-h`).

The final verse included in the narrative parameters of this dialogue is promissory in nature.[307] While v. 17 does mirror, somewhat, the actions taken in v. 10[308] it is not considered part of an adjacency pair because, as von Rad states, "The ceremony [in v. 17, *added by ET*] proceeded completely without words and with the complete passivity of the human partner!"[309] The only signs seen in v. 17 are fire and smoke, which represent the Divine.[310] There are no specific conditions required of Abram. All the responsibility lies with the Deity.[311]

---

[306] For example, Sarna comments, "For the first time in the history of religions, God becomes the contracting party, promising a national territory to a people yet unborn. This pledge constitutes the main historic title of the Jewish people to its land, a title that is unconditional and irrevocable, secured by a divine covenant whose validity transcends space and time." Sarna, *Genesis*, 115. Westermann explains, "Yahweh gives [Abram, *added by ET*] an assurance which consists in the enactment of a solemn oath (vv.9-18) divided into preparation (vv. 9-10) and execution (vv. 17-18)." Westermann, *Genesis 12-36: A Commentary*, 223. Williamson states, "Rather than being Yahweh's answer to Abraham's request for reassurance, vv. 9-11 merely paint the canvas for the audio-visual assurance of vv. 17-21." Williamson, *Abraham, Israel and the Nations: The Patriarchal Promise and Its Covenantal Development in Genesis*, 123. See also page 128.

[307] Williamson, *Abraham, Israel and the Nations: The Patriarchal Promise and Its Covenantal Development in Genesis*, 136.

[308] If the scholarly argument is focused on cult or covenant, than this pairing can be argued. As Williamson observed, "The theophanic symbols passing between the pieces bring to completion the entire ceremony that began in vv. 9-10, and thus function as the sign which Abraham had requested in v. 8." Ibid., 129. In v. 9 the Divine verbally identifies specific animals. In v. 10 Abram is described as taking 'all these' and dividing them specifically. The tenuous connection between these verses and v. 17 is the reference to the divided pieces in v. 17. However, the reference to divided pieces occurs in the narrative verses. With no other direct connective response, v. 17 is not considered part of the g-g` pairing.

[309] Von Rad, *Genesis: A Commentary*, 188.

[310] Westermann, *Genesis 12-36: A Commentary*, 228. Also see Sarna who states, "The principal party, here God, passes between the pieces. He is represented by the smoke and the fire, which are frequent symbols of the Divine Presence. As in a legal document, the nature of the instrument of transfer is defined, its promissory clause is specified as concerning a grant of land, and the extent of the territory involved is delineated in geographic and ethnographic terms." Sarna, *Genesis*, 117.

[311] Humphreys, *The Character of God in the Book of Genesis: A Narrative Appraisal*, 97.

The dialogue of Gen 15, taken as a whole unit, is "one of sharp exchange" where, according to Brueggemann, Abram "seeks to refute the promise and resist the assurance."[312] The adjacency pairs in this conversation bear this theory out, to a certain extent. The Deity's introductory statement is disputed by Abram on each of its promissory points. The demand for specifics is given by the Divine again point for point: the inheritor will be a direct descendant of Abram and this inheritor will become as numerous as the stars in the heavens. After Abram believes there is still room for a challenge to the Divine. A promise of a land inheritance is refuted with a request to know, with a surety. The Deity answers with language that does not leave anything to doubt for Abram. It is, however, interesting to note that this sign of knowledge does not come until after the commandment to sacrifice and the act of ritual Abram preforms. In this example of a Divine/human relational dialogue we see that the human demands attention be paid to the particulars of his immediate situation, requiring concrete verification of the grand divine promises.[313] These requests are answered with distinct and specific responses. Abram receives all that he requests of the Deity.

6. Genesis 32:25-31: Jacob's wrestle

a. *Adjacency Pairs and Turn Taking*

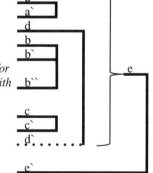

27a.   *And he said, Send me away because the dawn rises.*
27b1.   And he said, I will not send you away
27b2.   unless you bless me.
28a.   *And he said unto him, What is your name?*
28b.   And he said, Jacob.
29.   *And he said, Jacob, I will not say your name again for it is Israel because you persisted with Elohim and with men and have prevailed.*
30a1.   And Jacob asked and he said, Declare your name
30a2.   *and he said, Why do you ask this?*
30b.   *And he blessed him there.*
31.   And Jacob called the place Peniel because I saw Elohim face to face and my life was delivered.

---

[312] Brueggemann, *Genesis*, 141.
[313] Humphreys, *The Character of God in the Book of Genesis: A Narrative Appraisal*, 97.

b. *Analysis*

The final Divine/human relational dialogue[314] is ambiguous, confusing
and at the root of numerous problems for exegetes.[315] We will find, however, that through clear examples of turn-taking and adjacency pairs, for
all the confusion this passage generates, it is in fact, one of the more
straight forward dialogues to be examine.

The initial adjacent pairing of the Gen 32 dialogue comes in v. 27.[316]
The request to be sent away in v. 27a (שלחני) is directly responded to in
v. 27b1 (לא אשלחך) (a-aʻ). One participant asks to be released. The other
participant refuses to give the order. The adversarial quality of this first
pairing does not negate the pairing.

---

[314] For the sake of the Divine/human dialogue analysis we will continue under the assumption that the entity with whom Jacob is wrestling is of Divine origin. I do, however,
fully acknowledge that the attacker can be argued to be human. Brueggemann states,
"The adversary is identified only as 'a man,' which leaves all the options open."
Brueggemann, *Genesis*, 267. Also see von Rad, *Genesis: A Commentary*, 320. The
argument for a human adversary is often promoted to counter the concept that the
Deity would appear to a human in the form of an enemy. In the case for a human
attacker, the role is often given to Esau and the conflict, both physical and verbal, an
anticipation of the next day. Brueggemann, *Genesis*, 267. While the character of the
Divine in Gen 32 seems to be peculiar it is, in fact, not unknown to have a Divine
entity described as "lurking like a panther" (Hos 13:7). Gunkel, *Genesis*, 352. It
should also be noted that a Divine antagonist does appear in Exod 4 where the Deity
seeks to kill Moses and in Gen 22 where the Deity "tests" Abraham.

[315] Turner declares this passage a "masterpiece in which mystery and ambiguity cannot
be clarified by interpretation but are an essential part of its spirit." Turner, *Genesis*,
141. Also see Gunkel, *Genesis*, 349. Wenham, *Genesis 16-50*, 295.

[316] In the analysis of Gen 4 and 15 there are examples of adjacency pairs where dialogue
and narrative elements work in concert. With regard to the parameters discussion for
this dialogue the narrative vv. 25 and 26 are not considered part of the conversation.
This claim seems to be in direct opposition to most commentaries which certify vv. 25-33
as a complete event. Von Rad argues for a connection between vv. 26 and 27. He states,
"The words in v. [26, *added by ET*] are so strangely unrelated that one might think at
first, in view of the hopelessness of the fight, that Jacob had won the upper hand over
his antagonist (by a trick or fighting?). This interpretation would best suit the continuation, in v. [27, *added by ET*], where the antagonist asks Jacob to let him go." Von
Rad, *Genesis: A Commentary*, 320. The argument against inclusion is strengthened by
the fact that vv. 25 and 26, while setting the conversation stage, have no pairing within
the dialogue. The lame motif, so important to most commentaries, has no mention within
the verbal conversation and "remains under the surface of the entire dialogue" not
returning to the narrative until vv. 32-33. Coats, *Genesis*, 229. Brueggemann notes that
"after the wrestlers are exhausted in conflict, they are reduced to speech. Breathlessly,
they engage each other." Brueggemann, *Genesis*, 268. What had been a physical bout
becomes, what Humphreys calls, a "verbal contest" worthy of the preceding physical
sparing. Humphreys, *The Character of God in the Book of Genesis: A Narrative
Appraisal*, 194.

The second directly adjacent pair in this dialogue is contained in v. 28 (b-b`). There are no elements of emphatic demand or extra wording to indicate a respectful request. The Deity asks, "What is your name?" (מה-שמך) The answer is simply, "Jacob" (יעקב). The question and its corresponding response do not have grammatically significant identifiers. The response in v. 28b, however, finally allows the reader to distinguish one of the dialogue participants. There are, of course, arguments that the question is either rhetorical[317] or that it presumes the Deity does not know Jacob.[318] These discussions are applicable to the larger thematic issues but do not affect the adjacency pair.

Verse 29 (לא יעקב יאמר עוד שמך כי אם-ישראל) is an extension of the above b-b` pairing. Here the Deity restates and renames the dialogue partner (b-b`-b``). Most scholars see v. 29a as the beginning of the fulfillment of the covenant promise. The name change, they argue, announces Jacob's new character and destiny. Fretheim categorizes this verse as a blessing. He considers Jacob's new name a gift of God that has been mediated through a divine agent, empowering Jacob to experience and bring forth life and future well-being.[319] Within conversation analysis, however, there are no dialogue markers directly connecting the name change in v. 29 to Jacob's request to be blessed in v. 27b2. This theory comes most often from a multi-chapter narrative analysis.[320]

In actuality the next adjacent pair is contained in v. 30a1 and 30a2. Jacob now turns the table on his attacker and requests the name of his sparring partner (הגידה-נא שמך) (c-c`). Although the pairing of vv. 28a, b and 29 have revealed Jacob's new name, his attacker remains enigmatic in this new dialogue response (30a2) (למה זה תשאל לשמי). Jacob's request to know the assailant's name is, according to von Rad "embedded in this most urgent of all human questions, this question about the name, is all men's need, all his boldness before God."[321] The Deity's answer is in the form of a question. While classified as a response it is, in fact,

---

[317] Speiser explains, "The object [of identifying the question as rhetorical, *added by ET*] is to contrast the old name with the new and thereby mark the change in Jacob's status." Speiser, *Genesis*, 255.

[318] Gunkel, *Genesis*, 350.

[319] Terence E. Fretheim, *God and World in the Old Testament: A Relational Theology of Creation* (Nashville, Tenn.: Abingdon, 2005), 106.

[320] For example, Wenham argues that "Jacob's rebaptism as Israel is equally significant [to Abraham and Sarah's name changes, *added by ET*], for Israel is of course the name of the nation, and in granting it, Jacob's opponent reveals the true import of the encounter." Wenham, *Genesis 16-50*, 296.

[321] Von Rad, *Genesis: A Commentary*, 322.

an evasion.[322] For Brueggemann, the Deity stops short of what could be the ultimate gift of the Divine name.[323]

As if to avoid Jacob's question all together, the text immediately reports (v. 30b) the Deity's action of blessing Jacob where he stands (ויברך אתו שם). Looking for an adjacent pairing we now return to Jacob's first request in v. 27b2. In the final clause of v. 27b2, the second speaker, soon to be identified as Jacob, requests a blessing from the first speaker (כי אם-ברכתני). This request and its paired narrative action in v. 30b stand outside the discussion of names (d-d`), encompassing the verbal jockeying for identities. For some scholars the reason for the placement of Jacob's initial blessing request in v. 27b2 is due to the narrative description of the rising sun in v. 25.[324] Most argue that the dawn brings with it the ability to identify his opponent.[325] If Jacob is going to ask for a blessing, "one must assume that Jacob has discovered something of the divine nature of his opponent."[326] He takes advantage of the physical situation to demand a continuation of the verbal dialogue. He "invokes and petitions God to

---

[322] There are scholarly explanations for the circumvention, most of which center on the idea that if the Deity's name is known to humans they would have power over the Divine. Brueggemann contends that the Deity must remain hidden to be considered "intact" as a Divine being. Brueggemann, *Genesis*, 269. Also see Westermann, *Genesis: A Practical Commentary*, 229. Von Rad maintains that if a human knows the name of the Deity then the Deity can be summoned at will by the human. Von Rad, *Genesis: A Commentary*, 322. Brown, however, contends that refusal to surrender his name "reveals, paradoxically, his divine status (v. 30; see Judg. 13:18), for immediately thereafter Jacob pronounces the name of the site (v.31)." Brown, "Manifest Diversity: The Presence of God in Genesis," 12.

[323] Brueggemann, *Genesis*, 269.

[324] Barthes sees the request, dialogue, and its inclusive narrative, as a familiar episode like mythical narratives where the hero must overcome an obstacle or ordeal. Barthes, *Image, Music, Text*, 137. Speiser agrees, stating, "Such manifestations serve either as forecasts or as tests." Speiser, *Genesis*, 256. Indeed, for over a century "many have assumed the text reflects an original oral tradition relating a local legend of a night-time battle, in which a deity impedes the human from crossing the river but is compelled to give him a gift." Arnold, *Genesis*, 283.

[325] Speiser describes the passage as "a desperate nocturnal struggle with a nameless adversary whose true nature does not dawn on Jacob until the physical darkness had begun to lift." Speiser, *Genesis*, 256.

[326] Von Rad, *Genesis: A Commentary*, 321. Westermann describes Jacob's attacker as a "demon" and ascribes the timing of the blessing to the belief that demons only possess power during the light and lose it at daybreak. Westermann, *Genesis: A Practical Commentary*, 229. Even if you follow scholarship that defines the attacker as human, Turner explains, "Prior to this incident, Jacob believed that he faced a hostile Esau (32:11). Now, in the darkness, an aggressive combatant wrestles with him. Jacob had struggled with Esau in the womb; does he think he does so again at the Jabbok? Is this the reason why he craves a blessing and is so keen to know his assailant's name?" Turner, *Genesis*, 142.

make sure of his continued support as he moves back into the land and
prepares to meet Esau."[327] The demand for a blessing is answered in
v. 30b.

Scholars, however, continue to see the change of name from Jacob
to Israel as the blessing.[328] Speiser even goes so far as to state that, "no
blessing can be involved at this point [v. 30b, *added by ET*], since that
was already represented in the change of name."[329] For Sarna, the justification of the blessing is also the new name because it signals a "final
purging of the unsavory character traits" that Jacob, the trickster, has been
associated with.[330] Coats has a similar but slightly divergent description
of the name/blessing juxtaposition.[331] He argues that the focal interest of
the unit is the name change. The essence of the surrounding struggle, he
states, is some manner of the blessing. As the new name Israel suggests,
Jacob's success is not only in the physical struggle but in the adjacent
pairing of petition and counter-petition between the Divine and man. For
Coats, the blessing, while entwined with the name change, in fact, stands
in parallel to the name change as our adjacent pairs b, c and d suggest.

Jacob's final response (e-e`) to this strange encounter (v. 31) may
remind the reader of the conclusion of Hagar's Divine/human relational
dialogue.[332] Similar to Hagar, Jacob calls a name. While Hagar named

---

[327] Humphreys, *The Character of God in the Book of Genesis: A Narrative Appraisal*,
193.
[328] Steven L. McKenzie, "'You Have Prevailed': The Function of Jacob's Encounter at
Peniel in the Jacob Cycle," *ResQ* 23/4 (1980): 229. See also Victor H. Matthews and
Frances Mims, "Jacob the Trickster and Heir of the Covenant: A Literary Interpretation," *PRSt* 12 (1985): 193.
[329] Speiser, *Genesis*, 255.
[330] Sarna, *Genesis*, 227.
[331] Coats, *Genesis*, 229-30.
[332] Translation issues aside, scholars are in agreement that both passages (Gen 16 and 32)
carry the general meaning of seeing or being seen by the Divine and surviving. Humphrey's states, "In the story-world of Genesis [where, *added by ET*] God has engaged
humans directly, this is the first in which the encounter is clearly stated to have been
in terms of seeing. This may have been the case with Hagar in Genesis 16:13-14, but
the text in that instance is not clear. Several characters have spoken with God. Jacob
alone wrestles with him. Jacob alone clearly sees him. And Jacob survives — his life
delivered." Humphreys, *The Character of God in the Book of Genesis: A Narrative
Appraisal*, 195. Gunkel explains, "The general idea underlying this clause is the frequent notion in ancient Israel that whoever saw the deity must die (Judg 6:22; 13:22;
Exod 33:20) for so the deity guards his secret. He may well permit a human eye to
see his face, but he does not allow the human mouth to revel [sic, *added by ET*] his
secret. Consequently, whoever has seen God's face and remained alive experiences
particular good fortune (cf. Judg 6:23; 13:23; Deut 34:10)." Gunkel, *Genesis*, 351.
Sarna argues from a slightly different perspective. He states, "God explicitly tells
Moses, 'Man may not see Me and live!' This is the biblical way of expressing the

the Deity, Jacob names the location where he has encountered the Divine
‫(ויקרא יעקב שם המקום פניאל כי-ראיתי אלהים פנים אל-פנים ותנצל נפשי)‬.
Although there has been no direct reference in the dialogue of a face-to-
face motif,[333] Jacob claims such an experience due, in part, to the previous
conversational pairs. In Wenham's opinion the wrestling aspect and the
name change are not as important to Jacob as the fact that after encounter-
ing the Divine in face to face conversation, he has survived.[334] It is only
through the overall dialogue exchange (e) that we learn anything regarding this perilous and auspicious event (e`).

Within the Gen 32 Divine/human relational dialogue there are some
of the clearest examples of adjacency pairing we have seen. From a
relationship stand point this conversation is also interesting as the participants seem to manipulate the situation to their advantage, changing
the power structure within the dialogue as they progress through it. In
v. 27 Jacob is the stronger party, refusing to send away the Divine. In the
second exchange the Deity is in control and Jacob answers the Divine's
question simply and truthfully. The third pairing, according to Brueggemann, is an 'act of incredible boldness' on Jacob's part. The human
assumes priority and demands to know the Deity's name which is cir-
cumvented.[335] The blessing that is requested by Jacob in v. 27b2 is fulfilled by the Divine in v. 30b. The exact details of the blessing are
debatable but what is certain is that the blessing does, in fact, encompass
the patriarch's name change. The final adjacent pair is Jacob's evaluation
of the Divine/human encounter. He names the location Peniel because he
has survived his tumultuous face to face meeting with the Deity. As far
as Divine/human relationships go, this dialogue is one of the most
intense. The adjacent pairs are as sharp in contrast as the bond between
Divine and human. Surrounding the identity of each participant is the
bestowal of a blessing. The name of each individual may not be known
or even made clear but what is sure is that a blessing can only be issued
from the Deity.

---

intensity of the experience of the individual encounter with the Divine Presence — the
utterly overwhelming nature of the mysterious contact with the awesome majesty of
the transcendent yet immanent God." Sarna, *Genesis*, 228.

[333] Coats lists "one possible exception being the allusion to the face of God in 33:10."
Coats, *Genesis*, 230.

[334] Wenham, *Genesis 16-50*, 297.

[335] Brueggemann, *Genesis*, 268-69.

D. The Essence of Dialogue: Conclusions

Within these Divine/human relational dialogues we have seen all manner of what many would call bad human behavior. Persons who, due to improper and even immoral activities, are under condemnation, who lie and avoid responsibility for their actions. Individuals of respectability who doubt, demand, question and challenge the Deity they supposedly believe in. There are, however, two major themes that run through these dialogues.

First is the fact that the Deity, through dialogue, expresses a knowledge of the individual named within the conversation. Their situation and relationships are ever present in the adjacent pairs. The Deity's choice of question and response is not tangential. It is focused and poignantly specific to the individual human's situation. For the length of the conversation there is no other Divine/human personal relationship as important as that of the named individual.

Second is the idea that the human perspective must be expressed. Within each of these dialogues the human voices what amounts to their limited world view. The Divine does not belittle these relatively trivial concerns. Instead, the Deity, explicitly addressed almost every trepidation with a wider possibility — a future or perspective the human did not have the capacity to perceive.

Individual conversations also reveal some interesting truths. From the Cain dialogue we learn that regardless of the crime a human is still entitled to Divine patronage, though restricted that protection might be. The Hagar dialogue demonstrates the fact that even when no personal human relationships exist, relationship with the Deity is possible. Within the dialogues of chapters 17 and 18 we observed that the term "secondary character" is not a true moniker. Every individual, whether on stage or not, is known and identified as important to the Divine. A study of the visionary dialogue in Gen 15 indicated that first, belief and knowledge are different, second that questioning and challenging the Deity can build human understanding and finally, signs leading to sure knowledge only come after belief and acting on that belief. The final Divine/human relational dialogue confirmed that it is impossible to know the Deity as intimately as the Divine knows us. However, if you refuse to send the Deity away requests for blessings will be fulfilled.[336]

---

[336] Schwartz states, "God may be approached by approaching otherness in all its forms. This does not mean we will *fully* understand God; just that we will understand more about God or the ways God works in the world." Schwartz, "God the Stranger," 43.

CHAPTER 4

DIVINE/HUMAN RELATIONAL DIALOGUE

I began this thesis with the question, "Is it possible to find an interpersonal relationship model between lowly humans and the Divine as contained within conversation in Genesis?" My aim in this study was to develop a model of Divine/human relational dialogue that would then inform a model of the Divine/human relationship. Through the identification of latent elements and the use of form and narrative criticism it was possible to define and then extract relational dialogue from the surrounding narrative. While no rigid Divine/human relational dialogue formula could be established what has been discovered is a model with great applications to a better understanding of the overall Divine/human relationship.

For the purpose of this thesis "dialogue" was defined as verbal communication between two or more individuals, one of whom could be identified as the Deity, with interaction carried out for social purposes rather than as an exchange of goods and services. These conversations went beyond the typical "call and response" construction to include a "cooperative endeavor" in the form of social interaction between the Deity and an individual human. This interaction, our dialogue analysis proved, showed a Deity with an existing knowledge and relationship with the human conversational partner.

The examination of the initiation of dialogue disclosed simple and unassuming beginnings. There was no Divine "grand entrance" or dramatic upheaval in the life of the human to announce the commencement of the Divine/human verbal exchange. There may have been some previous human narrative action but it is the Deity who spoke first and with this first expression came acknowledgement of an existing relationship and recognition of the human condition. In each case the human's social, moral or subordinate status was no impediment to Divine/human relational dialogue.

One of the key elements under scrutiny in this thesis was the manner in which a proper name was used within the confines of relational dialogue. This study revealed that a name was more than its etymology. When used by the Deity, a name acknowledged the human individual's standing before the Divine and in the world. The named person was no longer impersonal but a complete individual before the Deity. This human was also shown to have a privileged relationship with the Divine separate from conventional society that surrounded them. Through the use of a name the importance of character, identity and destiny were revealed and it was established that the individual did not exist on the Deity's periphery.

The anticipated finding of this thesis was the discovery of a model of the Divine/human relationship. What was most interesting to me was the knowledge that, while it is impossible to know the Deity as intimately as the Deity knows us, engagement in Divine/human dialogue demonstrated there was no other personal relationship as important to the Divine as that of the named individual during the time of the conversation. On the human side of the dialogue each individual was able to openly express their limited mortal perspective without Divine ridicule and receive, for their effort, a divinely explained broader future. Divine patronage was not limited, as some scholars like to think, to only noteworthy individuals; murders, foreigners and tricksters conversed with the Deity, "secondary characters" took center stage, and speaking up or speaking back broadened the human faith and understanding of the Deity in whom they believed. The model of Divine/human relational dialogue shows that, regardless of Israel's[1] special relationship with the Deity, a Divine/human relationship begins on the level of the individual who is known by their Deity.

---

[1] Understood as a nation or the more modern concept of an organized religion.

BIBLIOGRAPHY

ABRAMS, M. H. *The Mirror and the Lamp: Romantic Theory and the Critical Tradition*. New York: Norton, 1958.

ALTER, Robert. *The Art of Biblical Narrative*. New York: Basic Books, 1981.

—. *The Five Books of Moses*. New York: W.W. Norton, 2004.

—. "In the Community: A Literary Approach to the Bible." *Commentary* 60 (1975): 70-77.

ANBAR, Moshe. "Genesis 15: A Conflation of Two Deuteronomic Narratives." *JBL* 101 (1982): 39-55.

ANDERSEN, Francis I. *The Sentence in Biblical Hebrew*. The Hague: Mouton, 1974.

ARNOLD, Bill T. *Genesis*. New Cambridge Bible Commentary. Cambridge: Cambridge University Press. 2009.

BAR-EFRAT, Shimon. *Narrative Art in the Bible*. 2nd ed. Sheffield: Almond, 1989.

BARTHES, Roland. *Image, Music, Text*. Translated by Stephen Heath. New York: Hill and Wang, 1977.

BARTON, John. *Reading the Old Testament: Method in Biblical Study*. Philadelphia, Pa.: Westminster Press, 1984.

BENWELL, Bethan, and Elizabeth STOKE. *Discourse and Identity*. Edinburgh: Edinburgh University Press, 2006.

BERLIN, Adele. *Poetics and Interpretation of Biblical Narrative*. Bible and Literature Series 9. Sheffield: Almond. 1983.

BLENKINSOPP, Joseph. *The Pentateuch: An Introduction to the First Five Books of the Bible*. 1st ed. New York: Doubleday, 1992.

BLUM, Erhard. "Formgeschichte — a Misleading Category? Some Critical Remarks." In *The Changing Face of Form Criticism for the Twenty-First Century*. Edited by Marvin A. Sweeney and Ehud Ben Zvi. Grand Rapids, Mich.: Eerdmans, 2003.

BOWMAN, Richard G. "Narrative Criticism: Human Purpose in Conflict with Divine Presence." In *Judges and Method: New Approaches in Biblcial Studies*, edited by Gale A. Yee. Minneapolis, Minn: Fortress, 2007.

BRETT, Mark G. *Genesis: Procreation and the Politics of Identity*. London: Routledge, 2000.

BRICHTO, Herbert Chanan. *The Names of God: Poetic Readings in Biblical Beginnings*. Oxford: Oxford University Press, 1998.

BRODIE, Thomas L. *Genesis as Dialogue: A Literary, Historical, and Theological Commentary*. Oxford: Oxford University Press, 2001.

BROWN, Francis, S. R. DRIVER, and Charles A. BRIGGS. *The Brown-Driver-Briggs Hebrew and English Lexicon*. Peabody, Mass.: Hendrickson, 2005.

BROWN, William P. "Manifest Diversity: The Presence of God in Genesis." In *Genesis and Christian Theology*. Edited by Nathan MacDonald and Mark W. Elliott. Grand Rapids, Mich: Eerdmans, 2012.

BRUEGGEMANN, Walter. *Genesis*. Atlanta, Ga.: John Knox, 1982.

—. *Theology of the Old Testament: Testimony, Dispute, Advocacy*. Minneapolis, Minn.: Fortress, 1997.

BURNETT, Fred W. "Characterization and Reader Construction of Characters in the Gospels." *Semeia* 63 (1993): 3-78.

BURNETT, Joel S. *Where Is God? Divine Absence in the Hebrew Bible*. Minneapolis, Minn.: Fortress, 2010.

CAMPBELL, Antony F. "Form Criticism's Future." In *The Changing Face of Form Criticism for the Twenty-First Century*. Edited by Marvin A. Sweeney and Ehud Ben Zvi. Grand Rapids, Mich.: Eerdmans, 2003.

—. "Preparatory Issues in Approaching Biblical Texts." In *The Blackwell Companion to the Hebrew Bible*. Edited by Leo G. Perdue. Oxford: Blackwell, 2001.

CASSUTO, Umberto. *A Commentary on the Book of Genesis*. Translated by Israel Abrahams. Jerusalem: Magnes, 1961.

CHILDS, Brevard S. *Exodus, a Commentary*. Old Testament Library. London: SCM. 1974.

—. *Introduction to the Old Testament as Scripture*. London: SCM, 1979.

CLAASSENS, L. Juliana M. "Laughter and Tears: Carnivalistic Overtones in the Stories of Sarah and Hagar." *PRSt* 32 (2005): 295-308.

COATS, George W. *Exodus 1-18*. Forms of the Old Testament Literature 2A. Grand Rapids, Mich.: Eerdmans. 1999.

—. *Genesis*. Forms of the Old Testament Literature 1. Grand Rapids, Mich.: Eerdmans. 1983.

COOPER, Alan. "Hagar in and out of Context." *USQR* 55 (2001): 35-46.

COTTER, David W. *Genesis*. Berit Olam. Collegeville, Minn.: Liturgical Press. 2003.

CRAIG, Kenneth M. Jr. "Questions Outside Eden (Genesis 4.1-16): Yahweh, Cain and Their Rhetorical Interchange." *JSOT* 86 (1999): 107-28.

CURTIS, Edward M. "Structure, Style and Context as a Key to Interpreting Jacob's Encounter at Peniel." *JETS* 30/2 (1987): 129-37.

DARR, Katheryn Pfisterer. *Far More Precious Than Jewels: Perspectives on Biblical Women*. 1st ed. Louisville, Ky.: Westminster John Knox, 1991.

DAVIDSON, Robert. *Genesis 12-50*. Cambridge Bible Commentary. Cambridge: Cambridge University Press. 1979.

DENNIS, Trevor. *Sarah Laughed*. Nashville, Tenn.: Abingdon, 1994.

DOZEMAN, Thomas B. "The Wilderness and Salvatin History in the Hagar Story." *JBL* 117 (1998): 23-43.

DREY, Philip R. "The Role of Hagar in Genesis 16." *Andrews University Seminary Studies* 40 (2002): 179-95.

EISSFELDT, Otto. *The Old Testament: An Introduction*. Translated by Peter R. Ackroyd. New York: Harper and Row, 1965.

FINLAY, Timothy D. *The Birth Report Genre in the Hebrew Bible*. Tübingen: Mohr Siebeck, 2005.

FLEISHMAN, Joseph. "On the Significance of a Name Change and Circumcision in Genesis 17." *JANES* 28 (2001): 19-32.

FOKKELMAN, J. P. *Narrative Art in Genesis: Specimens of Stylistic and Structural Analysis*. Assen: Van Gorcum, 1975.

—. *Reading Biblical Narrative: An Introduction*. Louisville, Ky.: Westminster John Knox, 1999.

FREEDMAN, David Noel. "Genesis." In *Eerdmans Commentary on the Bible*. Edited by James D. G. Dunn and J. W. Rogerson. Grand Rapids, Mich.: Eerdmans, 2003.

FRETHEIM, Terence E. *Abraham: Trials of Family and Faith*. Columbia: University of South Carolina Press, 2007.

—. *God and World in the Old Testament: A Relational Theology of Creation*. Nashville, Tenn.: Abingdon, 2005.

—. *The Suffering of God: An Old Testament Perspective*. Philadelphia, Pa.: Fortress, 1984.

FRYE, Northrop. *The Great Code: The Bible and Literature*. New York: Harcourt Brace Jovanovich, 1982.

GARCIA-TRETO, Francisco O. "Crossing the Line: Three Scenes of Divine-Human Engagement in the Hebrew Bible." In *Teaching the Bible*. Edited by Fernando F. Segovia and Mary Ann Tolbert. Maryknoll, NY: Orbis, 1998.

GORDON, Robert P. "The Ethics of Eden: Truth Telling in Gen 2-3." In *Ethical and Unethical in the Old Testament*. Edited by Katherine Dell. New York: T&T Clark, 2010.

GOSSAI, Hemchand. *Power and Marginality in the Abraham Narrative*. Lanham, Md.: University of America Press, 1995.

GOWAN, Donald E. *Theology in Exodus: Biblical Theology in the Form of a Commentary*. 1st ed. Louisville, Ky.: Westminster John Knox, 1994.

GUNKEL, Hermann. *Genesis*. Translated by Mark E. Biddle. Macon, Ga.: Mercer University Press, 1997.

—. *The Legends of Genesis: The Biblical Saga and Hisory*. New York: Schocken, 1964.

—. *Water for a Thirsty Land: Israelite Literature and Religion*. Translated by A.K. Dallas and James Schaaf. Edited by K. C. Hanson. Minneapolis, Minn.: Fortress, 2001.

GUNN, David M., and Danna Nolan FEWELL. *Narrative in the Hebrew Bible*. Oxford Bible Series. Oxford: Oxford University Press. 1993.

HA, John. *Genesis 15: A Theological Compendium of Pentateuchal History*. Berlin: W. De Gruyter, 1989.

HAMILTON, Victor P. *The Book of Genesis: Chapters 18-50*. Grand Rapids, Mich.: Eerdmans, 1995.

HATAV, Galia. "(Free) Direct Discourse in Biblical Hebrew." *HS* 41 (2000): 7-30.

HAYES, John H. *Methods of Biblical Interpretation: Excerpted from the Dictionary of Biblical Interpretation*. Nashville, Tenn.: Abingdon, 2004.

HAYES, John H., and Carl R. HOLLADAY. *Biblical Exegesis: A Beginner's Handbook*. Atlanta. Ga.: John Knox, 1982.

HERION, Gary A. "Why God Rejected Cain's Offering: The Obvious Answer." In *Fortunate the Eyes That See*. Edited by Astrid B. Beck and Andrew H. Bartelt. Grand Rapids, Mich: Eerdmans, 1995.

HOUSE, Paul R. *Beyond Form Criticism: Essays in Old Testament Literary Criticism.* Sources for Biblical and Theological Study 2. Winona Lake, Ind.: Eisenbrauns. 1992.

—. "The Rise and Current Status of Literary Criticism of the Old Testament." In *Beyond Form Criticism: Essays in Old Testament Literary Criticism.* Edited by Paul R. House. Winona Lake, Ind.: Eisenbrauns, 1992.

HUMPHREYS, W. Lee. *The Character of God in the Book of Genesis: A Narrative Appraisal.* Louisville, Ky.: Westminster John Knox, 2001.

JACOBSON, Richard. "The Structuralists and the Bible." *Int* 28 (1974): 146-64.

JANZEN, J. Gerald. *Abraham and All the Families of the Earth: A Commontary on the Book of Genesis 12-50.* Grand Rapids, Mich: Eerdmans, 1993.

JEANSONNE, Sharon Pace. *The Women of Genesis: From Sarah to Potiphar's Wife.* Minneapolis, Minn.: Fortress, 1990.

JOHNSTONE, Barbara. *Discourse Analysis.* 2nd ed. Malden, Mass.: Blackwell, 2008.

KAPELRUD, Arvid S. "The Covenant as Agreement." *SJOT* 1 (1988): 30-38.

KIM, Hyun Chul Paul. "Form Criticism in Dialogue with Other Criticisms: Building the Multidimensional Structures of Texts and Concepts." In *The Changing Face of Form Criticism for the Twenty-First Century.* Edited by Marvin A. Sweeney and Ehud Ben Zvi. Grand Rapids, Mich.: Eerdmans, 2003.

KINGSBURY, Jack Dean. *Matthew as Story.* Philadelphia, Pa.: Fortress, 1986.

KORPEL, Marjo C.A., and Johannes C. DE MOOR. *The Silent God.* Leiden: Brill, 2011.

LA SOR, William Sanford, David Allan HUBBARD, and Frederic William BUSH. *Old Testament Survey: The Message, Form, and Background of the Old Testament.* Grand Rapids, Mich.: Eerdmans, 1982.

LIPTON, Diana. *Revisions of the Night: Politics and Promises in the Patriarchal Dreams of Genesis.* JSOTSup 288. Sheffield: Sheffield Academic Press, 1999.

MATTHEWS, Victor H. "Hospitality and Hostility in Genesis 19 and Judges 19." *BTB* 22 (1992): 3-11.

—. "Hospitality and Hostility in Judges 4." *BTB* 21 (1991): 13-21.

—. *More Than Meets the Ear: Discovering the Hidden Contexts of Old Testament Conversations.* Grand Rapids, Mich.: Eerdmans, 2008.

MATTHEWS, Victor H., and Frances MIMS. "Jacob the Trickster and Heir of the Covenant: A Literary Interpretation." *PRSt* 12 (1985): 18.

MAYFIELD, Tyler D. *Literary Structure and Setting in Ezekiel.* Tübingen: Mohr Siebeck, 2010.

MAYS, James Luther. *The Harper Collins Bible Commentary.* Rev. ed. San Francisco, Calif.: Harper San Francisco, 2000.

MCKENZIE, Steven L. "'You Have Prevailed': The Function of Jacob's Encounter at Peniel in the Jacob Cycle." *ResQ* 23 (1980): 225-31.

MCKENZIE, Steven L., and Matt Patrick GRAHAM, eds. *The Hebrew Bible Today: An Introduction to Critical Issues.* 1st ed. Louisville, Ky.: Westminster John Knox, 1998.

MELUGIN, Roy F. "Recent Form Criticism Revisited in an Age of Reader Response." In *The Changing Face of Form Criticism for the Twenty-First Century.* Edited by Marvin A. Sweeney and Ehud Ben Zvi. Grand Rapids, Mich.: Eerdmans, 2003.

MEYERS, Carol L. *Women in Scripture: A Dictionary of Named and Unnamed Women in the Hebrew Bible, the Apocryphal/Deuterocanonical Books, and the New Testament.* Grand Rapids, Mich.: Eerdmans, 2001.

MILLER, C. L. *The Representation of Speech in Biblical Hebrew Narrative: A Linguistic Analysis.* Harvard Semitic Monographs 55. Atlanta, Ga.: Scholars Press. 1996.

MOBERLY, Walter. *Genesis 12-50.* Sheffield: JSOT Press 1992.

MOERMAN, Michael. *Talking Culture: Ethnography and Conversation Analysis.* Philadelphia, Pa.: University of Pennsylvania Press, 1988.

MUILENBURG, James. "Form Criticism and Beyond." *JBL* 88 (1969): 1-18.

NGAN, Lai Ling Elizabeth. "Neither Here nor There: Boundary and Identity in the Hagar Story." In *Ways of Being, Ways of Reading.* Edited by Mary F. Foshett and Jeffrey Kah-Jim Kuan. Saint Louis: Chalice, 2006.

NIDITCH, Susan. "Genesis." In *Women's Bible Commentary.* Edited by Carol A. Newsom and Sharon H. Ringe. Louisville, Ky.: Westminster John Knox, 1998.

NIKAIDO, S. "Hagar and Ishmael as Literary Figures: An Intertextual Study." *VT* 51 (2001): 219-42.

NOEGEL, Scott B. "A Crux and a Taunt: Night-Time Then Sunset in Genesis 15." In *The world of Genesis: Persons, Places, Perspectives.* Edited by Philip R. Davies and David J.A. Clines. JSOTSup 257. Sheffield: Sheffield Academic Press. 1998.

NOTH, Martin. *A History of Pentateuchal Traditions.* Translated by Bernhard W. Anderson. Chico, Calif.: Scholars Press, 1981.

NUNAN, David. *Introducing Discourse Analysis.* London: Penguin, 1993.

PERRY, T. Anthony. "Cain's Sin in Gen. 4:1-7: Oracular Ambiguity and How to Avoid It." *Prooftexts* 25 (2005): 258-75.

PHILLIPS, Elaine A. "Incredulity, Faith, and Textual Purposes: Post-Biblical Responses to the Laughter of Abraham and Sarah." In *The Function of Scripture in Early Jewish and Christian Tradition.* Edited by Craig A. Evans and James A. Sanders. JSNTSup 154. Sheffield: Sheffield Academic Press. 1988.

PLASTARAS, James. *The God of Exodus: The Theology of the Exodus Narratives.* Milwaukee, Wisc.: Bruce, 1966.

POWELL, Mark Allan. "Literary and Structuralist/Postmodernist Approaches Methods." In *Methods of Biblical Interpretation.* Edited by John H. Hayes. Nashville, Tenn.: Abingdon, 2004.

—. *What Is Narrative Criticism? A New Approach to the Bible.* London: SPCK, 1993.

RAD, Gerhard von. *Genesis: A Commentary.* Old Testament Library. Philadelphia. Pa.: Westminster Press. 1972.

RAMSEY, George W. "Is Name-Giving an Act of Domination in Genesis 2:23." *CBQ* 50 (1988): 24-35.

RAPPORT, Nigel, and Joanna Overing. *Social and Cultural Anthropology: The Key Concepts.* 2nd ed. London: Routledge, 2007.

REIS, Pamela Tamarkin. "Hagar Requited." *JSOT* 87 (2000): 75-109.

REVELL, E.J. *The Designation of the Individual: Expressive Usage in Biblical Narrative.* Kampen: Kok Pharos, 1996.

RHOADS, David M. "Narrative Criticism and the Gospel of Mark." *JAAR* 50 (1982): 411-34.

RICHTER, Wolfgang. *Grundlagen einer Althebräischen Grammatik.* St. Ottilien: EOS-Verlag, 1978.

RULON-MILLER, Nina. "Hagar: A Woman with an Attitude." In *The World of Genesis: Persons, Places, Perspectives.* Edited by Philip R. Davies and David J.A. Clines. JSOTSup 257. Sheffield: Sheffield Academic Press. 1998.

SAILHAMER, John. *The Pentateuch as Narrative: A Biblical-Theological Commentary.* Grand Rapids, Mich.: Zondervan, 1992.

SARNA, Nahum M. *Genesis.* JPS Torah Commentary. Philadelphia, Pa.: Jewish Publication Society. 1989.

SCHNEIDER, Tammi J. *Mothers of Promise: Women in the Book of Genesis.* Grand Rapids, Mich.: Baker Academic, 2008.

—. *Sarah: Mother of Nations.* New York: Continuum, 2004.

SCHWARTZ, G. David. "God the Stranger." *Horizons in Biblical Theology* 20 (1998): 33-48.

SEEMAN, Don. "'Where Is Sarah Your Wife?' Cultural Poetics of Gender and Nationhood in the Hebrew Bible." *HTR* 91 (1998): 103-25.

SIDNELL, Jack. *Conversation Analysis: An Introduction.* Chichester, West Sussex: Wiley-Blackwell, 2010.

SKINNER, John. *A Critical and Exegetical Commentary on Genesis.* 2nd ed. Edinburgh: T. & T. Clark, 1930.

SOGGIN, J. Alberto, and John Bowden. *Introduction to the Old Testament: From Its Origins to the Closing of the Alexandrian Canon.* 2nd ed. London: SCM, 1976.

SOULEN, Richard N. *Handbook of Biblical Criticism.* Atlanta. Ga.: John Knox, 1976.

SPEISER, E. A. *Genesis.* Anchor Bible 1. Garden City, N.Y.: Doubleday. 1964.

STECK, Odil Hannes. *Old Testament Exegesis: A Guide to the Methodology.* 2nd ed. Atlanta, Ga.: Scholars Press, 1998.

STERNBERG, Meir. *The Poetics of Biblical Narrative.* Bloomington, Ind: Indiana University, 1987.

SWEENEY, Marvin A., and Ehud Ben Zvi, eds. *The Changing Face of Form Criticism for the Twenty-First Century.* Grand Rapids, Mich.: Eerdmans, 2003.

TALSTRA, E. *Solomon's Prayer: Synchrony and Diachrony in the Composition of I Kings 8, 14-61.* Contributions to Biblical Exegesis and Theology 3. Kampen: Kok Pharos. 1993.

TERRIEN, Samuel. *The Elusive Presence: Toward a New Biblical Theology.* Religious Perspectives 26. New York: Harper and Row. 1978.

TEUBAL, Savina J. "Sarah and Hagar: Matriarchs and Visionaries." In *Feminist Companion to Genesis.* Edited by Athalya Brenner. Sheffield: Sheffield Academic Press, 1993.

TRIBLE, Phyllis. "The Other Woman: A Literary and Theological Study of the Hagar Narratives." In *Understanding the Word: Essays in Honor of Bernhard W. Anderson.* Edited by James T. Butler, Edgar W. Conrad, and Ben C. Ollenburger. JSOTSup 37. Sheffield: JSOT Press, 1985.

—. *Texts of Terror: Literary-Feminist Readings of Biblical Narratives.* Philadelphia, Pa.: Fortress, 1984.

TRIBLE, Phyllis, and Letty M. RUSSELL. *Hagar, Sarah, and Their Children: Jewish, Christian, and Muslim Perspectives.* 1st ed. Louisville, Ky.: Westminster John Knox, 2006.

TURNER, Laurence A. *Announcements of Plot in Genesis*. JSOT Supplement Series 96. Sheffield: JSOT Press. 1990.

—. *Genesis*. Sheffield: Sheffield Academic Press, 2000.

VAN SETERS, John. *Abraham in History and Tradition*. New Haven, Conn.: Yale University Press, 1975.

VAN SETERS, John. "The Pentateuch." In *The Hebrew Bible Today: An Introduction to Critical Issues*. Edited by Steven L. McKenzie. and M. Patrick Graham. 1st ed. Louisville, Ky.: Westminster John Knox, 1998.

VAN WOLDE, Ellen. "The Story of Cain and Abel: A Narrative Study." *JSOT* 52 (1991): 25-41.

—. *Words Become Worlds: Semantic Studies of Genesis 1-11*. Leiden: Brill, 1994.

—. *The Problem of the Hexateuch and Other Essays*. Translated by E. W. Trueman Dicken. New York: McGraw, 1966.

WARDHAUGH, Ronald. *How Conversation Works*. Oxford: Basil Blackwell, 1985.

WARNING, Wilfried. "Terminological Patterns and Genesis 17." *Hebrew Union College Annual* 70-71 (1999-2000): 93-107.

WENHAM, Gordon J. "The Religion of the Patriarchs." In *Essays on the Patriarchal Narratives*. Edited by A.J. Millard and D.J. Wiseman. Leicester: Inter-Varsity Press, 1980.

—. *Genesis 1-15*. Word Biblical Commentary 1. Waco, Tex.: Word. 1987.

—. *Genesis 16-50*. Word Biblical Commentary 2. Dallas, Tex.: Word. 1994.

WESTERMANN, Claus. *Elements of Old Testament Theology*. Translated by Douglas W. Scott. Atlanta, Ga.: John Knox, 1978.

—. *Genesis 1-11: A Commentary*. Translated by John J. Scullion. London: SPCK, 1974.

—. *Genesis 12-36: A Commentary*. Translated by John J. Scullion. Minneapolis, Minn.: Augsburg, 1985.

—. *Genesis: A Practical Commentary*. Translated by David Green. Grand Rapids, Mich.: Eerdmans, 1987.

WILLIAMSON, Paul R. *Abraham, Israel and the Nations: The Patriarchal Promise and Its Covenantal Development in Genesis*. Edited by David J.A. Clines and Philip R. Davies, Journal for the Study of the Old Testement Supplement Series. Sheffield: Sheffield Academic Press, 2000.

WYATT, N. "The Meaning of El Roi and the Mythological Dimension in Genesis 16." *SJOT* 8 (1994): 141-51.

PRINTED ON PERMANENT PAPER • IMPRIME SUR PAPIER PERMANENT • GEDRUKT OP DUURZAAM PAPIER - ISO 9706

N.V. PEETERS S.A., WAROTSTRAAT 50, B-3020 HERENT